GOVERNING METROPOLITAN TORONTO

A publication of the
Franklin K. Lane Memorial Fund,
Institute of Governmental Studies,
University of California, Berkeley

The Franklin K. Lane Memorial Fund takes its name from Franklin Knight Lane (1864–1921), a distinguished Californian who was successively New York correspondent for the San Francisco *Chronicle,* City and County Attorney of San Francisco, member and later chairman of the United States Interstate Commerce Commission, and Secretary of the Interior in the cabinet of President Woodrow Wilson.

The general purposes of the endowment are to promote "better understanding of the nature and working of the American system of democratic government, particularly in its political, economic and social aspects," and the "study and development of the most suitable methods for its improvement in the light of experience."

GOVERNING METROPOLITAN TORONTO: A SOCIAL AND POLITICAL ANALYSIS 1953-1971

By ALBERT ROSE

Published for the
INSTITUTE OF GOVERNMENTAL STUDIES

UNIVERSITY OF CALIFORNIA PRESS

Berkeley, Los Angeles, London

University of California Press
Berkeley and Los Angeles, California

University of California Press, Ltd.
London, England

Copyright © 1972, by
The Regents of the University of California

ISBN: 0-520-02041-3

Library of Congress Catalog Card Number: 72-157821

Printed in the United States of America

For My Family

FOREWORD

For almost two decades, Metropolitan Toronto has been enviously called the only "truly metropolitan government" in North America. Furthermore, Americans south of the Canadian border also consider it something of a "sport"—a reform that could be accomplished only under a parliamentary system, without plebiscites and other home-rule vetoes.

The combination of curiosity and adulation from this side of the international boundary has not produced a sophisticated understanding of what Metro has and has not accomplished. Instead, for several reasons, we tend to overlook the vitality, the variety, and the significance of Canadian adjustments to urbanization and metropolitanization since World War II. First, observers in the United States have tended to ignore all other relevant Canadian governmental policies and reforms, and have concentrated on the establishment of the Municipality of Metropolitan Toronto. Passing references have occasionally been made to Metropolitan Winnipeg. But there is little awareness and no discussion of other significant Canadian experiences: British Columbia's regional district, especially as it is evolving in Vancouver and Victoria, the newer regional governments in Ontario, and the regional urban communities in Quebec.

Second, the creation in the United States of a "truly metropolitan government," as exemplified by Toronto, we have held to be "unattainable." Thus we have not persevered in a close examination of the complexities of "metropolitan governance" as it involves multitudes of governments in a two-tier structure. Third, we have all too readily condoned our failure to create "truly metropolitan governments" like Toronto, because of the presumed "innate" incapacity

FOREWORD

of our constitutional system. In doing all this we have tended to overlook much in the Toronto experience that suggests relevant objectives, procedures, structures, negotiating techniques, and standards of evaluation.

Metropolitan Toronto can best be understood if it is studied in context as an indigenous Canadian institution, although one that is fully within the political traditions of the Western world. Albert Rose, a political scientist by background and Dean of the Faculty of Social Work, University of Toronto, is well qualified for this assignment. He has been a leading participant in the civic life of Metropolitan Toronto, and has long observed Toronto's experiments and considered them in the context of world-wide metropolitanism. He has told the story as only a knowledgeable Canadian could tell it, but he has also kept a constant eye on his neighbors to the south. And he knows us well.

No one can predict with any certainty how the remainder of the story will unfold. As long as the city, region, province, nation, and continent are changing, local government in Metropolitan Toronto will also be under pressure to adapt. Whether it will change further, and if so in what direction, at what rate and for whose benefit, are matters for continuing debate.

Using the levers of power afforded by a parliamentary system, leaders in Toronto and the Province of Ontario have restructured the government of this major Canadian metropolis twice in less than 20 years. Between the two principal reorganizations, its citizens and leaders have enlarged Metro's functions, debated its representational structure, argued over its performance, and worried about its future. Accordingly, the province has committed itself to further reviews of Metro's system of governance on a reasonably regular basis, presumably as long as major issues of organization, representation, and function either remain or recur.

An alternative approach to these issues may be represented by the consolidated, single-tier "uni-city" of Winnipeg, which went into operation January 1, 1972, replacing the 10-year-old two-tier Metropolitan Municipality of the City of Winnipeg and suburban municipalities. Winnipeg's new government will provide an opportunity to compare different models of metropolitan organization. Toronto and other Ontario regions are organized on the model of a two-tier federation of constituent municipalities. The proponents of amalgamation in Toronto are already using the new Winnipeg reform to provide fresh reasons for attack on Metro Toronto.

But it should be remembered that Winnipeg—like Indianapolis with its uni-government—is a relatively small and simple metropolitan community. Its order of magnitude is different from Toronto's. Thus the Winnipeg metropolis has only a half-million people, in a province that has a total population of just 900,000. Toronto has a population of 2.1 million in a province that is nearing 8 million. Perhaps, the greater adaptability and acceptability of a two-tier system permits a degree of flexibility and adjustment that may be essential in large and complicated metropolitan areas like Toronto.

Nevertheless, experience with Winnipeg's large council and small ward constituencies, the grouping of the latter into community committees, and the dual roles of regional and sub-regional representative which the Manitoba Act assigns the members of council, will undoubtedly affect the future thrust of regional, municipal, and neighborhood organization, not only in Canada but in the United States as well. Remoteness and unresponsiveness of urban governments and lack of civic participation have been problems in both nations. Accordingly, the most important feature of the Winnipeg reforms is probably the attempt to provide for a measure of municipal decentralization, in tandem with regional centralization. Will it work in the medium-size metropolis of Winnipeg? Can these objectives be achieved in huge, heterogeneous metropolitan areas? A careful reading of Canada's metropolitan experiments may be most helpful in dealing with these and other pressing questions of urban governance.

The principal motivation for creating Toronto's Metro was to correct serious inadequacies in basic municipal service facilities needed to accommodate the City's rapidly growing suburban population. Suburban financial difficulties and the desire to borrow upon the assessed valuation of the central city were also factors. As Albert Rose makes clear, housing needs and other social issues were not totally ignored in the thinking behind Metro's formation, but ideas relating to physical, fiscal, and service needs clearly dominated. Moreover these were the problems that Metro strove mightily to solve—especially during its first decade. The effort produced substantial accomplishments.

The very strength and success of these endeavors, and their consequent far-reaching influence on life in the Toronto region, have involved Metro ever more deeply in a host of controversial issues of housing, social reform, environmental concern, intergroup relations, protest movements, citizens' organizations, and other emerging new power conflicts. Like other political institutions and representatives of the "establishment," Metro has not yet fully learned how to deal with these manifold and sometimes mercurial challenges. But it is struggling.

This experience suggests that, contrary to the conclusion usually drawn by American and Canadian commentators, a metropolitan federation may need to concentrate initially on environmental problems and physical development, and grow into a viable organization before attempting to attack social problems. At the same time large numbers of people are increasingly impatient with any delay in addressing such problems as poverty, education, housing, social amenities and environmental quality. Basic questions of strategy and timing have enormous import for future developments in the United States.

In any event, the phasing of Metro's involvement in social issues was not primarily in the hands of the Metropolitan Council. Even more than in the United States, such decisions are made by a higher governmental entity—the provincial cabinet—which was responsible for Metro's creation and reorganization. It may well be that the province will decide to take direct responsibility for administering social services and regulatory functions—tasks that in other times and other places might be assigned to local government.

Already, the Province of Ontario is directly responsible for public housing, water quality control, and the assessment of real property. Moreover, it reviews many crucial local decisions and frequently modifies them or substitutes its own judgment for that of local and regional officials. Often this is done by quasi-autonomous agencies, such as the Ontario Municipal Board, which are not clearly responsible to a Minister.

Toronto has served as a model for other urban areas in Ontario. Thus the province has used the Toronto experience to help formulate new policies applicable elsewhere, and is implementing these policies by reorganizing local government in Ontario's other highly urbanized areas through the establishment of regional governments, similar in structure to Metropolitan Toronto. Already regional organizations have been created in Ottawa-Carleton, the Niagara peninsula, York County (adjacent to Metropolitan Toronto on the north), and in the cottage (second home) region of Muskoka.

All these reorganizations have been two-tier in structure. Ontario's only single-tier reorganization has been the consolidation of the two upper Lake Superior cities of Port Arthur and Fort William and their suburban fringes into the new Municipality of Thunder Bay. Now under consideration are proposals to organize regional governments on the east (Oshawa) and on the west (Peel-Halton) of Metropolitan Toronto, as well as in the Kitchener-Waterloo area, Hamilton-Burlington area, and Sudbury area in Northern Ontario. The Brant area and the rural Haldimand-Norfolk area are still being studied.

For the past five years policy decisions have been progressing simultaneously both with respect to regional and provincial economic development, and with respect to regional governmental reorganization. These activities have centered in the province's Department of the Treasury and Economic Development, and the Department of Municipal Affairs, respectively. Developments in each program will have a decisive effect on the objectives and behavior of the other. Because there has been little outward evidence of provincial coordination of the two programs, local and regional officials have been confused and apprehensive. (As Americans, we are of course already aware that "outward evidence" may tell us little about what is happening in a system of Responsible Government.)

Now, however, the two programs are more likely to be coordinated as a result of the proposed transfer of the Department of Municipal Affairs into a new "Super-Ministry" of Finance and Intergovernmental Affairs. This change will put the two programs under the same minister, Darcy McKeough, now Treasurer and Minister of Economics, who was Minister of Municipal Affairs when most of the current regionalization of local government was being implemented.

What will happen to Canadian local government in the next decade? Can the province allow local governments the luxury of making their own mistakes, even after they have been reorganized into regional municipalities? There will inevitably be great pressure on the province to exercise directly whatever powers may be necessary to achieve the announced objective of the Design for the Development of a Toronto-Centered Region: "(1) . . . a more even distribution

FOREWORD

of people in Ontario, (2) the improvement of the quality of life for those people, and (3) better use of the natural environment." Alternatively, or perhaps jointly with direct provincial administration, there could be an extension and tightening of central tutelage over local administrators.

Possibly the most significant aspect of the new super-ministry is the inclusion of the phrase "Intergovernmental Affairs" in its title. In the United States, at least, it is becoming apparent that the governance of large metropolitan areas is a complicated exercise in intergovernmental relations. The same forces that lead to the involvement of federal, state, and local governments in the affairs of the metropolis are also operating in Canada. The way these influences should be structured and interrelated is under debate. Clearly, however, the role of local government in planning, making policy, and administering the community and the metropolis depends partly upon the ability of local officials to command and to be worthy of consultation by and collaboration with their regional, provincial and federal governmental partners.

Will the reorganization of local government into regional municipalities enhance the stature of local officials and increase their ability to participate in intergovernmental affairs? If so, a major consequence of the reform may be a political strengthening of local government. Will reorganization also improve the capacity of the region, the province, and the federal government to cope more effectively with the urban demands of the 1970's? If so, then regionalization must be viewed as an even more significant and complicated affair.

Thus, as Albert Rose demonstrates, Metropolitan Toronto is not merely a group of local governments that have been federated in order to meet regional needs more effectively than before. It also represents a major new sub-provincial locus of activity, decision-making, and power. The new locus was created by a devolution of power from the province. Such relationships, however, are never static. Thus it remains to be seen whether the regionalization of local government will enhance its prestige and influence, and lead to further shifts in responsibility.

Metro deserves to be examined for at least two reasons. First, it is a straightforward effort to weld together in a large urban area the fragmented local governmental jurisdictions that have common problems and need each other's support. Second, urban governance is not only a local or regional phenomenon, it is also part of a state and national complex. Accordingly the Province of Ontario affords a classic demonstration of the pivotal position that state (provincial) governments obviously can, probably should, and in some instances actually do occupy in the urban governance enterprise. Creation of a metropolitan government represents a significant redeployment of state (provincial) power in the region.

Herein lies the most important single lesson for the major urban states in the United States of America, as well as for our federal government. How soon they will learn this, and with what necessary modifications, remains to be seen. Minnesota, for example, has already acted with remarkable foresight in creating the Metropolitan Council of the Twin Cities region. In 1971 California seemingly came within a hair's breadth of creating an analogous environmental and regional planning agency for the San Francisco Bay Area. For some time the federal government has been vigorously promoting regional councils of governments (COG's), which nevertheless remain pale wraiths when compared with Toronto's Metro. This contrast helps emphasize the potential lessons we can learn from what is going on in Toronto and Ontario.

Looking beyond Canada and the United States, the study and attempted restructuring of urban governmental institutions are seen as a thriving enterprise in many parts of the world. In an effort to analyze and evaluate that experience, the Institute of Governmental Studies has commissioned many research ventures in various metropolitan regions. The first fruit of this effort was Donald L. Foley's recent book on the government of London. With his volume on Toronto, Albert Rose has made an important contribution to what hopefully will be a many-volume series on the problems of organizing urban governance in selected metropolitan regions.

STANLEY SCOTT	VICTOR JONES
Editor, Lane Fund	*Coeditor, Lane Studies*
Publications	*in Regional Government*

Berkeley, California
March 1972

CONTENTS

Foreword vii

Preface xxi

Chapter I
INTRODUCTION 1
Origin and Growth 1
A Financial and Commercial Center 3
Population Composition and Change 4
Early Concern with Planning and Housing 6
Housing: World War II and After 10
Regional Planning and Metropolitan Reorganization 11

Chapter II
PRELUDE TO METROPOLITAN GOVERNMENT 14
Formidable Urban Difficulties 14
A Call for Metropolitan Government 16
Further Study of the "Metropolitan Problem" 17
Toronto's Request for Amalgamation 20
The Ontario Municipal Board and the Metro Bill 21

Chapter III
METROPOLITAN GOVERNMENT IN TORONTO: THE FIRST SIX YEARS, 1954–1959 23
Auguries of Success 23
The Functions of Metro 25
Functions of the Area Municipalities 26
Coming into Being 27
The Approach to Urban Growth and Development 28
   Housing and Planning Problems Acknowledged 28
   Extension of Physical Services Emphasized 29
   In Summary 30
First Review of the Metropolitan Form of Government, 1957–1958 32

CONTENTS

Representation: First Point of Attack	33
Chairman Gardiner's Submission	33
The Metropolitan Council's Submission	35
Statements of the Metro Commissioners	37
Report of the Metropolitan Toronto Commission of Inquiry	40
Support for Federation	41
Representation and the City-Suburban Split	42
Role of the Executive Committee	43
The Metro Chairman	43

Chapter IV
CITY AND REGIONAL PLANNING, 1954–1959 — 45

The Metropolitan Toronto Planning Board	46
Early Difficulties	47
The Role of Regional Planning: Ambiguous Expectations	48
Assistance Instead of Control	49
Planning Problems in the City of Toronto	50
The Draft Official Plan of the Metropolitan Toronto Planning Area, 1959	53
Contents of the Plan	54
Additional Plans	56
Eight Underlying Principles	57
Local Planning Boards in Metropolitan Toronto	60
The Roles of the Local Boards	61
The Special Position of the City	63

Chapter V
HOUSING AND URBAN RENEWAL, 1954–1962 — 65

Slum Clearance and Public Housing: Whose Responsibility?	66
A Federal-Provincial Authority for Metro	67
The Case of Lawrence Heights	69
A Threat to a Way of Life	70
Anticipated Impact of Service Needs	71
The Chairman's Support	71
Completion and Subsequent Experience	72
Lessons of Lawrence Heights, and Moves Toward a Metropolitan Program	73
Staff Inadequacies and Appointed Advisors	74
Housing Policy: A Multilevel Program	74
Suburban Opposition	75
A Dismal Record and Its Causes	77
Toward a Single Housing Authority	78

Chapter VI
METROPOLITAN GOVERNMENT IN TORONTO: THE SECOND SIX YEARS, 1960–1965 — 80

New Studies of Metropolitan Reorganization	83

Report by the Metropolitan Committee of Heads of Departments   84
Report on the Metropolitan Toronto System of Government   86
Major Political Developments in Metro, 1962–1965   88

Chapter VII

THE REORGANIZATION OF METROPOLITAN TORONTO, 1963–1967   97

The Major Issues in Metropolitan Reorganization   98
  The Nature of the Reform   98
  Inequities in Representation and Additional New Problems   98
  Inadequacies in Welfare Administration   100
  A Renewed Drive for Amalgamation   102
  A Royal Commission   102
Submissions to the Royal Commission on Metropolitan Toronto   103
Recommendations of the Royal Commission   105
  Reorganization of Metropolitan Toronto   105
  The Metropolitan Council and Proposed City Councils 106
  Metro's Boundaries and the Fringe Areas   107
  Metropolitan Planning   107
  Metropolitan and Local Services   109
  Education   110
The Statement by the Prime Minister of Ontario   113
  One City and Five Boroughs   114
  Composition of the Metro Council   114
  The Next Review   118
Metropolitan and Local Services   119
Education   119
1966: Year of Transition   121
Bill 81: The New Municipality of Metropolitan Toronto Act   122

Chapter VIII

REGIONAL PLANNING AND PROVINCIAL POLICY ON REGIONAL GOVERNMENT   124

The Future: Social Problems Loom   124
The Past: A Decade of Physical Development   126
  Water Supply   127
  Water Pollution Control (Sewage Disposal)   128
  Transportation   129
The Official Plan of the Metropolitan Toronto Planning Area   130
Trouble in Transportation Planning: The Case of the Spadina Expressway   134
  Initial Plans and the Start of Construction   134
  Hints of Future Problems   136
  "A Plate of Spaghetti" and Housing Demolitions   136
  "Stop Spadina, Save Our City . . ."   137
  Metro Halts Construction   138

The Municipal Board Supports the Project	138
"A Good Place to Stop"	139
A Profound Shock	139
Four Main Issues	140
Wide Ramifications	143
Provincial Policy on Regional Government	144
A Series of Regional Studies	144
Ontario's Policy and Metro's Future	145
Guides for Regionalization	146
Design for Development: The Toronto-Centered Region	148
Three Zones	149
Development Principles	150
Goals for the Region	150
Decentralize, If Possible	151
Hemming in Metro? Stimulating Growth Elsewhere?	152
Regionalization Throughout Ontario	154

Chapter IX
CONCLUSIONS: THE ISSUES OF 1970 AND AFTER   155

The Role of the Metro Chairmanship	157
The First Chairman: What Metro Needed	157
The Second Chairman: New Forces Impinge	157
Emphasis Still Physical and Fiscal	159
Area-wide Election or Choice by Council?	159
The Third Chairman	160
The Boundaries of Metro, and Geographic Scope of the Planning Area	162
The New Toronto	163
Metro-Ontario Conflict?	164
An Expanding Metro: F. G. Gardiner	165
A Unitary Versus a Two-Tier Concept of Metropolitan Government	167
Governmental Interaction with Neighborhood Groups	167
Urban Renewal	168
Traditional Citizens' Organizations	168
A New Force: Neighborhood Groups	169
Financing Local Action	170
Formidable Forces	171
The Entrance of Political Parties?	171
Early Efforts	172
The 1969 Election	172
The Outcome Undecided	174
Deficient Machinery for Setting Future Priorities	174
Policy Ad Hoc-ery	175
Rapid Rotation and Lack of Mutual Concern	176
The City's Position Within Metro	177
Toronto's Comparative Decline	177
The City's Turn for Help	178

A Success: Reconstruction of Toronto's Educational Plant	179
Trouble in the Sewers	179
Urban Renewal: An Unclear Future	180
Concluding Comments	181
Eyes on Toronto	181
The Metropolitan Concept: From the Outside Inwards	181
An Equal Deal for the City	182
A "Have-Not" Municipality	183
The Quality of Life	184

Glossary   185

Notes   189

Index   197

Tables

1. Population Changes in the City and Its Five Largest Suburbs, 1946–1950	18
2. Development of Planning Activities, Metropolitan Toronto Planning Area, 1953 and 1957	51
3. Population Distribution by Municipal Units, 1941–1971	115

Maps

1. Toronto's Place on the Continent	91
2. A Century Ago: 1867	92
3. The End of Annexation: 1914	92
4. The First Reorganization: 1953	93
5. The Second Reorganization: 1967	93
6. Metropolitan Toronto Planning Area: 1953–1970	94
7. Metro Expressways Existing and Proposed: 1959	95
8. Spadina Expressway: A Good Place to Stop?	96

PREFACE

THE INITIATION of a federal system of metropolitan government in the Greater Toronto area on January 1, 1954 aroused great interest, not only in North America but throughout the world. As a consequence, Metro Toronto has been figuratively under a microscope since its very beginning. Much has been written concerning its growth and development, its strengths and weaknesses, and its probable future directions.

It may be surprising that this book is the first comprehensive analysis of Metro written by a native of Toronto. Until very recently the study of local government did not attract the interest of many scholars within Canadian universities, particularly the University of Toronto. Outstanding exceptions include John Dakin and the late James Milner. An Institute of Local Government has been in operation at Queen's University in Kingston, Ontario, for the past two decades however, and scholars at Carleton University in Ottawa have devoted considerable attention to local government.

This book is the work of a native son who assembled data as a participant observer. It introduces some unique biases that should be admitted candidly at the outset. An interested person who has spent most of the past half-century in the City of Toronto cannot regard with detachment the changes in its government and its fantastic rate of urbanization. It is not merely that one sometimes remembers the past with nostalgia. One cannot help asking whether changes that have apparently destroyed the past—historical buildings, distinguished architecture, traditional neighborhoods, and examples of successful neighborhood development—have really been necessary,

PREFACE

even though Toronto must now accommodate a population three or four times as large as it was 35 years ago.

The research role of participant observer introduces other biases. The writer has been involved for 25 years in efforts to improve the system of government in the Metropolitan Area of Toronto. In 1948 he was appointed Research Director for the Committee on Metropolitan Problems of the Civic Advisory Council; and he compiled the reports of the council concerning possible solutions to the problems of metropolitan growth in Toronto. These were published between 1948 and 1951. In 1952 he was made Chairman of the Community Planning Association of Canada (Ontario Division). In 1955 he was appointed to the Metropolitan Toronto Housing Authority, the first and most substantial metropolitan-wide housing authority in Canada, and served on that body as Vice-Chairman for nearly eight years. In 1964, with the formation of the Ontario Housing Corporation, which incorporated the Metropolitan Toronto Housing Authority, the writer became a member of the Board of Directors of this new provincial corporation and continues to occupy that position. During this period, public housing in Metropolitan Toronto has expanded from less than 3,500 to nearly 25,000 dwelling units.

These statements are made to suggest that a participant can perhaps be too close to the day-to-day operation of the phenomenon he is observing to be completely objective. The scholar from outside the community, who interviews the major participants in the drama and then returns home to write his analysis, can sometimes be more impartial, though it is doubtful whether he could be more knowledgeable. A participant observer may also become rigid in his views and unwilling to reexamine his positions on major issues, even though these may be opposed by responsible politicians, scholars, planners, and newsmen.

It is essential to emphasize, therefore, that in the years before the creation of Metropolitan Toronto this writer believed that a federal system of government, such as the form deemed appropriate for Toronto by the Government of Ontario, was a far better solution to the growth and development problems of this metropolitan area than a unitary system.

For at least the past 20 years, the City of Toronto has formally taken the position that "amalgamation" of the 13 traditional municipalities of Greater Toronto was the preferred solution for the dilemmas of metropolitan sprawl and the insufficiencies of municipal services in a rapidly expanding metropolis. The writer has believed in the utility of a federation of municipal governments despite the criticism of certain associates, and their insistence that one large city divided into appropriate wards and directed by a Mayor elected by the voters, in a population of more than two million, would afford the only intelligent solution.

Despite his general approval of the form of metropolitan government and its application during the past 18 years, the writer is not uncritical of certain important aspects of Metropolitan Toronto's experience. In fact the two major themes of this book are fundamental criticisms of the manner in which the Metropolitan Council has functioned. The first is that physical planning and physical development have dominated the program, budgeting and financing of metropolitan-wide activities in the Toronto area to the neglect of social planning, social development, and the social and human concerns of a substantial proportion of its residents. This contention has been the subject of several papers and addresses by the writer.[1]

For more than 12 years Metropolitan Toronto disappointed a great many of its supporters by its almost exclusive preoccupation with the extension of physical hardware designed to open up vast rural areas to urban settlement. Thus the tenth annual report on Metropolitan Toronto published in 1963 was almost entirely concerned with water supply, sewage disposal, problems in private and public transportation, and physical planning.[2]

Even now in the early 1970's it still seems that physical planning is much easier to accomplish than social planning, and that the Metropolitan Council would much rather continue to demand an expansion of its territory than devote itself to improving the social facilities and human resources of its substantial downtown core, essentially the entire 35 square miles of the pre-1967 City of Toronto.

The second major theme is that the central city in the Metropolitan Area of Toronto may now be experiencing serious neglect at the hands of the Metropolitan Council. This despite the undeniable fact that City residents have paid dearly in supporting the growth of Metropolitan Toronto. The "metro concept," as explained by the first Chairman of the Metropolitan Council, Mr. F. G. Gardiner, assumed that all the residents of a metropolitan area, whether in the central city or in the fringe areas and semi-rural suburban municipalities, must combine their resources to ensure the survival and healthy development of the whole metropolis.

Initially, the City of Toronto fought vigorously against federation, especially when it was clear that the City would contribute more than 60 percent of the taxable assessment of real property in the entire area. Before 1954 Toronto was a relatively affluent municipality, but once the federal system was established its councillors had no choice but to participate, and its residents had no choice but to pay. The participation and the payment were willingly accomplished because it was expected that when the time came for help to flow from the expanding and increasingly affluent suburban municipalities back to the hard-pressed central city, a similar sense of responsibility would prevail.

In the analysis that follows, the writer will argue that the metro concept is not working in reverse. The City of Toronto is in grave danger of becoming a deprived municipality—not so much with respect to its commercial image, nor the face it presents to visitors and tourists, but with respect to the quality of the environment provided for its less affluent citizens. True, the City continues to go forward in a vast building program under private auspices. But as a consequence, poor, low-income families and single elderly persons are being denied the possibility of independent living in the costly areas beyond the City boundaries, and they are even in great danger of being denied access to the central city itself.

Any comprehensive analysis of Toronto's 18 years of metropolitan government owes a great deal to other students of the subject. The first important article the writer read was by Winston W. Crouch.[3] The pioneer researchers who visited Metropolitan Toronto and wrote earlier studies of major importance include John G. Grumm[4] and Frank Smallwood. Smallwood spent many months in Toronto in 1963 in order to publish his analysis of a study sponsored by the Bureau of Municipal Research. The writer had the privilege of meeting Grumm only briefly, but he had many contacts and discussions with Smallwood, whose contribution to the subject is acknowledged.[5] The writer was also influenced by the work of Eric Hardy and the late James B. Milner. James Milner was one of Canada's pioneers in the teaching and practice of community planning law, and his contributions to the development of the administration of

PREFACE

housing and planning procedures in Metropolitan Toronto, and indeed throughout Canada, are sorely missed. In later years the writer came to know Harold Kaplan, whose book remains the definitive study of the subject.[6]

It is appropriate and essential to express appreciation to Victor Jones and to Stanley Scott of the Institute of Governmental Studies at the University of California, the instigators of this book. It was during a sabbatical year in 1962–1963, spent on the campus of the University of California, Berkeley, that the author was encouraged by these scholars to continue his research and writing program concerning Metropolitan Toronto. In 1966 he was invited to participate in the Franklin K. Lane Project, and this book is one of a number generated by that activity. In the several drafts that have been prepared, the author has been assisted by many persons, and he would like to thank in particular his secretary, Mrs. Gwen Collins, who typed the manuscript and made many invaluable editorial suggestions.

A. R.

Toronto, Ontario
January 1972

CHAPTER I

INTRODUCTION

IN 1970, more than two million persons resided within the political boundaries of Metropolitan Toronto. Only half that many lived there on January 1, 1954, when the original 13 constituent municipalities were brought together to form the Municipality of Metropolitan Toronto. About one-quarter of the 1970 population, 450,000 persons, had not yet been born. Another estimated 500,000 have come from abroad since the inauguration of a metropolitan form of government. Another large group would be described by social scientists as "in-migrants," usually native-born or long-resident Canadians who have moved to the urban center from small towns or rural areas in Ontario, or from relatively underdeveloped parts of Canada, particularly from the Maritime Provinces.

Whatever the combination of factors, the total impact is of tremendous importance to Toronto. Perhaps it is because so many people are new residents, that few Torontonians appear to be seriously concerned with their local government, its progress during the previous 18 years, or its new form in the revised political framework that came into being on January 1, 1967. It seems that fewer and fewer residents feel an allegiance to one of the local municipalities. Many residents are indifferent whether the metropolis is composed of one huge city, four cities and a metropolitan government, or the present pattern of five boroughs, one city, and the Municipality of Metropolitan Toronto.

ORIGIN AND GROWTH

It was not always so. Toronto, the capital of the Province of Ontario and the second largest city in Canada, derived its name from the one given by the Huron Indians to their country; it probably means "land of plenty." As early as 1750, the French had established a fortified trading post on the present site of Toronto. In 1787 the British purchased the site from the Mississauga Indians, and in 1793 settlement began, with its establishment as the capital of the newly formed Province of Upper Canada. The new capital, renamed York, was captured by American forces during War of 1812, and the parliament buildings and archives were burned in 1813. By 1820 the residents numbered about 1,250, but as a result of large-scale immigration the population grew rapidly and commerce became more important than administrative functions.

In 1834 the Town of "muddy" York resumed its original name and was incorporated as the City of Toronto, with a population of more than 9,000. In the second half of the nineteenth century this city became the leading financial, commercial, and manufacturing center of the Province of Ontario (formed in 1867), and it gradually became the focal point of the emerging railway network. The Census of 1901 listed the City's population at about 208,000. Immigration continued from the 1880's until the beginning of World War I in 1914, by which time the City had grown to 400,000.

Until 1920 most of those who settled in Toronto chose to reside within the City boundaries. Particularly in the years between 1880 and 1910, a series of villages and small towns had developed adjacent to the incorporated city, and the City of Toronto expanded considerably through a number of formal annexations. By 1920, however, this process was almost complete; although several new municipalities were created and began to expand during the 1920's, the process of annexation fell into disuse.[1]

On one hand, the City of Toronto and its administration were fully occupied in digesting the areas incorporated within its boundaries by annexation. Moreover, the persons who deliberately chose to move into such new municipalities as the Town of Leaside and the Village of Forest Hill did so to create the kind of local municipal environment they sought, and so they resisted further encroachment by the central city. Their strength and the weakness of the City created a local system that, by the beginning of World War II, included the City and 12 municipalities adjacent to or surrounding it. The total metropolitan population revealed in the Census of 1941 was 892,179. Of these, 73.5 percent resided within the boundaries of the City proper.²

Almost from the beginning of its settlement, the City of Toronto gained an unfortunate reputation, which has survived up to the present. For the most part, the earliest settlers were British citizens sent from England to develop the civil and military administration of Upper Canada. They were soon joined by Anglican clergymen, businessmen, and merchants. They constituted a social and political elite which by the 1830's was regarded by some members of the community as a representation of all that was undesirable in the British colonial administration of that day.

Newcomers of lower social classes and those who were not of the civil and ecclesiastical establishment worked hard throughout this period to achieve a system of responsible self-government for the British colonies of North America. In both Upper and Lower Canada (Quebec) abortive rebellions erupted in 1837–1838, but they did lead to a full-scale investigation of the situation in these colonies by Lord Durham, who recommended in his report of 1840 the union of Upper and Lower Canada. The Union Act was passed by the British Parliament in 1841. In the midst of these developments Toronto was for many Canadians the center of British power and exclusiveness, as well as the center of economic power and domination over the hinterland. This combination of apparent attributes caused the City to be seen as a smug, Anglo-Saxon, Anglo-dominated center of political and economic power, and despite the substantial immigration from Europe in the late nineteenth and early twentieth centuries, this notion persisted until the end of World War II.

A FINANCIAL AND COMMERCIAL CENTER

Toronto never became a great industrial center. Although many manufacturing enterprises developed in the course of time, the emerging metropolis has been primarily a center of financial enterprise and commercial distribution rather than a center for the production of goods. Paradoxically, the three most powerful banks (the Royal Bank of Canada, the Bank of Montreal, and the Bank of Nova Scotia) among the ten chartered banks in Canada did not have their headquarters in Toronto. Yet Toronto rivaled Montreal and to some extent, as in the case of the development of its Stock Exchange, has surpassed it in economic importance.

Although Montreal has always exceeded Toronto in population, both within the central city and the wider metropolitan area, Toronto's economic importance to Canada must not be underestimated. Income declared for personal income tax purposes in Toronto in 1965 was $4.3 billion; in Montreal the comparable figure was $3.8 billion. The figures for 1968 were, Toronto $6.047 billion, Montreal $4.972 billion.[3] It is clear from federal data that the individual and corporate residents of the Metropolitan Area of Toronto contribute a substantial percentage of the total federal revenues.

One significant consequence of Toronto's rise as a commercial and financial center has been the perpetuation of its image as a proud, exclusive, and unfriendly urban area. For the past century, at least, it has been known in many editorial pages and public halls throughout the nation as "Hogtown." While this can be dismissed as an indication of the traditional rural debtor psychology, nevertheless this general opinion of Toronto has persisted, despite fundamental changes in the composition of its population.

POPULATION COMPOSITION AND CHANGE

Questions concerning religion, nationality, or ethnic origin have been included in the Canadian Census to the present day, in part because French Canadians have insisted on this method of identifying their group, and in part because Jewish Canadians have been equally interested in knowing their number. These census data for 1941 show that 81 percent of the population of Greater Toronto traced their origins to the British Isles. Nearly 80 percent of the residents of Toronto at that time considered themselves to be Protestant (various denominations of Protestantism are published in the census material); the Roman Catholic population was a mere 14.2 percent, and the Jewish population approximately 5.8 percent.[4]

By 1951, following five years of significant immigration, these patterns had begun to change. In 1951 Torontonians numbered 1,117,470. The percentage indicating that they were of British origin had dropped to 69.[5] Moreover, there had been an important increase in the number of persons who gave Italian or German as their nationality. The denominational pattern had begun to change as a

INTRODUCTION

result of immigration, but the proportion who said that they were Roman Catholics did not yet exceed 20 percent. Although the number of Jewish persons had increased by some 7,000, the percentage was relatively stable.

The census data published as a result of the enumeration of June 1961 revealed the full force of the immigration subsequent to 1946.[6] Within the City of Toronto the proportion of residents of British origin had dropped to 52 percent. On the other hand, those of Central or Southern European origin had increased to more than 35 percent. The figures collected on the "period of immigration" indicated that 196,000 residents of the city proper had come to Canada since the end of World War II. Similar trends occurred within the metropolitan area as a whole, but were not as marked as those in the central city. This was because many newcomers came first to the urban core, while many of the longer-term residents of British origin and Protestant affiliation moved to the new suburban areas adjacent to the City. Still, for the metropolitan area as a whole, the proportion of British origin was only 60 percent in 1961. Since 1951 the Italian segment had grown from 28,000 to 140,000; those of German origin from 19,000 to 80,000; those of Polish origin from 27,000 to 59,000; and a mixture of nationalities listed as "Other Europeans" —Hungarian, Portuguese, and so on—had grown from 41,000 to 190,000.[7]

Changes in the patterns of religious affiliation were even more striking. By 1961 the City's population who considered themselves Protestants had dropped to 62 percent, while the Roman Catholic percentage had increased to 34.7 in the City, and to 27 in the Metro area. The Jewish population had failed to keep pace with the rapid increase in Metro's population, although its proportion was still a little more than 5 percent of the total. Other religious denominations had appeared in Toronto after 1946, notably the Buddhists, but none of these were of numerical significance.

Although Toronto has continued to be regarded with grave suspicion by the residents of other parts of Canada, particularly western Canada and small towns and rural areas in central and eastern Canada, it is obvious that the Toronto of 1948–1953 (when the great debate concerning the establishment of metropolitan government was waged) was not the Toronto of the nineteenth century, or even that of the first third of the twentieth century. Changes in national origin and religious affiliation are perhaps the most identifiable part of the basic changes that have occurred.

More fundamentally, Toronto is no longer simply a central city, which in fact, lost population between 1931 and 1951. It is also a rapidly expanding urban agglomeration that increases in total population by about 50,000 per year. The great debate over political organization in the early post-war years was not, therefore, a debate concerning the people and the patterns of the past, but took place before the arrival of the newcomers and the development of the new patterns that emerged during the 1950's and 1960's.

EARLY CONCERN WITH PLANNING AND HOUSING

If the national image of Toronto was that of a self-satisfied community based upon wealth and exclusiveness, the residents of the City have failed to see the appropriateness of these views. As we have seen, in the early part of the nineteenth century the City was not only the center of British colonial administration and of economic power based upon privilege but also, in equal measure, the center of resistance to traditional colonial administration and advancement derived from birth and position. Although Toronto expanded rapidly during the second half of the nineteenth century, there is some evidence that its citizens were by no means satisfied with the quality of its urban development. Thus for example, Professor Masters has noted that in 1873 serious concern was expressed over the unhealthy conditions existing in certain areas, partly as a result of the prevalence of outside toilets adjacent to wells supplying water.[8] At the time, the City had a population of about 60,000.

By the turn of the century Toronto was a city of more than 200,000. As expansion began on the City's outer fringes during the next 25 years, the deterioration of the urban core began to be recognized. For example, in October 1909 one of the principal speakers at the Canadian Conference of Charities and Corrections strongly condemned existing conditions in Toronto, where the conference was held. Her comments might have been made at any time during the 1950's and 1960's:

We are told that we have no slum district in Toronto and know nothing about the tenement house; but we do know that there is a great deal of overcrowding, and the effect on the children is something that we will realize better later on. I fear that Toronto is breeding a class of criminals that will keep it busy to take care of in the next few years, if nothing is done. . . . Children rooming with parents is a serious evil. I could tell you of scores of cases where father, mother, and children sleep in one room. . . . In these homes there is a lack of proper sanitary conditions. . . . How can children grow up decently in homes like these! [9]

Public concern with these problems was indicated by the organization of the Bureau of Municipal Research in June 1914. In its first year the bureau published two bulletins on housing conditions. In December 1918, after two years of study, the bureau published a substantial and comprehensive report on a major downtown area known as "The Ward." [10] This report provided a revealing picture of physical deterioration in an urban environment, and of the consequent social, hygienic, and economic effects upon the residents and the City as a whole. One of the appendices was entitled "Slum Conditions of Toronto" and consisted of the concluding chapter of a report by the Medical Officer of Health in July 1911. This is also expressed in language that is still appropriate today.

It must be apparent that we are confronted with the existence of congested districts of insanitary, overcrowded dwellings, which are a menace to public health, affording hot-beds for germination and dissemination of disease, vice, and crime. Municipality after municipality has been called upon to pay the penalty for neglected slums. The portion of this paid by human life and human suffering cannot be as easily computed as the tax for hospital, prison, and reformatory maintenance. We are more willing to supply this accommodation than to endeavour to stamp out the gardens of vice and crime and the very hot-beds of disease. What we want is prevention, not cure. We can scarcely hope for people to rise much above their environments.[11]

In its annual reports the bureau often noted that its publication on "The Ward" had made seemingly little impact on the housing situation. During the prosperous years of the 1920's the bureau continued to advocate the appointment of an advisory planning commission or the creation of a City Planning Board as the only way to achieve a number of objectives, including slum clearance.[12]

The long years of economic depression after 1929 slowed down the "flight to the suburbs," and all but two of the 12 suburban municipalities fell into default on their debenture obligations. Even a severe depression—and suburban difficulties—did not lessen the concern of many influential citizens and organizations with living conditions in the center of the City. Indeed, the fact that larger numbers of families were forced, through sheer economic necessity, to crowd together in the most inadequate housing inspired greater effort towards positive action.

The City of Toronto celebrated its centennial in 1934. In proposing a toast to the City of Toronto at a major centennial function, the Lieutenant-Governor of Ontario, Dr. Herbert A. Bruce, delivered an address that led directly to one of the most comprehensive and significant investigations of urban housing conditions in Canada. He pointed out in part:

Toronto is a city enviably situated, a city of fine residential areas, of beautiful buildings, of high standards of citizenship. That is how we see it; but I fear, in all candour one must confess that this city in common with every large city has acquired inevitable "slum districts."

These areas of misery and degradation exert an unhappy environmental influence upon many of our citizens. You will probably say: "But Toronto has few such areas and they are not of great extent!" I say, and I think you will agree with me, that Toronto wants *none* of them and that the Toronto of the future which we would like to contemplate *will* have none of them.[13]

These remarks made a profound impression. Shortly thereafter a committee was appointed to enquire into housing conditions in the City of Toronto, with special reference to the quality of accommodation, rents paid by tenants, and environmental conditions. The committee's appointment was a major indication of one of the attributes of Toronto that belie its image throughout other parts of Canada. Its citizens have always been sufficiently concerned to band together in what is now called "citizen participation in urban renewal." The Lieutenant-Governor's Committee to Study Housing Conditions in Toronto, which reported late in 1934, did in fact identify the most seriously deteriorated neighborhoods and larger areas within the City proper, an identification that helped guide public policy for the next 30 years.[14]

Until the Bruce Report was published, neither the federal government nor the provinces had displayed serious interest in the possibilities of public housing as a social or economic measure.* Federal

---

* The first federal legislation in the field of housing was not passed until 1935, and the first National Housing Act was not passed until 1938. Provincial legislation in housing matters as such did not exist, except in Nova Scotia.

housing legislation did not exist. Some housing had been constructed under the auspices of provincial governments for two or three years following the First World War, but interest waned after 1921. The City of Halifax was involved in a housing program after the disastrous explosion of 1917.* There is little else to relate.

After 1934 this void began to be filled, at first slowly and then more rapidly. In 1935 the Parliament of Canada passed the Dominion Housing Act, a part of the so-called "Canadian New Deal." In fact, it was the only piece of major social legislation of that program not ultimately adjudged ultra vires, beyond the legal power of the federal government of Canada.† In 1936 the Toronto City Council passed a standard-of-housing by-law, which became the model for certain local by-laws (codes or ordinances) in other cities in Canada and in the United States, notably Baltimore.[15] In the same year, the City Council created an advisory committee on housing matters, and in September 1937 this committee presented a "housing program" calling for the replacement on the site of 4,000 obsolete dwellings. Within the Department of Public Welfare of the City of Toronto, a Housing Division was created in 1938.[16]

Moreover, in that year the first National Housing Act was passed by the federal parliament. Although this legislation was inhibited by the outbreak of war in September 1939, the act did contain the seeds of much housing legislation passed in the post-war period. It included provisions for mortgage loans to enable individuals to buy their own homes; one section permitted local municipalities to participate with the federal government in rudimentary programs of

---

* The collision of two ships in Halifax harbor in April 1917 led to an explosion that leveled a substantial portion of the waterfront area. On part of the devastated area some of the first public housing, which exists today, was built by action of the governments of Canada and Nova Scotia, to provide housing for persons who had lost their homes in the explosion.

† In terms of constitutional responsibilities, housing has been interpreted by the Judicial Committee of the Privy Council in Westminster to be a responsibility of the provincial governments, by virtue of their power over "property and civil rights" in Section 92 of the British North America Act of 1867. The local governments in Canada are generally considered to be "the creatures of the provinces" and thus receive their power over housing and urban development through provincial legislation. In 1935, however, the Dominion Housing Act was ruled within the powers of the Government of Canada by virtue of the latter's responsibility for "peace, order and good government" in Section 91 of the BNA Act.

slum clearance and public housing; and it included other sections that were expanded in 1944 and thereafter to give Canada the broad federal-provincial housing legislation it has now enjoyed for more than 20 years.

HOUSING: WORLD WAR II AND AFTER

Although the Second World War put a damper upon normal private house building activity, and also curtailed certain intergovernmental housing programs, the pressure within the City of Toronto for action with respect to slum clearance and public housing activities did not cease. Many citizens in a large number of voluntary associations continued to urge local government participation in those programs that were still feasible in the midst of a major war. In particular, a housing shortage of crisis proportions was evident by 1941, and the pressures to create "housing for war workers" resulted in a federal-municipal program. Interestingly enough, these houses were built (in three groups of 200 dwellings each) not in the City of Toronto but in the suburban municipalities to the west, northwest, and east of the city proper. The Commissioners of Building and Welfare and the City Solicitor also reported in 1941 that 17,000 families were "doubled up"; a year later the Commissioner of Buildings and the City Solicitor reported that there was a need for 2,000 new dwelling units annually but that only 550 had been created in 1941.

In the field of physical planning, more than 20 years of effort by the Bureau of Municipal Research, the Board of Trade (a chamber of commerce), and many voluntary citizens' organizations were rewarded by the establishment of the City of Toronto Planning Board on June 1, 1942. In its second annual report, December 31, 1943, the City Planning Board issued a "Master Plan for the City of Toronto and Environs," in which three blighted residential areas were designated for redevelopment.[17] An intensive study was made of one of these areas in east central Toronto, and in 1947 this became the site of Regent Park North, the first redevelopment project in a major Canadian metropolis.

A year later, in its third report, the board included an analysis and plans for three slum clearance and redevelopment projects. During the previous year more than 300,000 persons visited a major display, one of the first of its kind to be held in the City of Toronto,

INTRODUCTION

at which the City Planning Board and its private planning consultants presented models of certain aspects of the City's future, which they visualized during the first decade or two following the assumed victorious end of the war.

REGIONAL PLANNING AND METROPOLITAN REORGANIZATION

The broader aspects of regional planning were not neglected during these early years. As early as 1923 the Government of Ontario circularized the municipalities of Greater Toronto concerning the passage of a "Toronto Metropolitan Act" which would have created the "Metropolitan District of Toronto" embracing the City and suburban municipalities within the County of York.[18] The new district was to be provided with all the powers given to county councils. In the early 1930's the County of York set up a Metropolitan Area Committee, which submitted an interim report in January 1934, but appears to have been disbanded thereafter.

A year later the newly formed Department of Municipal Affairs of the Province of Ontario commissioned Professor A. F. W. Plumptre of the University of Toronto to prepare a report on the metropolitan area. This report was submitted in June 1935.[19] Three years later the provincial department set up "The Committee for the Study of Municipal and Related Problems in Toronto and Its Neighbouring Municipalities." The committee canvassed the municipalities by questionnaire and collected a great amount of detailed information. Its work appears to have been interrupted by the onset of the war, and the study was not resumed in the post-war period.

Thus in both housing and planning, a good deal of background had been laid for the vigorous discussion that began before the war was formally ended in August 1945 and continued without cease for nearly a decade. Clearly the creation of a metropolitan form of government in the Toronto area was not an accident, but was the culmination of a long history of citizen and official concern with generally poor housing conditions, with grossly inadequate housing for families of low income, with inadequate attention to physical planning, and with an almost total absence of federal and provincial legislation in these fields.*

* Until recently the federal government has been extremely reluctant to move aggressively in the field of housing and urban development, primarily because

Although a good deal was accomplished in the first five years following World War II, undoubtedly one motivating factor in the creation of the Municipality of Metropolitan Toronto was the hope that this form of regional government would go far towards meeting the housing needs of a metropolitan population, and do so in a more adequately planned environment.

Before the formation of Metro Toronto in 1953, the existing structure of government in the metropolitan area—a central city and 12 suburban municipalities, the latter within the County of York—was incapable of providing for the physical needs of a rapidly growing urban community. It cannot be argued, therefore, that the chronic shortage of housing was the *prime* factor leading to the formation of metropolitan government. The rapid post-war expansion of the need for water supplies and sewerage, educational facilities, traffic improvements, and arterial extensions were among the most important aspects of the demand for an enlarged physical plant in an urban area that was otherwise threatening to degenerate into chaos.

This analysis of the growth and development of metropolitan government and regional planning in the Toronto area will demonstrate that *physical development* seems more readily adaptable to metropolitan organization than does *social development*. Of course, metropolitan organization provides not only new geographic dimensions as politics and public administration, but new social dimensions as well. Still, an enlarged governmental administration seems initially most likely to facilitate the resolution of problems that are physically based. Progress on such problems of physical growth and urban development is more rewarding politically and more visible than progress with social problems. Thus the former is more likely to excite the imagination of the electorate because it takes tangible form in new housing, new developments, new schools, new highways, and other new facilities that are most likely to be found on the fringes and in the new suburbs of the expanding metropolis, where middle- and upper-income populations reside. On the other hand, problems

---

of the constitutional restraints inherent in the interpretation of the British North America Act. In 1970, however, the Prime Minister announced that he would form a new department within the federal government, to be known as the Ministry of State for Urban Affairs. Apparently a way around the constitutional dilemmas has been found.

in social development are much more difficult to solve and tend to appear in the heart of the central city, where low-income families and poor housing conditions are concentrated.

It is one of the basic themes of this study that in the process of solving the physical problems of a modern metropolis, the Municipality of Metropolitan Toronto has reduced the position of the central city, upon which it was founded, to that of a "have-not" municipality. Regional planning in Metropolitan Toronto made great strides in the years 1953–1970, using the "financial anchor"—as Metro's first Chairman, Mr. F. G. Gardiner, put it—of the City of Toronto's favorable tax base and solid economic potential. During those 17 years, however, Toronto's own physical services deteriorated sadly, while Toronto taxpayers have paid a very substantial share (about 60 percent) of the total cost of equipping 200 square miles of developing urban territory for a resident population that will total about 3 million persons by 1980.

CHAPTER II

PRELUDE TO METROPOLITAN GOVERNMENT

H<small>INDSIGHT MAKES</small> it clear that the Toronto Metropolitan Region was ready for "take-off" at the end of World War II.[1] Although the area experienced many of the familiar problems characteristically referred to as "metropolitan sprawl," "metropolitanitis," and so on, the major portents for constructive growth and reorganization were favorable. The total population of the commonly designated metropolitan area was approaching one million, and a significant influx was anticipated when the overseas armed forces were demobilized.

Release of an enormous pent-up demand for durable consumer goods was the most likely economic forecast. This demand was nowhere more evident than in the field of housing. The production of dwelling units in the Toronto region had declined by more than 50 percent in the decade following 1929, and almost no new construction was possible during World War II.[2] Moreover, an undetermined element within the population was composed of persons who had come to Toronto to work in war production activities. Very few returned to the small towns or rural areas from which they came. These facts added up to a strong demand for housing, and a short supply.

FORMIDABLE URBAN DIFFICULTIES

On a negative and more realistic side, the orderly process of urban development in the Toronto region at that time faced formidable difficulties. The respected Bureau of Municipal Research published a White Paper on December 20, 1945, entitled *Where Are Toronto and Its Metropolitan Area Heading?* [3] The bureau pointed out that the City and its suburbs were "one social and economic unit and any attempt to treat them as a series of independent units cannot but lead to grave failure in the end." The bureau's analysis pointed to the fact that the population of the City of Toronto was becoming stationary. From 1929 to 1939 its population did increase from some 606,000 to 649,000. There was a further "official" increase to 676,887 in 1944, but available information was not adequate to determine how much immigration had occurred in comparison with military enlistments and other departures.[4]

Meanwhile the 12 suburban municipalities had been growing at a much more rapid rate. From 1926 to 1945 the suburban population doubled from a little less than 126,000 to more than 263,000.[5] The City was already considered built up, and many persons had moved out to the suburban areas, particularly to the newly formed and carefully planned small towns and villages that had become prime residential areas since the war. The bureau concluded that "if properly planned, the area of the municipal corporation of Toronto could accommodate—with dignity and the necessary amenities and with adequate provision for business and industry—a much larger population than at present. Toronto now [1945] has only slightly over 30 persons per acre of land area." [6] By contrast, population in the suburban areas then averaged a little less than two persons per acre.

The financial picture was even more dismal after 15 years of deep economic depression and wartime neglect. Total assessed values liable for taxation for general purposes declined slowly but steadily throughout the entire period. In fact, assessments were some 7.5 percent lower in 1945 than in 1935. The decline was consistent through the three components—land, buildings, and business assessments. Partly for these reasons, but more particularly because the level of municipal services within the City was typically far superior to that in the newly emerging fringe areas, Toronto's 1944 per capita taxation was more than 37 percent higher than the average in the 12 suburban municipalities.[7] The only bright spot in the financial picture was the decline in per capita net general and educational debt of more than 56 percent within the City of Toronto. Moreover, the per capita net debt for the City, not including public utilities, was less than half the average among the suburban municipalities.

A CALL FOR METROPOLITAN GOVERNMENT

This White Paper was important, not only because it expressed the concern of a civic organization that derived its membership from many leading business and professional enterprises, but also because it was among the first modern statements calling for the development of regional planning and a metropolitan form of government in the Toronto region. Previously, in the spring of 1944, the bureau had published three White Papers on community planning. In the second of these (dated March 1, 1944) the following were listed as metropolitan services: education, transportation, police, fire, public health, water service, sewers and sewage disposal, traffic arteries, and community planning.

The bureau's second White Paper also argued that the boundaries of the municipality of the City of Toronto were purely artificial political lines, having no relation whatever either to the boundaries of the Toronto economic area or to those of the Toronto community. It called for two alternative courses: the annexation of satellite municipalities to the City, or the establishment of an overriding municipality governed by an elective council, similar to the London County Council, with responsibility for the administration of obviously metropolitan services and having the responsibility for city planning through a single board. The White Paper forecast the bureau's later stand in favor of "amalgamation," that is, the creation of a unitary form of metropolitan-wide government. The paper concluded ". . . there seems no good reason why the Greater Toronto area needs more than one local government. If the various municipalities in the area had had independent existence for 200 or 300 years, the objection to unification might be understood. No doubt vested interests—real or fancied—lack of imagination, and inertia will prevent at least for a time the establishment of unitary local government for the Toronto area. A second best solution of the problem of local government in the Toronto area, that of a borough system, would be better than no solution at all."

On January 1, 1946, the Metropolitan Area of Toronto consisted of the central City of Toronto and 12 adjacent or nearby local municipalities, all within the County of York. Five of the 12 municipalities were townships, a title stemming from the original local municipal division of the counties in the early nineteenth century. Four were towns, and three were incorporated villages. Although the Municipal Act of Ontario, dating from 1849, laid down certain specifications for municipalities with such titular designations, these requirements had long since fallen into disuse in the Toronto area. At the beginning of the post-war period all but two of these municipalities had fewer than 25,000 residents, although two of the larger townships approximated that population. At that time five of the municipalities had fewer than 10,000 persons and one had just over 10,000 population.

At the end of World War II, only the City of Toronto had a formal planning board, organized in 1942. Soon, however, the Toronto and York Planning Board was established, representing the first crude attempt at regional planning in the area. The creation of this board, chaired by Frederick G. Gardiner—Reeve (Mayor) of the Village of Forest Hill and later the first Chairman of the Municipality of Metropolitan Toronto—together with the enormous growth in population of the suburban municipalities, made it inevitable within three or four years that there would be no further annexation by the City of Toronto and no unitary form of government.[8]

FURTHER STUDY OF THE "METROPOLITAN PROBLEM"

The rapidity of the expansion within the major suburban municipalities may be seen in Table 1. This massive growth led the City and some suburban leaders to sponsor an intensive study of the problems of the metropolitan area conducted by a special Committee of the Civic Advisory Council of Toronto. The council had been formed in 1945, by representatives of a number of civic organizations and various departments within the University of Toronto, to offer research facilities and the views of well-informed citizens at little or no expense to local government in Greater Toronto. In 1948 the council created a Committee on Metropolitan Problems to assume this special assignment. Notably, the City, at a meeting in June 1948, undertook to finance the entire study, and to make the findings available to all municipalities within the metropolitan area. Thus To-

Table 1
Population Changes in the City and Its Five Largest Suburbs, 1946–1950

Municipality	1946	1950	Percent Change
Toronto (City, 22,287 acres)	696,555	667,487	− 4.2
East York (Township, 3,647 acres)	44,773	60,155	+34.3
Etobicoke (Township, 27,312 acres)	21,274	44,137	+107.4
North York (Township, 44,689 acres)	30,114	62,646	+108.0
Scarborough (Township, 45,012 acres)	28,444	48,146	+69.2
York (Township, 5,050 acres)	85,324	95,659	+12.1
Total, five suburbs	209,929	310,743	+48.0

SOURCE: Civic Advisory Council of Toronto, Committee on Metropolitan Problems, *First Report*, Section Two, Statistical Appendix (Toronto: April 1950), p. 28.

ronto recognized that the rapidly developing suburbs had grown less concerned with the solutions to metropolitan-wide problems with each passing year.

This study was the first overall examination of the Metropolitan Area of Toronto, initiated by the City and the suburban municipalities acting together. The method of carrying out the study was unique for Canadian cities, with the task placed in the hands of a volunteer committee of citizens, assisted by a research staff. The first report of the Committee on Metropolitan Problems of the Civic Advisory Council was issued in November 1949. It dealt with the difficulties facing the City and its traditional suburban municipalities in a period of extraordinary population growth and urban development. A companion volume presenting the statistical data was issued in April 1950. The *Final Report,* recommending alternative solutions, was published in March 1951. These early studies emphasized the economic and social interdependence of the 13 municipalities within the Toronto Metropolitan Region. They also pointed out that many of the suburban municipalities could not provide essential local services for their residents, were it not for the fact that nearly one hundred inter-municipal agreements had been signed between the City of Toronto and one or more suburban municipalities (or, in a few cases, between two or more of the fringe municipalities).

The studies submitted by the Civic Advisory Council were well publicized in the major newspapers and discussed within many local councils and civic organizations. Their principal impact was the recognition that the so-called "metropolitan problem" is a two-sided phenomenon. There are direct pressures within the City for capital expenditures in terms of housing, improved service installations, public transportation facilities, traffic improvements, redevelopment of blighted areas, and so forth. In addition, there are indirect pressures emanating from the entire metropolitan area. Thus the residents of the suburbs use City facilities—streets, arterial highways, shopping centers, public transportation services, recreational facilities. These suburban users are usually as vocal as City residents in requesting improved facilities. Capital and current expenditures of the central city were bound to rise as a result of these twin pressures.

At the same time, the settlement of new urban areas on the fringe brought a whole series of problems for these relatively small or underdeveloped municipalities. In particular, they were faced with unusual difficulties in the provision of basic municipal services, such as water supply, sewage and garbage disposal facilities, police and fire protection and, especially, educational facilities. The rate of expansion was unusually rapid, and the small metropolitan municipalities had to meet the levels of their neighboring communities in services. They would have avoided this competition had they been distinctly separated from the metropolitan area.

Particular emphasis was placed on the difficulties inherent in expanding educational facilities. These improvements involved the most serious problems of physical planning and of capital and operational financing. Demands for educational provisions of every kind —elementary schools, nursery schools, libraries, and community centers—had become urgent in the suburban municipalities. The latter were in no position to meet these demands adequately with available resources.

Although the studies helped elucidate these developments, their impact was not great at the time, and there was little positive reaction from the suburban municipalities. Spokesmen for the residents of the more fortunate fringe municipalities usually argued that their citizens were well provided with municipal services, that their tax rates were relatively low, and that all of this could be maintained within the confines of a single municipality. Most elected and appointed officials, however, emphasized their desire to cooperate, which meant that they wanted to "wait and see" what was likely to happen as a consequence of the City of Toronto's increasing interest in physical expansion, and the Province of Ontario's interest in regional government.

TORONTO'S REQUEST FOR AMALGAMATION

Although the City of Toronto had sparked the efforts of the Committee on Metropolitan Problems, the City Council did not wait for the committee's final report before it initiated an application to the Municipal Board of the Province of Ontario for an order "amalgamating" the municipalities within the traditional Metropolitan Area of Toronto. The Municipal Board, a quasi-judicial body with the power to order or deny applications for annexation of part or all of one municipality by another, received the application in 1950, and scheduled hearings during 1951 and 1952.

The City of Toronto presented its case for a unitary form of government. With only one exception, the other municipalities strongly opposed the City's application by engaging the best available lawyers. Although some alternative proposals were offered, most of the 11 opposing municipalities merely favored the preservation of the status quo, appearing to hope that in some mysterious fashion the problems would solve themselves, probably through the extension of existing municipal agreements. In this connection several municipalities favored the creation of special administrative commissions for the provision of specific services, and pointed to the success of the Metropolitan Police Commission in London (England), the Port of New York Authority, the Greater Winnipeg Water District, the Vancouver Metropolitan Health Board, and even the Toronto Transportation Commission.

In summary, the case against the City of Toronto's amalgamation plea was described by the writer in 1954 in the following words: "a federal, rather than a unitary approach to the solution of political, social and economic problems is more democratic and is consistent with the Canadian pattern; in any event the City of Toronto has a poor record as far as planning is concerned and the local municipalities should not be entrusted to an administration with a long history of neglect of some of its most profound problems; finally, every effort should be made to preserve local interest and citizen participation in the affairs of our municipalities and this will be less likely if a huge city is created." [9]

THE ONTARIO MUNICIPAL BOARD AND THE METRO BILL

These several arguments apparently carried considerable weight with the Ontario Municipal Board and its parent, the Government of Ontario. In January 1953 the board issued its report, formally entitled *Decisions and Recommendations of the Board,* in the matter of an application by the City of Toronto and the Town of Mimico described as Applicants, with the remaining 11 municipalities described as Respondents.[10] The board rejected the City's application. While it admitted that it had not been asked to propose a solution to the problems of the Metropolitan Area of Toronto, the Chairman, Mr. Lorne R. Cumming, Q.C., indicated that the board favored the creation of a metropolitan government in the form of a two-tier system of local government. Mr. Cumming was highly respected in the fields of municipal government and physical planning. He had been the Solicitor of the City of Windsor, and was active in municipal organization and in the Community Planning Association. He was also the author of several papers on important aspects of planning, including zoning.

One month later, in February 1953, the Prime Minister of Ontario personally introduced Bill 80, "An Act to Provide for the Federation of the Municipalities in the Metropolitan Area." The act set up an interim metropolitan administration on April 15, 1953. It came into full force on January 1, 1954, although certain arrangements concerning public transportation were not made final until the middle of that year.

Bill 80 was actually a compromise between the opposing views concerning the future of the metropolitan region, but it was certainly an almost complete rejection of the unitary, "one big city," approach. The act created a new political unit, the Municipality of Metropolitan Toronto (soon familiarly known as Metro), with a Metropolitan Council consisting of 12 representatives from the City and one, the Mayor or Reeve, from each of the suburban municipalities.

The first Chairman of the Metropolitan Council, Mr. Frederick G. Gardiner, was initially appointed by the Government of Ontario, and was, therefore, the only Metro councillor not designated to represent a specific geographic constituency. From January 1, 1955, it was possible for his successors to be elected either from within the Metropolitan Council or from outside that body. In fact, Mr. Gardiner was elected for a second term and served with further elections until the end of 1961. The act also provided for a Metropolitan School Board with the same pattern of representation, half of the elected members from the City school authorities, although the chairman was elected from within the board from the very beginning.

The most significant feature of this political experiment was that the 13 local councils continued to serve the City of Toronto and the 12 suburbs, which were now to be known collectively as the "Area Municipalities." Certain functions of all local councils were assumed by the Metropolitan Council, but otherwise the municipalities continued as before. Thus, the solution chosen in 1953 for the Metropolitan Area of Toronto enabled the municipalities to continue their traditions, to preserve their identity, and to administer local services, while uniting with all the other Area Municipalities to provide services that were considered metropolitan in nature and scope.

CHAPTER III

METROPOLITAN GOVERNMENT IN TORONTO: THE FIRST SIX YEARS, 1954–1959

METROPOLITAN TORONTO was created in 1953 amid a series of most favorable portents. The Conservative Party had governed the Province of Ontario for a full decade, including the closing years of a successful war and the continuation of an unprecedented prosperity. This government, widely believed to possess an anti-urban bias because of its numerical domination by representatives of rural areas and small urban communities, took the unprecedented step of creating a metropolitan form of government for more than 1,100,000 persons, approximately one-fifth of the total population of the province.

AUGURIES OF SUCCESS

Despite the boldness of its action, the provincial government had several important assurances that its political venture had a reasonable chance to be effective. First, the Province of Ontario had acted on the very strong recommendation of its own advisory quasi-judicial body, the Ontario Municipal Board, a group allegedly beyond being swayed by mere political considerations. We have already noted the reputation and substantial prestige of its Chairman, Mr. Lorne R. Cumming.

Second, the province chose the method of indirect election to the Metropolitan Council, a device that was the basis of county government throughout Ontario. There was nothing radical or revolutionary in this scheme, no new constituencies were drawn, and no direct elections were required. Rather, the elected heads of the suburban municipalities, Toronto's Mayor and two senior controllers, and the senior alderman from each of the nine wards in Toronto, were to sit on the Metropolitan Council.

Third and perhaps most important of all, the province appointed as the first Chairman of the Metropolitan Council a man who clearly commanded respect from those elected to public office. Mr. Frederick G. Gardiner was a distinguished lawyer and a powerful figure within the Conservative Party, not only in the Province of Ontario but also at the national level.* The new Chairman had been the senior elected official of one of the constituent municipalities (Forest Hill Village) and Chairman of the Toronto and York Planning Board. In these capacities he had been a powerful opponent of the consolidation of the municipalities in the Toronto Metropolitan Region. But he now admitted frankly that he had been mistaken, and believed that the problems within the area could be dealt with only on a metropolitan-wide basis.

Representation on the Metropolitan Council was not merely indirect, and well balanced in that sense, but was also evenly distributed between the apparently conflicting interests of the City of Toronto and the 12 suburban municipalities.† The Metropolitan Council was composed of 24 representatives, 12 from the City and 12 from the suburbs. The appointed Chairman was therefore in a most important and interesting position: presumably he was the senior political figure within the metropolis, yet he was not elected either within a municipality or by the electorate at large. He was obviously the senior administrative official, yet his duties were not spelled out in the Municipality of Metropolitan Toronto Act, and although he was an appointed official, it was not clear whether his role was that of a Mayor or of a city manager. The pattern to be taken in the development of the Chairman's role would be left open. Mr. Gardi-

* Mr. Gardiner was the Chairman of the Conservative Party convention that nominated John G. Diefenbaker in 1957.

† Indirect representation was considered to be a form of balance in 1953, in that each of the 12 traditional suburban municipalities elected its Mayor or Reeve to represent it on the Metropolitan Council. At that time the notion of one representative each was not challenged on the basis of population distribution, nor was any local unit excluded from the metropolitan federation.

ner's position was all the stronger because he was clearly the choice of the Prime Minister of Ontario. It was apparent that both men were eager to have the new system work well. In introducing Bill 80 the Prime Minister emphasized that the problems of the Toronto metropolis were grievous and, by implication, a thorn in the side of the provincial government. He admitted that the proposed solution was an experiment, and promised that the development of the new metropolitan form of government would be reviewed no later than five years from the date of its initiation on January 1, 1954.

THE FUNCTIONS OF METRO

The distribution of functions between the metropolitan government and the local government, as laid down in the original Municipality of Metropolitan Toronto Act of 1953, may be described very simply. The following functions were assigned to Metro:

1. *Water Supply.* Construction and maintenance of pumping stations, treatment plants, trunk mains, and reservoirs for the wholesale distribution of water to the 13 Area Municipalities.

2. *Sewage Disposal.* Construction and maintenance of trunk sewer mains and sewage treatment plants to provide a metropolitan sewage disposal system capable of accepting sewage on a wholesale basis from the Area Municipalities.

3. *Roads.* The designation of highways as metropolitan roads, and the establishment of an arterial system of highways. Financing to be split evenly with the province.

4. *Transportation.* The former Toronto Transportation Commission became the Toronto Transit Commission, with responsibility for public transportation throughout the metropolitan area.

5. *Education.* The Metropolitan School Board was given responsibility for coordinating educational facilities in the metropolitan area, and charged with paying a grant to each of the 13 local school boards (the latter continued in existence for primary, secondary, and vocational school pupils).

6. *Health and Welfare.* The Metropolitan Council was given responsibility for the provision of homes for the aged, the maintenance of wards of Children's Aid Societies, post-sanatorium care for tuberculosis patients, and the hospitalization of indigent patients.

7. *Justice.* The Metropolitan Council must provide and maintain a courthouse and jail.

8. *Housing.* The Metropolitan Council was given all of the powers of a municipality in the fields of housing and redevelopment.

9. *Planning.* The Metropolitan Planning Board was created, with authority extending beyond the metropolitan area, encompassing all adjoining townships. It was charged with preparing an official plan for this larger metropolitan planning area.

10. *Parks.* The Metropolitan Council was empowered to establish metropolitan parks.

11. *Finance and Taxation.* The Metropolitan Council was made responsible for the uniform assessment of all lands and buildings in the 13 municipalities. On the basis of the total assessment, the requirements of the metropolitan government are levied against each Area Municipality at a uniform mill rate. The local government then collects the metropolitan tax requirement, as well as its own requirement, from its taxpayers. All responsibility for debenture financing was given to Metro to exercise both for itself and on behalf of any local government in the area. Moreover, the Metropolitan Corporation was required to assume the school debenture debts of each municipality, and acquired all assets of the local municipalities needed for metropolitan services.

FUNCTIONS OF THE AREA MUNICIPALITIES

The following functions were assigned to the local municipal councils:

1. *Water Supply.* Local distribution systems and retail sale of water to consumers.

2. *Sewage Disposal.* Local sewage collection.

3. *Garbage Collection.* Left entirely with the Area Municipalities.

4. *Roads.* The construction and maintenance of local streets and sidewalks.

5. *Police.* Left entirely with the Area Municipalities.

6. *Fire.* Left entirely with the Area Municipalities.

7. *Education.* The local board of education would continue, and must finance the cost of any standard of educational service above the level of metropolitan grants, if it desired to go beyond the basic standard.

8. *Health and Welfare Services.* Public health in the municipal or health unit, unemployment relief, maintenance of non-wards, social work services.

9. *Housing.* The local councils retained all their powers with respect to housing and redevelopment.

10. *Planning.* Local planning boards could be continued or created, and expected to plan in conformity with the overall metropolitan plan.

11. *Parks and Recreation.* Creation and maintenance of local parks.

12. *Finance and Taxation.* On the basis of the uniform assessment the local council would collect the revenues required to provide local services.[1]

COMING INTO BEING

During the nine months following April 15, 1953, the Municipality of Metropolitan Toronto and its administrative structure came into being, under the guidance of the first Chairman. During this preliminary period, the role of the Chairman was crucial to the ultimate success of the metropolitan administration. Mr. Gardiner interpreted his role as a combination of metropolitan Mayor and city manager. The various administrative departments of the metropolitan government were set up in the first year, and the most important administrative appointments were made. At the time, two of the most competent administrators in North America were serving in the Treasury and Assessment Departments of the City of Toronto, and these men became the finance and assessment commissioners, respectively, of Metropolitan Toronto.* The Clerk of the County of York became the Clerk of the new Metropolitan Corporation. All three continued to serve in these posts for more than a decade. The continuity of these long-term public administrators must not be underestimated when judging the public acceptance and stability of the new government in Greater Toronto.

Four standing committees of seven persons each were created: for housing and welfare; works; roads and traffic; and planning and parks. During the first year the Chairman also recommended setting up an executive committee, which within two years assumed many of the

---

* Mr. G. Arthur Lascelles, Finance Commissioner, had an international reputation and served for a time as President of the Municipal Finance Officers Association. Mr. Alfred J. B. Gray, Assessment Commissioner, was acknowledged to be the ranking authority on property assessment in Canada, and he also had an international reputation.

functions of a board of control or a cabinet. This executive committee, for which no provision had been made in the Municipality of Metropolitan Toronto Act, was at first composed of five persons: the Metropolitan Chairman and four members elected by the Metropolitan Council from within its own membership. These annual internal elections soon became a matter of controversy and a source of tension between the City and the former suburbs.

THE APPROACH TO URBAN GROWTH AND DEVELOPMENT

Ontario's action, incorporating the first metropolitan municipality in North America, was taken for a variety of reasons. By the early 1950's the three large townships, in which the most substantial physical development and growth of population were occurring, had reached a virtual deadlock in the performance of normal municipal functions required for urban growth. These townships, as well as other municipalities in the area, lacked sufficient pure water and facilities for sewage disposal, and what was worse, the prospects for expansion appeared dismal. Further, the problem of providing educational facilities for large numbers of children of new residents seemed overwhelming. Moreover, there can be little doubt that the impasse in the provision of housing accommodations, and the stagnation of community planning in the Toronto region, were among the most important considerations. In October 1953, in one of his first speeches after assuming office, Chairman Gardiner told the American Society of Planning Officials that "we had to be driven by intolerable inconvenience and the threat of financial difficulties before we took the steps necessary to solve our problems." [2]

HOUSING AND PLANNING PROBLEMS ACKNOWLEDGED

The actions of several municipalities in restricting and occasionally even halting the approval of plans for subdivisions and the issuing of building permits during the years 1948–1951 were considered by many to be important factors precipitating the creation of Metro. Certainly in the early post-war period the division of jurisdiction between the municipalities made it extremely difficult to initiate programs of publicly assisted or subsidized housing. The report of the Ontario Municipal Board of January 20, 1953, stated: "The responsibility of municipalities with respect to the serious shortage of housing in the metropolitan area was one of the controversial questions raised in the hearing and some of the respondents, through their counsels, contended that the provision of any type of subsidized or publicly assisted housing should not be considered a proper function of municipal government. In particular, the activities of the City in providing emergency housing and in the undertaking of the Regent Park redevelopment project were the subject of some criticism." [3]

On the subject of regional planning, i.e., the direction and control of the physical development of the entire metropolitan area, the report of the Ontario Municipal Board was clear: "As previously stated, the present division of jurisdiction with respect to community planning and the control of land uses is considered by the Board to be a most serious weakness of the present system of local government. No intelligent or efficient extension of municipal services throughout the metropolitan area can be expected in the absence of a comprehensive metropolitan plan of development and some centralized control of major land uses." [4]

Undoubtedly, therefore, one of the prime objectives sought in establishing Metro was to move toward a solution to dilemmas in the fields of housing and community planning. It is interesting that Mr. Gardiner, in his early speech to ASPO, listed housing as a service for which Metro was responsible. He said:

"The Metropolitan Corporation [Metro] will have all of the powers of a municipality with respect to the provision of housing and redevelopment, which is one of the major problems which remain to be solved. Our housing requirements are not less urgent than those which pertain in your metropolitan city." [5]

EXTENSION OF PHYSICAL SERVICES EMPHASIZED

Nevertheless, during the first years, Metro did not make a direct attack on the related problems of housing and metropolitan planning. Instead, with the full support and leadership of the Chairman, the Metropolitan Council took the view that the main contribution of the new government should be to provide all those *basic physical services* that would make it possible for private and public enterprise to build housing for the expanding population.

In an address to the Institute of Public Administration of Canada on September 9, 1954, Chairman Gardiner devoted most of his remarks to the physical program contemplated for Metropolitan Toronto, and to its anticipated costs. He spoke of a $45 million program to increase water supplies over the next five years, referred to a $60 million program for sewer construction, and discussed Metro's 1954 educational expenditures of $31 million gross ($23 million net expenditure with $8 million recovered from the provincial grant) paid toward the attainment of "a reasonable standard of education" throughout the metropolitan area. He dwelt on the financial details of Metro's $56 million budget for the calendar year 1954, of which $35 million was derived from direct taxation and $21 million from provincial grants.

For the first time, Chairman Gardiner used a phrase he was to repeat again and again over the coming years—"the metropolitan concept." He concluded his address to the institute in these words: "I can say to you today that the Metropolitan Council members have recognized the challenge that was presented to them; they have adopted the *metropolitan concept;* the system is working and is working well." [6]

IN SUMMARY

In summary, what worked and worked well during the first five or six years of Toronto's metropolitan government was the implementation of a vast program of urban development, based upon the carefully planned extension of water and sewer services northward from Lake Ontario into the three huge underdeveloped suburban municipalities of Etobicoke, North York, and Scarborough. As these services became available after 1954, vast new areas (previously rural) were opened up to urban development. There were substantial increases in the number of subdivision plans filed with local planning boards, and ultimately approved by the Minister of Planning and Development on the advice of his Community Planning Branch. Most of these new neighborhoods comprised only single-family dwellings on individual lots, whose required minimum frontage was soon increased to 50 feet from the previous 25 to 40 feet. With the construction of sewage facilities, the problem of septic tanks and water contamination disappeared from the Township of North York within three or four years. Problems of financing urban growth and development remained.

Prior to 1954 not one firm in Metropolitan Toronto was building as many as 100 dwellings per year, but a house-building industry emerged during the first five years of metropolitan government. A number of smaller firms amalgamated, and by the end of the 1950's many organizations were completing 100 dwellings or more each year, and at least one was building between 250 and 500 units. As a consequence of the fortuitous combination of National Housing Act mortgage financing for homeowners, and the expansion of physical services by the Metropolitan Corporation, the housing problem was truly solved, at least for those who could afford to buy the typical two- or three-bedroom bungalow that dominated suburban construction in North America during the 1950's.

In response to firm but polite criticism soon forthcoming from the Metropolitan Toronto Branch of the Community Planning Association of Canada, from various private planning consultants, and from employed municipal and metropolitan planners alike, the members of the Metropolitan Council insisted that "first things must come first." A well-received newspaper cartoon of the day showed Chairman Gardiner seated on a bulldozer demonstrating his concept of planning as he scattered the members of the Community Planning Association in all directions. The cartoon was a reasonably accurate reflection of the Chairman's belief that the solution to the serious post-war housing shortage was creation of a physical environment within which private enterprise could flourish and provide single-family detached dwellings for prospective homeowners.

This was the era of the North American glorification of home ownership as the mark of assumption of individual and civic responsibility by family heads. No mention was made of tenants, who were thought of as "second-class citizens" and, in the view of politicians, likely to be individuals and families of doubtful initiative and stability, but in any case with low incomes. It is not argued that the members of the Metropolitan Council created the atmosphere in which these concepts took root and flourished in Toronto; the concepts themselves were widespread throughout the United States and Canada. Nevertheless, those who played major roles in the unfolding of Metro after 1954 gave tremendous encouragement to the prevailing fashion. To be sure, they were not entirely remiss in their attention to housing for low-income groups, and in the development of a formal planning organization for Metropolitan Toronto. But their view was, to repeat, "first things first." *

FIRST REVIEW OF THE METROPOLITAN FORM
OF GOVERNMENT, 1957–1958

Although the Government of Ontario had agreed in principle to review the experience of the Municipality of Metropolitan Toronto no later than five years from its inception, opposition to metropolitan activities was so vigorous that the first formal inquiry was initiated by an Order-in-Council on May 2, 1957 (OC-15120/57).

The Prime Minister of Ontario appointed a Metropolitan Toronto Commission of Inquiry with the following terms of reference:

(1) To inquire into and report upon (a) the composition, organization, and methods of operation of the Metropolitan Council and the Metropolitan School Board, established pursuant to the Municipality of Metropolitan Toronto Act, 1953, as amended; (b) the extent to which the Metropolitan Municipal Government and organization established by the said legislation had succeeded in meeting the need for a better local government in the said area and accomplishing the objectives for which it was established; and (2) To make such recommendations with respect to the matters inquired into as may be considered desirable.

Opposition to the creation of a metropolitan form of government —voiced during the hearings before the Ontario Municipal Board in 1950–1952—continued after the formal creation of the Metropolitan Council on January 1, 1954. From the early years of the post-war period, the three major newspapers in Toronto—the *Daily Star,* the *Telegram,* and the *Globe and Mail*—were united in their opposition, and strongly advocated a unitary form of government for the metropolitan area. They favored the application of the City of Toronto for "amalgamation" in 1950, and criticized the introduction of Bill 80 in the spring of 1953. The latter they considered to vitiate or deny the social and economic unity evident throughout the area. Moreover, once the Municipality of Metropolitan Toronto was created, these newspapers, together with the councils and many ratepayers' associations in the suburban municipalities within Metro,

---

* Experienced planners viewed the need to provide housing and undertake community planning as implicit, rather than explicit. The matters most often explicitly mentioned were financial competence and the supply of hardware, that is, public works.

embarked upon a program of moderate harassment or, at the very least, continuous criticism.*

REPRESENTATION: FIRST POINT OF ATTACK

During the middle 1950's, as the 12 suburban municipalities continued rapid growth and urbanization, the first and most logical point of attack was representation within the Metropolitan Council. It was not entirely strategic, however, to limit the argument to the issue of equity between the suburbs and the City. Thus the discussion also compared the equities of representation *among* the 12 municipalities themselves. The villages and towns were dwarfed by the larger townships. None of the villages and towns had more than 15,000 population. One had only 9,000. On the other hand, the three large townships began to grow rapidly, and by 1957 the populations were 182,942 in North York, 151,885 in Scarborough, and 110,306 in Etobicoke.[7]

CHAIRMAN GARDINER'S SUBMISSION

The nature of the overall criticism of Metro may be gleaned from the submission by Chairman Gardiner to "The Commission Appointed by the Lieutenant-Governor in Council of the Province of Ontario to Inquire into the Affairs of the Municipality of Metropolitan Toronto." Mr. Gardiner appeared on June 15, 1957, with a brief which, he stated, presented his personal views and not necessarily those of the members of the Metropolitan Council.

His statement dealt with three fundamental questions, as follows: "(1) Is the Metropolitan Council as presently constituted calculated to give adequate representation by population to the thirteen municipalities and if not in what manner may a more satisfactory result be accomplished? (2) What would constitute reasonably adequate compensation to the members of the Metropolitan Council? (3) Should the Chairman of the Council A. be elected at large by those entitled to vote in the Metropolitan Area? B. be one of the members of the Council elected in a local municipality? *OR* C. is the present

---

* The councils of the suburban municipalities and a variety of citizens' groups opposed the development of Metro's responsibilities, but for very different reasons from those put forward by the major newspapers. The newspapers espoused amalgamation, while the suburban councils abhorred amalgamation, and feared the expansion of Metro's functional responsibilities as an indirect method of achieving what they did not want, i.e., a unitary form of government.

system of an annual election of a chairman who may or may not be an elected member of the Council satisfactory?" [8]

The Chairman's submission was largely confined to the three questions noted, but his discussion of the first question occupied about three-quarters of his entire presentation. He described Metropolitan Toronto as a federal system of municipal government. He felt that the Municipality of Metropolitan Toronto Act defined the powers of the Municipality of Metropolitan Toronto, and the Municipal Act defined the powers of the local Area Municipalities. The Metropolitan Corporation had no general power; its powers were specifically conferred by the special act of incorporation and the amendments thereto.

The Chairman knew that there were substantial population differences between federal and provincial constituencies, yet each, whatever its size, was represented by one member. Thus the residents of Metropolitan Toronto were not strangers to a system that accepted wide divergence from a strict representation by population, and that did not recognize the principle of "one man, one vote." In sum, Chairman Gardiner simply argued that the City of Toronto must have a number of representatives and voting strength equal to the total combined representation of the suburban members: "This submission is founded upon the fact that the population in the City of Toronto is relatively equal to the total population of the twelve suburbs and that the total assessment in Toronto is approximately 54 percent of the total in the area with the excellent tax base of approximately 61 percent industrial and commercial compared to 39 percent residential." [9]

After this pronouncement Mr. Gardiner offered the view that there were only two ways in which a system of more reasonable representation by population could be established. First, it would be possible to establish a number of metropolitan electoral districts from each of which a member would be elected directly to the Metropolitan Council, wherein he would possess one vote. The second plan would be to preserve the current system, but "with the provision of a multiple-vote system *so that upon important questions*" [emphasis supplied] there would be representation by population.

Chairman Gardiner discussed each of these plans. He found that a serious defect in the system based on a number of metropolitan electoral districts would be created. This defect, he felt, rested in the clear loss of liaison between the local municipal councils and the Metropolitan Council: "This, in my view, is sufficiently serious to condemn such an arrangement." Yet to his submission he attached a map indicating how 18 metropolitan electoral districts might be established, each with a reasonably comparable total population.

It was clear that Mr. Gardiner favored the second plan, namely a multiple system of voting in the Metropolitan Council, as then established. This system was already in operation in county councils, where multiple votes were recorded on the basis of population. Such multiple voting would be applied whenever a recorded vote was called on important questions. He argued that since almost all the business of the Metropolitan Council was conducted on the basis of voice votes, and it was only occasionally that the "yeas" and "nays" were recorded, there could be no serious objection to a system of multiple voting.

The submission went on to suggest an allocation of votes whereby the 12 representatives of the City of Toronto would have a total of 28 votes, and the representatives of the 12 Area Municipalities would have a range from one vote for the Reeve of each of the least populous municipalities to as many as four votes for the Reeve of each of the four largest townships—again, a total of 28 votes for the 12 suburban councillors. The Chairman would cast the deciding vote in the event of a tie. Mr. Gardiner concluded: "The system recommended maintains the automatic liaison between the local councils and the Metropolitan Council which in my view is essential and at the same time provides representation by population on important questions."

THE METROPOLITAN COUNCIL'S SUBMISSION

The Metro Council made perhaps the second most important submission to the Commission of Inquiry. It presented a 160-page document reporting in substantial detail on the operation of the metropolitan form of government since 1953–1954. In a nutshell, the Metro brief contained "a statement of the conditions which came into administrative operation on January 1, 1954, and the situation as it will exist on December 31, 1957, after a four-year period of metropolitan administration." [10] The brief began with a complete review of metropolitan organization, indicating both the names of the various departments initiated in 1953, and those added after that date. The list provides an important historical record, and is reproduced in full:

METRO DEPARTMENTS
(*By Date of Initiation*)

1953
Assessment Department
Audit
Clerk's
Legal
Personnel
Roads
Treasury
Welfare and Housing
Works
Metropolitan Toronto Planning Board
Metropolitan Toronto School Board
Toronto Transit Commission
Juvenile and Family Court

1954
Courts of Revision (i.e., Assessment)
Traffic Engineering Department

1955
Civil Defence Committee
Parks Department

1956
Property Department

1957
Board of Police Commissioners
Licensing Commission
Magistrates' Court

The agencies listed as additions in 1957 represent the first substantial change in the powers of the Metropolitan Corporation after its inauguration. In the years 1955–1956 the whole question of a metropolitan police force was under active study by a special committee of the Metropolitan Council, chaired by Mr. C. O. Bick, the Reeve of Forest Hill Village. The committee's report made a clear recommendation for the amalgamation of the 13 police departments within the Metro Area. Subsequently, early in 1957 the Municipality of Metropolitan Toronto Act was amended, transferring this function to Metro. The Metro police function was organized as in large Ontario cities, where the police must be supervised by a Board of Police Commissioners appointed by the municipality, and usually consisting of two or three magistrates, the Chief of Police, and the Chairman of the municipality. From 1957 through 1966 the Police Commission, as it is familiarly called, consisted of Magistrate C. O. Bick as Chairman—the title of Magistrate was conferred upon him as he assumed these responsibilities in 1957—two other magistrates, the Metro Chairman, and the Mayor of Toronto.

Also in 1957 the overall responsibility for licensing in all classifications throughout the 13 municipalities was transferred to Metro. The new Licensing Commission was created under the amended legislation and chaired for the next decade by the former Reeve of York Township, Mr. Fred Hall, who was also made a magistrate for these purposes. In that year all of the Magistrates' Courts formerly maintained by the City of Toronto and some of the other municipalities were transferred to Metro.

STATEMENTS OF THE METRO COMMISSIONERS

Following the report on organization and administration, the Metro brief to the Commission of Inquiry consisted of a series of reports from the various appointed senior civil servants within the Metropolitan administration: the Commissioner of Finance, the Commissioner of Assessment, the Commissioner of Works, the Commissioner of Roads, the Commissioner of Welfare and Housing, and so on. Each reported in turn throughout the balance of the comprehensive brief.

The Commissioner of Finance expressed the strong view that the exclusive power given to Metro to issue debentures for its own purposes, for the Area Municipalities, for the various boards of education, and for the Toronto Transit Commission, had already relieved the difficult and dangerous financial problems facing the region's municipalities in the years prior to 1954. By mid-1957 more than $201 million of debentures had been issued, about 35 percent for metropolitan purposes in general, and the remainder for the purposes of the Area Municipalities and their boards of education. The commissioner also estimated that the savings in interest cost on the bonds issued during the four years 1954–1957 was more than $21.5 million. To this could be added reduced interest payments on short-term loans, saving perhaps another three to four hundred thousand dollars. He stated: "The exclusive debenturing power of the Metropolitan Corporation has made possible the development of a metropolitan capital works programme for the next ten years and the integration of that programme with the anticipated capital requirements of the area municipalities and their Boards of Education." [11] In addition, the assumption of responsibilities formerly carried by the Area Municipalities had relieved them of an estimated gross expenditure of just short of $17 million in 1957. About 85 percent of this went into policing and the operation of the Magistrates' Courts.

Each of the reports offered by the Metro Commissioners emphasized physical expansion and the expenditure of money to provide the Commission of Inquiry, and ultimately the public, with some idea of the scope and magnitude of the operations of the Metropolitan Corporation. The Commissioner of Assessment reported that more than $406 million in new assessment had been added from January 1954 to April 1957, partly as the result of an increase of 40,000 new properties, or 13 percent since the beginning of 1954.[12] The total assessment upon which the metropolitan levy was apportioned was:

1954	$2,474,696,765
1955	2,705,146,354
1956	2,952,196,368
1957	3,183,122,850

The growth in assessments, together with the confidence engendered by the performance of the new metropolitan administration, provided a favorable financial atmosphere within Metropolitan Toronto from the time of the earliest issuance of bonds over the signature of Chairman Gardiner and Finance Commissioner Lascelles.

The various reports dealing with municipal services issued by the appropriate commissioners pounded away at the inadequacies of the years 1950–1953—and sometimes dated these inadequacies back beyond World War II—by comparison with the demonstrable progress made after 1953. It is difficult to find fault with these arguments. Unquestionably, the production and supply of water to the 13 Area Municipalities, as well as the collection of sanitary drainage from the systems of each of the municipalities, and its treatment before discharge into receiving waters, were well organized so quickly that the early post-war threats to public health and safety were soon forgotten. Still, many problems remained to be solved, and when compared with the total effort of the first full decade or more, it is now clear that the big expansion of water supply and sewage disposal facilities was barely underway at the end of four years. Nevertheless, the facts on improvements in the first four years were impressive.

The report of the Commissioner of Planning is of substantial help in understanding the long and tedious history, and the still incomplete development, of the Metropolitan Toronto Official Plan. The preparation of such a plan was spelled out specifically in the Municipality of Metropolitan Toronto Act of early 1953. On August 24, 1953, the Minister of Planning and Development of the Province of Ontario "designated" the area of the Metropolitan Corporation, plus its 13 surrounding municipalities, as the Metropolitan Toronto Planning Area, under the jurisdiction of the Metropolitan Toronto Planning Board.

In brief, the concept of regional planning was recognized from the very beginning. The Metropolitan Planning Area consisted of some 720 square miles, one-third of which were located within the boundaries of Metropolitan Toronto itself. In all, 26 municipalities were included in the planning area. In 1953, however, only eight of the 26 had Official Plans in existence. Ten more Official Plans were in force by the end of 1957, or had been submitted to the Minister for approval.[13] These new plans, as well as those for four small municipalities not authorized to prepare such programs, were developed with the assistance of the Metropolitan Planning Board. The commissioner reported that an Official Plan for the area would be substantially completed by the end of 1957. In fact, a draft Official Plan was published in 1959.

In those early years the major work of the Metropolitan Planning Board consisted of examining all subdivision applications issued within the overall Metropolitan Planning Area. During the first three and a half years of operation 1,114 such subdivision applications were received in which more than 116,000 residential lots were specified. Only 42 percent of this total was actually recommended for approval.[14] The Board thus became the ultimate judge of the appropriateness and validity of applications for urban development throughout the 720-square-mile area. Its recommendations were often resisted strenuously, however, by local planning boards and developers, who could appeal to the Ontario Municipal Board for a final decision.

In a real sense the board was not then, and is not even today, a true regional planning board with substantial authority over the process of urban growth and development throughout the metropolis. Nevertheless it played a significant role in directing attention to physical planning throughout the entire planning area during those early years. Thus the number of local planning boards increased from 14 in 1953 to 20 by the spring of 1957, and the number of staff engaged in planning rose from 32 to 122 persons.

In his portion of the Metro brief, the Commissioner of Planning recommended that the tremendous amount of work involved in processing subdivision applications, and in considering applications for the amendment of Official Plans throughout the planning area, should be strengthened by additional zoning powers. During the four-year period, 194 applications for amendments to Official Plans had been processed, and in the years 1955–1956 this work constituted 40 percent of all such applications the Department of Planning and Development received from the entire province.[15] The Commissioner of Planning pointed out that Metro had no direct zoning powers, other than the usual powers relating to metropolitan roads. Accordingly, he suggested that additional responsibilities for land use controls would enable the Metropolitan Planning Board to discharge its functions far more appropriately than in the past.

REPORT OF THE METROPOLITAN TORONTO COMMISSION OF INQUIRY

The "First Report" of the Commission of Inquiry, issued on March 14, 1958, consisted of 27 mimeographed foolscap pages and a list of exhibits.[16] No other report was ever issued. It must be noted that the Commission of Inquiry was chaired by Mr. Lorne R. Cumming, Chairman of the Ontario Municipal Board, and included four members of the provincial legislature. All five members signed the report. Both the composition of the commission and the contents of the report confirmed the views of those who had, from the beginning, regarded the review as proceeding toward a foregone vote of confidence. From the first announcement of the Commission of Inquiry, critics of the metropolitan form of government were not slow to point out that it would, indeed, be extremely difficult for Cumming, the "father" of Metro, to disown his own "child" in the fourth year of its existence.

In fact, the commission held 32 public hearings from mid-September to early December 1957 and received 46 briefs and written submissions. These included representations from the Metropolitan Council, as described above, the Metropolitan School Board, 10 of the 12 local councils, and 8 of the 10 boards of education. The exhibits filled 32 volumes and totalled 900,000 words.[17] The Chairman stated:

It is proposed, therefore, to include in this first report a number of findings and conclusions of a general nature which have been reached with respect to the value of the fundamental principles which were applied in the existing legislation as tested and applied during the past four years of actual operation, and, secondly, to offer certain specific recommendations for legislative amendments which might be considered and adopted during the present session of the legislature." [18]

This statement was followed by a clear indication that there would be a second (and final) report presenting a comprehensive review of the "remarkable accounts of the Metropolitan government and organization in each of its various fields of jurisdiction during its short period of existence to date." As noted, the second report was never issued.

SUPPORT FOR FEDERATION

Under the heading "General Findings and Conclusions," the commissioners reported that they had been greatly impressed by the evidence of continued and widespread acceptance and support of the principle of federation of autonomous local governments in the Toronto area. The report stated:

It is quite evident that, notwithstanding previous differences and doubts, the experience of the past four years has shown beyond question that the application of the principle of federation was a sound and practical approach to an acceptable and workable solution of the complex problem of providing adequate municipal services in the Toronto Metropolitan Area. . . .

It has been shown beyond question that with the development of a wider understanding of the basic principles of the legislation on the part of the citizens, together with the able and constructive leadership of the Metropolitan Chairman and persistent and sincere efforts of the elected representatives, great progress has been made in removing the serious obstacles to the economic growth and development of the area which seemed insurmountable under the former outdated system of rigidly divided jurisdictional areas and in equally rigid and unbalanced distribution of taxable resources.[19]

The commissioners were convinced of the soundness of the original decisions taken in 1953. Not surprisingly, they found that in both principle and detail the allocation of power and responsibilities—to the Metropolitan Council, the Metropolitan School Board, the local councils and the boards of education—had been overwhelmingly supported. In the evidence placed before them, they found no suggestion that any substantial changes should be made. They acknowledged, however, that the additional powers assigned the Metropolitan Council by amendments effective January 1, 1957, were more controversial. Thus the briefs did not fully support the unified Metropolitan Police Force and the Metropolitan Licensing Commission. But because "such evidence as was available was admittedly conflicting and inconclusive," the commission considered it too early to reach conclusions on the 1957 changes. In fact, the commissioners stated: "Moreover, your Commission does not consider it proper at this time to submit any recommendations as to the procedure which should be adopted by the legislature in considering future requests for any addition to the powers of the Metropolitan authorities." [20]

REPRESENTATION AND THE CITY-SUBURBAN SPLIT

With respect to the composition and organization of the Metropolitan Council and the Metropolitan School Board, the commissioners reported "a surprising amount of satisfaction with the present type of Council and School Board and an unwillingness to make any drastic change in the existing organization at the present time or in the immediate future." The report considered this the most significant feature of the evidence, and "seemed to your Commission [to represent] a surprising amount of satisfaction." While admitting that there were some criticisms of the existing form of council and representational formula, the report stated: "On the whole evidence, however, your Commission finds that there is no serious objection to the present form of Council notwithstanding such theoretical and academic arguments, and that in particular all the municipalities are content with the arrangement by which the political power is divided equally between the central city and the area municipalities as a group *in recognition of the position of the central city as the strong financial anchor of the federation.*" [emphasis supplied] [21] Not surprisingly, therefore, the commission found no immediate need for any extensive reform in the organization of the Metropolitan Council and the Metropolitan School Board.

The Report of the Commission of Inquiry dealt with other matters arising from the early experience of the administration of metropolitan government, issues which to some extent have persisted to the present day. First, the commission heard a good deal of evidence that proceedings within the Metropolitan Council were seriously influenced by a so-called "City-suburban split." Many briefs alleged that sharp divisions between City and suburban representatives hampered the progress of the metropolitan administration. The report rejected this allegation both on the matter of fact and the imputation of obstruction. It stated that "only once has an exact division occurred on only one issue of the many hundreds that have been decided in the history and proceedings of the Council." [22]

ROLE OF THE EXECUTIVE COMMITTEE

On a second question, however—the position of the executive committee within the structure of metropolitan government—the commissioners agreed with the briefs of the City of Toronto and the Township of York that there was "a somewhat doubtful position of the Executive Committee appointments pursuant to the powers contained in Section 11 of the original Act." The commissioners recommended, therefore, that this situation be clarified by including in the Municipality of Metropolitan Toronto Act a specific authority for the appointment of an executive committee. They went even further in recommending that a two-thirds vote of the Metropolitan Council be required to overrule certain recommendations of the executive committee. They also recommended that the Chairman of the Metropolitan Council be made the Chairman and a member of the executive committee, together with four to six additional members appointed from the Metropolitan Council, one-half to come from the City of Toronto and the other half from the Area Municipalities.[23] It was also suggested that there should be additional remuneration for the members of the executive committee.

THE METRO CHAIRMAN

The third question addressed was the method of selecting the Chairman of the Metropolitan Council. The Commission of Inquiry recommended no change in the position or the method of selection, stating:

The Commission is of the opinion that this important provision must be retained in its present form so long as the legislation continues to provide for an equal division of political power between the City and the outer area municipalities, and that unless and until the existing legislation is amended to provide for the direct election by an overall Metropolitan vote of a substantial number of the members of the Metropolitan Council, there is no advantage to be gained by requiring candidates for this vitally important position to undergo the expense and uncertainty of a political campaign extending over the 240 square miles of the Metropolitan Area.[24]

The report went further, to argue that advocates of direct election of the Metro Council Chairman "misconceive the true nature of the office." In the view of the commission, the Chairman should be far more than an impartial presiding officer with a vote to cast in the event of an equal division of the Council: "He should be the Chief Executive Officer responsible for continuous and detailed supervision and correlation of the work and activities of all the administrative departments in accordance with the policies adopted by the elected body. . . . His duties and responsibilities should correspond closely with those of the General Manager of a large corporation." [25]

In these words the commission raised two of the questions that have concerned the elected representatives and the general public since the metropolitan government was established. The first issue concerns the nature of the office itself. The commission clearly felt that the Chairman was akin to a city manager. In this event his position should be appointive rather than elective. But the question of electing the Chairman was also tied to the division of representation between the City and the suburbs on the Metropolitan Council.

This seems to represent a curious contradiction, in that there appears to have been greater satisfaction with appointment of the Chairman when the Metro Council was proportionately less representative of population distribution. On the other hand, in 1967, when the Metropolitan Council membership was changed to correspond closely to population distribution, including 12 representatives from the City and 20 from the five newly created boroughs, the question of the election of the Chairman was a very lively issue. During the years 1963–1966, the issue received a great deal of attention from the press. The Prime Minister of Ontario allegedly stated that for the first term, 1967–1969, no change would be made in the method of electing the Chairman. Apparently the matter is still open.

CHAPTER IV

CITY AND REGIONAL PLANNING, 1954–1959

THE FIRST formal structure for town planning in the Toronto area appeared when the City of Toronto Planning Board was established on June 1, 1942. This recognition of the need for physical planning under local auspices preceded by four years passage of the first planning legislation by a Canadian province, to wit, the enactment of Ontario's Planning Act of 1946.[1] By 1950, when the City of Toronto applied formally to the Ontario Municipal Board for an amalgamation order for the metropolitan area, the City was far ahead of most of the 12 traditional suburban municipalities in its attention to planning, zoning, and neighborhood development. True, the Town of Leaside, with a 1950 population around 15,000, had been laid out (about 1911) by a group of railway planners who drew a sharp distinction between residential, commercial, and industrial areas. Moreover, the Township of Etobicoke, with a 1950 population of more than 40,000, had recently engaged a planning consultant and was in the throes of completing a draft Official Plan. But for the most part, formal planning machinery did not exist throughout the metropolitan area. The rapid expansion of urban development was in serious danger of proceeding in chaotic fashion when the Ontario Municipal Board began to take evidence on the City's amalgamation request in the summer of 1951.

Previously it was emphasized that the "Decisions and Recommendations of the Board," dated January 20, 1953, devoted attention to the necessity for metropolitan-wide consideration of physical planning. Clearly the board hoped that the recommended metropolitan governmental administration would be far more able than any local governmental administration within the area to exercise a regional judgment in devising appropriate land use controls and in controlling the shape and pace of urban development in Metropolitan Toronto.*

THE METROPOLITAN TORONTO PLANNING BOARD

The Municipality of Metropolitan Toronto Act of 1953 stated: "When the Minister has approved an official plan adopted by the Metropolitan Council (a) any official plan then in effect in a subsidiary planning area affected thereby shall be amended to conform therewith; (b) no official plan of a subsidiary planning area shall be adopted that does not conform therewith; (c) no public work, as defined in The Planning Act, shall be undertaken, and no by-law shall be passed, by any municipality or local board within The Metropolitan Toronto Planning Area, that does not conform therewith." [2]

The language in this section (179) of the original act was continued without change in all revisions and consolidations of the legislation during the ensuing 13 years. The original act and its revised versions through 1965 also included a specific description of the task of the new Metropolitan Toronto Planning Board. The original legislation (Section 181) stated: "The scope and general purpose of the official plan for the Metropolitan Toronto Planning Area shall include (a) land uses and consideration generally of industrial, agricultural, residential, and commercial areas; (b) ways of communication; (c) sanitation; (d) greenbelts and park areas; (e) public transportation; and such other matters as the Minister of Planning and Development may from time to time define under The Planning Act."

Clearly the Government of Ontario considered the preparation of an approved Official Plan for the Metropolitan Toronto Planning

---

* It is the considered judgment of town planners that the primary control of private land use in Ontario is the traditional zoning by-law. In the case of Metropolitan Toronto, only the local municipalities were given this power, except adjacent to metropolitan roads where the Metropolitan Council could exercise similar power. It could be argued, therefore, that the division of power between Metropolitan Toronto (with its authority to adopt an Official Plan to which all local plans would have to conform), and local municipalities (who exercise zoning control), did not give Metro control of land use.

Area to be a matter of the utmost importance for the development of the region. By 1959 the first draft Official Plan was presented to the Metropolitan Council and the councils of the Area Municipalities. In 1969, however, ten years later, an Official Plan for the Planning Area did not yet exist in a form that would meet the approval of the Minister of Municipal Affairs, who had become the responsible minister.*

EARLY DIFFICULTIES

In 1954, and after, it was difficult to translate the recommendations of the Ontario Municipal Board and consequent provincial legislation into reality in the field of town and regional planning. Chairman Gardiner began by hiring away from the City of Toronto its chief planning official, Mr. Tracy LeMay, the Secretary-Treasurer of the City of Toronto Planning Board. Mr. LeMay was an elderly public servant with more than 40 years of employment with the City. Prior to the development of the planning board, his title had been City Surveyor. His training in town planning was thus a matter of practical experience rather than formal education in the newly emerging discipline of town and regional planning.

In moving to the new metropolitan administration, Mr. LeMay took with him many of the experienced members of his staff, and as a consequence their departure left the City of Toronto with little or no staff for its own planning board. Mr. LeMay employed as his assistant a young Canadian graduate in political science with an additional year of planning education, Mr. Murray V. Jones, whose total planning experience was comprised of three years as Secretary-Treasurer of the Township of Toronto Planning Board in Peel County, to the west of Metropolitan Toronto. At that time, the Township of Toronto encompassed a vast area of some 100 square miles and a population of about 20,000.

In a word then, both the Metropolitan Toronto Planning Board (MTPB) and the City of Toronto Planning Board began practically from scratch in 1954. The new Metropolitan Corporation had to build a planning staff, which was charged with the responsibility

* Because no plan has ever been submitted to the Minister for his approval, it is not technically correct to state that he would or would not approve of the draft Official Plans, and amendments thereto, which were prepared during the decade 1959–1969.

of developing an Official Plan for an area of 240 square miles, the largest task of its kind ever to face a formal planning organization in Ontario, or for that matter anywhere in Canada. At the same time, the largest component of the Metropolitan Area of Toronto (in terms of population and degree of urbanization), the central city, was left without a trained or experienced planning staff.

Moreover, Mr. LeMay died within the first year of metropolitan government. His assistant, Mr. Jones, who later became the first Metropolitan Commissioner of Planning, was not fully in accord with Chairman Gardiner's philosophy of urban physical expansion without full regard for the principles of town and regional planning. The future of the City of Toronto Planning Board was also in doubt, until Mr. M. B. M. Lawson, a graduate of the new town planning program at the University of Toronto, was appointed as the City's senior planning official in 1954. Within the framework of local government in the City, Mr. Lawson faced many of the same problems as Mr. Jones, particularly the problem of acceptance of planning as an important arm of governmental administration. This background is essential to an understanding of the evolution of Metropolitan Toronto's regional planning function and machinery.

THE ROLE OF REGIONAL PLANNING: AMBIGUOUS EXPECTATIONS

In his submission to the Commission of Inquiry in 1957, the Commissioner of Planning stated that work on the Metropolitan Official Plan would be substantially completed by the end of that year. The commissioner devoted most of his submission, however, to tracing the history of planning in the Greater Toronto area and describing the work of the Metropolitan Toronto Planning Board during the previous three and a half years. The commissioner stressed that the Ontario Municipal Board in 1953 had emphasized the distinction between the Metropolitan Toronto Planning Board's responsibility to prepare a plan of metropolitan development and to exercise control of "major" land uses, and the local municipality's responsibility to provide detailed plans for the orderly development of the various communities. Nevertheless, most persons who were familiar with the development of public intervention in the fields of housing and town planning in Metropolitan Toronto expected that the Metropolitan Council would exercise a good deal of authority, through its control of subdivision plans prepared within the Area Municipalities. In fact, it appears that the Metropolitan Council expected no more from its planning board than a cursory review of local plans of subdivision and their approval prior to submission to the Community Planning Branch of the Department of Municipal Affairs of the Government of Ontario.

It is, of course, impossible to state with certainty the various expectations held by members of the Metropolitan Council with respect to the activities of the MTPB. In the early days of metropolitan government, only a few members of the Metropolitan Council had direct experience with the activities of a local planning board. It cannot be assumed that the 12 metropolitan councillors from the City of Toronto were all experienced in this respect, since the City of Toronto Planning Board had been largely free from political membership during the first post-war decade. Suburban members of the Metropolitan Council were even less experienced. The senior planners of the MTPB certainly assumed that the Council expected from its planning board what the Municipality of Metropolitan Toronto Act required it to do, which was a great deal more than reviewing local subdivision plans. Nevertheless, the concept of an Official Plan was far more remote than the concept of "subdivision control" through a review of local plans.

ASSISTANCE INSTEAD OF CONTROL

Since there was uncertainty with respect to Metro's control over local planning, it was apparently decided that planning assistance to local municipalities would be provided by the MTPB, plus reviewing, examining and advising on the revision of by-laws on subdivision control and zoning. The Area Municipalities had relied extensively on the work of private planning consultants in the first decade of the postwar period. These were soon dropped in favor of assistance from the expanding technical staff of the MTPB. There was very little controversy concerning planning controls, and most of the work of the staff of the board was devoted to activities that were metropolitan-wide in nature, particularly in transportation planning and traffic engineering.

The rapid growth of planning activities in the Metropolitan Toronto Planning Area is outlined in Table 2, based on the presentation of the Commissioner of Planning, and appearing in the Metropolitan Council's 1957 brief to the Commission of Inquiry. The staff of the Metropolitan Toronto Planning Board devoted a great deal of attention in these first few years to aiding planning work in the smaller Area Municipalities that lacked a formal planning organization or the services of a planning consultant. Services included help with Official Plans, assistance in the preparation of zoning by-laws, community studies, and assistance in subdivision design, financial and school studies, traffic and transportation services, and traffic generation studies. By 1957, in addition to the City of Toronto Planning Board, formal planning organizations existed in all of the larger Area Municipalities (with only one exception) in Metropolitan Toronto, as well as in two of the large fringe municipalities in the outer ring of the Planning Area. For all of these municipalities the role of the MTPB was purely advisory. Nevertheless, the board wielded considerable power by virtue of the fact that its advice on planning, zoning and subdivision questions was given great weight by the Minister of Municipal Affairs and the Ontario Municipal Board. For some time only on rare occasions did these bodies of final jurisdiction fail to accept the advice of the board.

PLANNING PROBLEMS IN THE CITY OF TORONTO

The major problems facing the local planning boards were not all the same. Within the large, rapidly developing suburban municipalities the planning problem was essentially that of insuring appropriate land uses. In the terminology of the mid-1950's, the major planning problem facing the City of Toronto, however, was "urban redevelopment" and, a little later, in more fashionable terminology, "urban renewal."

Still, this was by no means the heart of the difficulty facing the City of Toronto Planning Board. The essential problem was to develop a set of roles and responsibilities appropriate to a central city, and yet not in conflict with the overall jurisdiction of the Metropolitan Toronto Planning Board. The City of Toronto Planning Board was required to prepare an Official Plan for the City. This plan would have to conform to the Metropolitan Toronto Official Plan, expected within the first few years of metropolitan government. But it was no easier for the City of Toronto to develop and gain

Table 2
Development of Planning Activities, Metropolitan Toronto Planning Area,
1953 and 1957

	1953		1957	
	Met. Area[e]	Fringe Area[f]	Met. Area	Fringe Area
No. of local Official Plans (year end)	3[a]	4	5[a]	12
No. of local planning boards	6	8[b]	8	12
No. of local boards with permanent staffs	4	1[b]	4	2
Total Planning Board budgets[c]	$116,400[d]	$30,800	$745,700[d]	$80,300
Total Planning Board staff	29	3	111	11
Total population	1,173,000	91,000	1,390,000 (est.)	130,000 (est)
Per capita Planning Board expenditures	0.10¢	0.34¢	0.54¢	0.62¢

SOURCE: Municipality of Metropolitan Toronto, *A Submission by the Council to the Commission of Inquiry* (1957), Report of the Commissioner of Planning, p. 125.
[a] Plus partial Official Plan in East York (240 acres).
[b] Plus Malton Planning Board (merged to Toronto Township Planning Board in 1957).
[c] Does not include expenditures on zoning administration in Toronto and Toronto Township.
[d] Including Metropolitan Toronto Planning Board.
[e] "Metropolitan Area" refers to the Municipality of Metropolitan Toronto encompassing the City and 12 suburban municipalities.
[f] The "Fringe Area" consists of 480 square miles governed by 13 additional municipalities within the Metropolitan Toronto Planning Area but outside the political boundaries of the Municipality of Metro Toronto.

approval for an Official Plan than it was for the Metropolitan Toronto planning organization.*

Throughout the entire post-war period the City of Toronto clearly was in a special position, because its major planning problems were fundamentally different from those of most Area Municipalities. The

* This is not meant to imply that the Metropolitan Toronto Planning Board had restricted the freedom of maneuver of the City of Toronto Planning Board. Wherever possible the MTPB attempted to avoid the City's planning issues, despite the difficulty of doing so in such matters as urban renewal planning. Thus the fact that the City of Toronto found the development of an Official Plan difficult was not attributable to the Metropolitan Toronto Planning Board. But it was not until the mid-1960's that the City of Toronto Planning Board seriously attempted to prepare an Official Plan.

distinction is both as simple and as complicated as the distinction between the concepts of "development" and "redevelopment," or between "planning" and "re-planning." In the suburban areas of Metropolitan Toronto urban growth was occurring on "raw land," for the most part, i.e., land that lacked basic physical services because it was substantially rural before World War II. On the other hand, in the City the principal problems were slum clearance, urban redevelopment, and the prevention of further blight through the newly emerging techniques of housing rehabilitation and conservation of neighborhoods. These techniques, which are the essence of urban renewal, were sufficiently clear that the City of Toronto Planning Board applied to the federal housing agency, Central Mortgage and Housing Corporation, for a grant to undertake a comprehensive study, described in Part V of the Housing Act of 1954 as an "urban renewal study." It was the first such major study in Canada, and was undertaken by the board in 1955 to be completed a year later.[3]

In its report, *Urban Renewal: A Study of the City of Toronto,* the board pointed out that "at a conservative estimate, 8 percent of the city's residential area now needs to be replaced and up to an additional 40 percent may require redevelopment or thorough-going improvement during the next 25 years." The urban renewal study did include a section entitled "Area Map," which indicated "improvement" areas, and gave examples of small areas "where most of the structures are sound, but some are doubtful." It was assumed that the cost of any rehabilitation required for these buildings would be less than the cost of clearing and rebuilding an equivalent number of residences.

Alternative proposals for environmental improvement were worked out on various assumptions. Under one set of assumptions, all properties were to be taken over as an investment by private enterprise, or by a public housing agency or limited dividend company, for the purpose of providing low-rental housing. This last is an example of public rehabilitation. Other proposals assumed that separate ownerships would be maintained, improvements to public property being modest enough to avoid excessive disturbance for the property owners, and yet sufficient to stimulate them to undertake voluntary rehabilitation.

A major and continuing contribution of the City of Toronto urban renewal study was its identification and designation of so-called

"Planning Areas." "A Planning Area," the report stated, "should be large enough to be treated independently in considering its future requirements and the impact of large-scale changes, yet small enough to have identity as a residential district or a commercial area."[4] Two of these areas, the Don Planning Area and the Spadina Planning Area, have since witnessed much of downtown Toronto's redevelopment of the past decade.

On completion of the 1956 urban renewal study the City Planning Board instructed its staff to make studies of certain sub-areas within the two major planning areas noted above. The urban renewal study had stated that the "priorities for public expenditure on redevelopment projects and neighbourhood improvements could . . . result from adequate, up-to-date studies of every district in the city."[5] By September 1957 the board had prepared two draft examinations entitled "Redevelopment Study Area No. 1" and "Redevelopment Study Area No. 2"[6] In the first of these reports an area bounded by Dundas, Parliament, Queen, and Jarvis Streets was examined, and in the second study an area bounded by Dundas, Spadina, Queen, and Bathurst Streets was given careful examination.

By 1959 the City of Toronto Planning Board was ready with a number of proposals for consideration by the Toronto City Council. During the 1960's, these proposals have encompassed a series of urban renewal projects that have caused a modest degree of change in the landscape of downtown Toronto. In the process, they have made available some 3,000 public housing units.

THE DRAFT OFFICIAL PLAN OF THE METROPOLITAN TORONTO PLANNING AREA, 1959

In 1959 the long and eagerly awaited Official Plan was issued by the Metropolitan Toronto Planning Board.[7] The plan was a formidable document whose extreme unwieldiness and high price ($50) drew more initial attention and debate than the contents of the report itself.

In retrospect, it seems clear that the production of a "Regional Plan" within five years of the formation of the Municipality of Metropolitan Toronto was a prodigious feat. There was literally no planning staff until late in 1954, and throughout the entire period, the staff was heavily engaged in a number of other activities. Unfortunately, within the first week or two of its publication the Official

Plan—described in the very first sentence of its Introduction as a "draft of the Official Plan"—was sharply criticized by a number of elected officials in the Area Municipalities.

More surprising was its virtual dismissal by both elected and appointed officials outside the government of Metropolitan Toronto itself. Many municipal politicians opposed the draft Official Plan, not only on substantive grounds but also because the plan was viewed as a further incursion of the Metro into local prerogatives. Some planners think that most local politicians and some officials gave lip service to "planning" but were not ready for the Official Plan when it materialized. Perhaps they did not fully understand what it meant to have an Official Plan, and to adhere to it.

It is hard to escape the conclusion that very few people have ever read the entire 1959 document, "submitted in conformance with paragraph 181 of the Municipality of Metropolitan Toronto Act of 1953." The staff of the MTPB very wisely forecast that this would be the tenor of the document's reception. Accordingly it encouraged discussion, consideration, and constructive criticism of the plan, with a view to its revision and ultimate submission to the Minister of Municipal Affairs for approval. Clearly, the staff that prepared this enormous and impressive document considered it no more than an interim report, and proceeded immediately to the preparation of a revision, which began to appear in draft sections in 1962.

The draft Official Plan of the Metropolitan Toronto Planning Area covered an area of approximately 720 square miles; that is, it attempted to forecast the growth of and establish principles that would govern the orderly development of both the 240-square-mile Municipality of Metropolitan Toronto, and an area twice as large in a broad semicircle extending from Lake Ontario on the west (in the County of Peel), across the top of Metro to the north, and thence southerly again, reaching Lake Ontario on the east of Metro in Ontario County.

CONTENTS OF THE PLAN

In addition to an Introduction, which contained a statement of the "scope and purpose of the Official Plan" and an eleven-page summary to be read by the hard-pressed politician and other students of the subject, the report included 13 chapters with 272 closely printed pages. These constituted the text of the Official Plan itself and were followed by 58 plates that were, in fact, maps of every description covering physiographic features, topography, the distribution of population, the distribution of employment, a Low Rent Housing Plan, the fundamental Land Use Plan, and the like.

The Official Plan gives a history of the physical and political development of the City of Toronto and, ultimately, the Metropolitan Area of Toronto, from its beginning in the year 1615. The major chapter titles will be familiar to all students of planning, and certainly to those who have studied T. J. Kent, Jr.'s *The Urban General Plan*.[8] The report deals with population, employment, housing, land use, transportation, water supply, waste disposal and storm water control, schools, parks and public open spaces, financial resources, and finally the administration of the Official Plan. The most important theoretical sections of the document are Chapter II, General Concept of the Plan; Chapter III, Planning Districts; and Chapter VII, Land Use. The writers begin their description, under the heading of Scope and Purpose, with the following statement:

The Official Plan is designed as a guide for official policy and private action in the development of the Planning Area during the next twenty years. This is about as far ahead as realistic assumptions can be made. On the other hand, most public and private investments made today are intended to serve for several decades and should therefore fit into the pattern of the Planning Area as it may be expected to be about the year 1980.

The image of the Planning Area in 1980, presented in this plan, does not claim to be an exact *prediction of what will be,* nor is it intended to be a binding *prescription of what shall be.* It is an *image of what is likely to be* if the public and private individuals and organizations, responsible for the development of the area, pursue their interests in a rational way within the framework of existing institutions. It presents a working hypothesis of desirable future development which seems possible of achievement on the basis of presently known trends. As such, it serves as a frame of reference for all detailed planning, both public and private. Any development which corresponds to this plan will be in reasonable balance with all other developments presented in the plan.[9]

The authors emphasize their belief that "there is no precedent in Ontario, or indeed, anywhere in Canada or the United States, for an Official Plan for a large metropolitan area."[10] The report also states: "the development of an Official Plan for a large metropolitan area is a pioneering effort. No precedent exists for the relation of such a plan to the planning activities of the area local municipalities." Whether or not this argument can be accepted as the whole truth, its curious repetition might be explained as an additional effort to forestall anticipated criticism, given the existing political relationships within the Metropolitan Council. Many members of Metro Council, particularly those elected from outside the City, saw the Official Plan as a form of further political centralization and interference with local autonomy.

ADDITIONAL PLANS

The report states that although the plan presented in massive form is the basic document of the Official Plan, four additional documents would be published *after the adoption* of the plan by the Minister of Municipal Affairs. These "supplementary documents" were described as (1) district plans; (2) a transportation plan; (3) a financial plan; and finally (4) an urban renewal plan.

Detailed plans were said to be under preparation for each of the 20 planning districts into which the Planning Area had been divided. The district plans were intended to be the main instruments in coordinating local Official Plans and zoning bylaws with the Metropolitan Toronto Official Plan. The transportation plan was described in conventional terms and was designed particularly to examine the relationship between private transportation facilities and public transit. The *Report on the Metropolitan Toronto Transportation Plan* was in fact published by the Planning Board in December 1964.[11] There is no similar record, however, that a financial plan was developed separately as a part of the Official Plan.* The report did indicate that such a plan would be prepared in cooperation with the Metropolitan Finance Commissioner and would project a detailed capital and current budget for the years 1960 and 1965, and fairly general estimates for the period 1965–1980. Five-year capital projections were certainly brought before the Metropolitan Council every year from the late 1950's on, but their relationships to the Official Plan were rather obscure.

* Apparently it was not considered necessary or appropriate, as time passed, to place a Financial Plan formally in the Official Plan. The reasons for this were twofold: first, the Financial Plan would require amendment each year; and second, these annual amendments would require the approval of the Minister of Municipal Affairs. It is possible that these technicalities went a long way toward explaining why the Metropolitan Council ultimately did not formally adopt the Official Plan. (See Chapter Eight, pp. 133–134.)

The urban renewal plan was, however, fulfilled just as described in the 1959 document: "A Plan for the renewal of older sections of the Metropolitan Area will be prepared upon completion of the Metropolitan Urban Renewal Study, which the Metropolitan Toronto Planning Board has been directed by the Metropolitan Council to undertake. This Plan will deal with the overall renewal needs of the area over the next 20 years." [12] A number of reports constitute what might be termed "The Metropolitan Urban Renewal Plan" and these appeared for the most part during the years 1964 to 1966.[13]

EIGHT UNDERLYING PRINCIPLES

In 1959 the Official Plan was designed to achieve orderly development of a metropolitan area and its environs by virtue of the application of eight underlying principles:[14]

"1. In order to minimize the time, cost, and inconvenience of the journey to work, a substantial amount of industrial and other employment should be available in locations easily accessible to residents of every section of the area." This first basic principle is clearly a key factor in defining the distribution of land uses, and in proposing the development of transportation facilities linking the various land uses. In several places, the report states that "while the need to commute should be kept to a minimum, the possibility of commuting should be at a maximum."

"2. The central areas should be intensively developed with a complete range of commercial and cultural services, accessible to each other by pedestrian movement and to all other parts of the area by efficient means of mass transportation. The centre should be the visually attractive symbol of the entire metropolitan community." The report does not make clear its definition of "the centre." If the central area was the heart of the urban core of downtown Toronto, obviously the responsibility for its development lay with the City of Toronto and its planning board. If "the centre" was a much larger area within the City of Toronto, the metropolitan responsibilities in the fields of public transportation and arterial roads would, obviously, play an important role.

"3. Most people want to enjoy, to some degree, the advantages both of city and country. Therefore, all residential areas should have easy access to large green belts and open areas as well as to the urban centres. At selected locations within these open areas, there should be provision for residential developments of a semi-rural type, not requiring urban services." Although this principle seems to suggest the desirability of the inauguration or perpetuation of the gentleman farmer in Metropolitan Toronto, it was actually the basis of the report's suggestion that the main center of the area should be supplemented by several outlying sub-sectors each serving about a half million people. Hopefully such secondary centers would develop around the locations of major shopping facilities, and would in turn be surrounded by residential centers of relatively high density.

"4. Every area opened up for new development should be related to existing facilities and should be fully supplied with public utilities, transportation, shopping, schools, parks, playgrounds, churches, and other neighbourhood facilities. Older areas offering opportunities for renewal should be the object of special area plans. New as well as older sections should offer a wide range of housing types suitable for families of different sizes and of different income levels, and should be identifiable communities; without, however, being isolated from the larger metropolitan community." Clearly the planners in the Metropolitan Board in the late 1950's favored all good things and were against sin. There is certainly nothing in this fourth principle that anyone could object to, and probably nothing that any undergraduate planning student would fail to remember in an examination.

"5. While the plan aims at achieving stability by determining the environment within which each individual development will proceed, it should also allow for orderly growth beyond 1980 and the developments foreseen by then, by reserving areas for future development and for expansion of transportation facilities and public utilities." The federal and provincial governments in partnership had purchased several vast tracts of land in the three large townships surrounding the City of Toronto during the years 1950–1953. This almost unbelievable act of foresight has been attributed to two men, the President of the Central Mortgage and Housing Corporation, and the Deputy Minister of Planning and Development at that time.*

---

* The two were Mr. David B. Mansur, first President of CMHC, who served in that capacity from 1945 to 1954, and Mr. Arthur Bunnell, who worked on one of the first transportation planning studies in Toronto and who ultimately be-

The tracts were assembled at something less than $1,000 per acre, and have played an important role in the development of Metropolitan Toronto. One such area is now in the process of installing basic municipal services, water mains, sewage facilities, and the like, and may become a close-in satellite community of some 60,000 by the mid-1970's.

"6. Public and private transportation should be coordinated in a transportation system, with the private automobile serving primarily for dispersed trips and public transportation concentrated in space and time. The most highly concentrated movements to and from the centre, especially during peak periods, require rapid rail service on its own right-of-way. Roads should be classified according to function; major arteries within the municipality of Metropolitan Toronto should be assumed by the Metropolitan Corporation." The sixth objective, like the fourth, opts for high principles and all good things. In reality the conflict between the forces behind the development of public rapid transit, and those favoring better facilities for private transportation through the building of expressways, has been seen by Harold Kaplan as one of the central difficulties in the entire development of Metro Toronto since 1953.[15]

"7. The natural features of the area—the lake front, the ravines, and the escarpment—should be utilized to the maximum extent." During the 1960's the seventh principle was grasped with ease by members of the Metropolitan Council. Important progress was made in parks and recreation, with Metro taking over the Toronto islands, Toronto's major natural recreational facility. These islands in Toronto Bay can be reached only by a system of ferry boats operated by the Toronto Transit Commission. By the late 1960's, the commission was much closer to the Metropolitan Council in its operation than the former Toronto Transportation Commission had been to the City of Toronto. Moreover, planning for the waterfront, extending from the far east to the far west of Metropolitan Toronto's Lake Ontario shoreline, became a very live issue in the late 1960's. By 1970 a major controversy was developing over the division of responsibilities among the Metropolitan Council, and the City and the boroughs fronting on Lake Ontario.

---

came the senior planning official in the Province of Ontario during World War II.

"8. Within the limits set by these goals the need of the individual area municipalities for a favorable assessment balance should be taken into account." Although it was hoped that the creation of a Metropolitan Assessment Department and a uniform system of evaluation throughout Metro Toronto would reduce the competition between the Area Municipalities for industrial and commercial assessment, this hope was quickly shattered. In the early 1960's it was quite clear that at least two of the three major areas of rapid population growth within the metropolis were as sorely out of balance, in terms of assessed valuation, as they had been in the years immediately following World War II.

It is interesting to note that in the development of what came to be called the "proposed Official Plan," issued in December 1965, the terms "principles" and "policies" appear in various drafts, as well as the final document.[16] Some of these principles bear a close resemblance to those just described. Some are not so familiar, however, and it is apparent that the intervening period saw subtle changes in emphasis for political reasons and reasons associated with technical planning considerations. These matters will be considered later.

LOCAL PLANNING BOARDS IN METROPOLITAN TORONTO

It will be recalled from Table 2 that in 1953, 6 of the 13 municipalities within the traditional metropolitan area had appointed planning boards in accordance with the Ontario Planning Act of 1946, as amended. In the fringe area 8 of the additional 13 municipalities had such boards. By 1957 the number of planning boards within the inner metropolis had grown to 8 and in the outer fringe the number had increased to 12. Seven years later, during the hearings before the Royal Commission on Metropolitan Toronto, the second Commissioner of Planning, Eli Comay, pointed out that all but 4 of the 26 Area Municipalities had planning boards.[17] Three of the smaller municipalities within Metro—the Village of Swansea, the Village of Forest Hill, and the Town of New Toronto—had continued to develop without such planning organizations. One small municipality, the Village of Port Credit in the fringe area, was also without a planning board. By 1964 some 12 of the 26 municipalities including the 6 large metropolitan municipalities—the City of Toronto, the Townships of North York, Scarborough, Etobicoke, York, and East York—employed permanent planning staffs.

THE ROLES OF THE LOCAL BOARDS

In a very real sense the urban development of Metropolitan Toronto since 1953 may be visualized in an analysis of the roles and responsibilities of local planning boards. One extreme view saw these organizations become redundant with the creation of the Metropolitan Toronto Planning Board in 1954. At the other extreme, it was alleged that the "real" planning must take place within the Area Municipalities, and that the role of the MTPB would perforce be that of a large regional advisory body preparing grandiose "official plans," without much contact with the reality "on the ground" and in the marketplace.

There has always been another view, holding the detailed work of planning for the growth and development of a vast metropolis to be beyond the capacity of any one planning organization. In this view, if the MTPB were to be given sole responsibility for planning throughout the area, this would have required the creation of district planning offices or subregional planning boards to deal with the mass of daily planning routine. The writer spent many hours in a number of capacities before local planning boards in Metro Toronto, and must emphasize that the amount of work to be undertaken and the number, variety, and importance of decisions to be made by the appointed planning boards have at times seemed almost overwhelming. Certainly, no single metropolitan planning board could have dealt with the flood of applications that came before such townships as Etobicoke, North York, and Scarborough from the mid-1950's to the mid-1960's.*

Thus in the traditional suburban municipalities, the local planning boards were and are clearly responsible for encouraging orderly *development* within the framework of a local Official Plan. As early

---

* It is conceivable, of course, that a planning board made up of appointed members receiving an appropriate honorarium could have handled this work, if they chose to meet for several hours five or six times a week. It is the view of the writer that the expansion of Metro Toronto became so controversial with the trend towards multiple housing in the 1960's that every application was disputed.

as 1953, before the inauguration of Metro, 3 municipalities within the metropolitan area had already developed an Official Plan. In addition, a partial Official Plan had been approved for a portion of a fourth municipality. By 1957 this number had grown to 5 (in addition to the aforesaid partial Official Plan) and the number of municipalities in the outer fringe of the metropolitan area with such approved plans had grown from 4 to 12. By 1964 the Royal Commission on Metropolitan Toronto learned that these numbers had risen to 18–8 within the 13 Metro municipalities and 10 in the fringe areas.*

The emphasis upon *development* both in the Metro area (outside the City of Toronto) and in the fringe Area Municipalities, was made necessary by the rapid growth in population and by the almost total absence of land for residential housing within the built-up City of Toronto. Furthermore, most persons on both the demand and supply sides of the equation conceived of housing primarily in the form of a single or semi-detached house for an individual family. Until the end of the 1950's the possibility that multiple housing in the form of apartment buildings might accommodate the growth in population was scarcely discussed. For all these reasons the planning boards, particularly in the 3 large townships surrounding the City, were in a much simpler and easier position than the City of Toronto Planning Board. They were dealing with vast areas of raw land, sometimes larger than the original City itself, and had the clear responsibility to separate out the respective land uses, and to plan communities whose populations would first reach 100,000, and then a quarter of a million each. In fact, the Chairman of the Metropolitan Council predicted before the Royal Commission on Canada's Economic Prospects, 1955–1980, that Metropolitan Toronto would have a population of about 2.8 million by 1980, with at least a half a million in each of the three largest townships.[18] This is not to suggest that it is easy to plan vast areas "from scratch," but the tasks are less difficult than those faced in the built-up central area of the modern metropolis.

* There is an obvious inconsistency here with respect to the fringe area municipalities. The number "12" for 1957 was reported by the Commissioner of Planning before the Committee of Inquiry in 1957; the number "10" for the fringe area was reported by the second Commissioner of Planning before the Royal Commission in 1964.

THE SPECIAL POSITION OF THE CITY

The City of Toronto Planning Board was, indeed, in a special position from the time of its revitalization in 1954. In short, its task was the replanning or redevelopment of the central city itself, an area of 35 square miles with a population of just less than 700,000. When the Municipality of Metropolitan Toronto was created, only one piece of public urban renewal had been accomplished in that area, namely, the clearance and rebuilding of the Regent Park North area, some 42.5 acres designated as a slum by the early 1930's. A second project immediately to the south, which would have added no more than 27 acres to the total, was under discussion at the time, and more than a dozen neighborhoods within the City were literally crying for attention.

As has been indicated, the planning board did undertake one of the first urban renewal studies in Canada. As a consequence of this study a number of additional urban renewal programs have been designated, planned, or accomplished during the past 12 years. Nevertheless, the task facing a central city planning board like Toronto's can scarcely be underestimated. The major role of the City's board, in addition to the familiar task of preparing an Official Plan, was *redevelopment,* and later, urban renewal.

The City planning staff saw its role in terms of district planning, and to this end it began a series of studies in the late 1950's which resulted in the following reports: The Plan for the Annex (1959); The Plan for Downtown Toronto (1963); The Don Planning District Appraisal (1963); The Eglinton Planning District Appraisal (1964); and Proposals for a New Plan for Toronto (1966). The great virtue of these district or neighborhood studies was that they gave the members of the appointed board and the professional planning staff opportunities to stimulate citizen participation. First, copies of the reports, often in digest form, were distributed to every household or business within the district planning area. In all cases, this distribution was followed by a series of public meetings within the neighborhood. Thus there was at least an attempt to maintain contact with the residents of smaller areas or communities within the City. It is often alleged that, in the modern metropolis, only the local suburban planning boards have been able to keep in touch with the "grass roots level." But in Metropolitan Toronto the City of Toronto Planning Board probably provided at least enough, if not more than enough, information to the residents of neighborhoods to enable them to envision the kind of local community in which they might be fortunate enough to live within the next decade or two.

Nevertheless, by 1970 the City Council had not acted on most of the different plans prepared by the planning board. Moreover, in the light of new approaches to citizen participation developed during the past three or four years, the manner in which the City of Toronto Planning Board conceived "citizen participation" was soon to be considered a mere gesture. The strength of these new movements was not, however, directed toward the district plans. Rather, the movements tended to counter significant proposals for urban renewal emanating from the planning board, particularly after 1965.

CHAPTER V

HOUSING AND URBAN RENEWAL, 1954-1962

O NE OF THE FACTORS leading to the formation of Metropolitan Toronto was the proven incapacity of the 13 municipalities to deal with the difficult questions of providing decent and adequate housing accommodation for their expanding populations. In the light of this fact, clearly underlined in the report of the Ontario Municipal Board of January 1953, it is remarkable that the Municipality of Metropolitan Toronto Act failed to assign substantial responsibility in the fields of housing and urban redevelopment to the newly created metropolitan administration. Instead, Metro was treated like any other local government. Thus Part XIII, Section 17 of the Act, "Housing and Redevelopment," reads as follows:

(1) The Metropolitan Corporation and the Metropolitan Council have all the powers conferred on the Corporation or Council of a municipality under the Housing Development Act [passed originally by the Government of Ontario in 1948] or any other Act with respect to housing or building development, housing projects, temporary housing accommodation and redevelopment areas, and with respect to any other matter concerned with the provision or improvement of housing accommodation.

(2) Nothing in (1) shall be deemed to limit or interfere with the power of the area municipalities with respect to the matters mentioned in sub-section (1).[1]

Therefore, in 1953 the Government of Ontario must have decided that the need for housing and slum clearance had been overemphasized, particularly for the lowest third of the income distribution. Alternatively, it was also felt that a sufficient number of powers and responsibilities had been conferred on the new Metropolitan Council, and that the Area Municipalities should retain housing and urban renewal, at least for some time, in order to provide local governments with a raison d'être.* As early as January 1, 1947, the City of Toronto had conducted a plebiscite on the question of clearing and redeveloping Regent Park North. Following the success of this referendum, the City had created the Housing Authority of Toronto as early as May of that year. The authority also had the powers of a limited-dividend housing company to operate in the middle-income field, under the then Section 16 of the National Housing Act, 1944.

SLUM CLEARANCE AND PUBLIC HOUSING: WHOSE RESPONSIBILITY?

To many elected and appointed officials, the emphasis upon slum clearance and public housing within the central city seemed most appropriate: The needy were clearly discernible within the urban core, whereas in the suburban municipalities there were very few "poor families," and very few families in need of public housing. The social situation in the suburbs was considered to be entirely different from that prevailing in the City of Toronto. To some extent this was a perfectly correct attitude, because no family could move beyond the City of Toronto unless housing were available in the form of single or semi-detached houses for sale. In the heart of the City, however, the housing stock developed over nearly a century had a sponge-like quality enabling it to soak up a vast number of migrants from foreign lands, as well as from rural areas and small towns throughout Canada. In large measure these trends have continued to the present day.

Chairman Gardiner of the Metropolitan Council did begin his administration, however, with many references to the need for more housing throughout the metropolitan area, particularly for relatively low-income families. In his view the "metro concept" meant that public housing should not be located only within the City of Toronto itself. He believed that all the municipalities within the new metropolitan federation must share in the capital and operating sub-

* An additional interpretation might be that in those years elected representatives showed very little interest in the whole matter of public housing. If it was considered at all as a function of local government, it would have been linked very closely to the notion of public welfare, and thus might be tolerable under the circumstances, provided that very substantial contributions for capital costs and operating subsidies were made by the senior levels of government.

sidies required for such accommodation, and should also expect to receive publicly provided housing within their borders. The Chairman's sincerity was unquestionable, and as early as 1955 he was actively promoting a new authority within the appropriate federal and provincial departments to coordinate public activity in housing and urban renewal within Metro.

For many reasons it was not possible to transform the Housing Authority of Toronto into a metropolitan-wide authority. The gist of the difficulty lay in the manner of appointment and the inclusion of elected representatives on the City's own authority. After the inauguration of a federal-provincial partnership in public housing with the amendment of the National Housing Act in 1949, a number of so-called federal-provincial housing authorities were created, from St. John's, Newfoundland, to Vancouver, British Columbia.

More than a dozen such authorities had been appointed in the Province of Ontario, and were responsible to a federal-provincial partnership through the Housing Branch of the Ontario Department of Planning and Development. These authorities were composed of five, seven, or nine "public-spirited citizens" (none of whom were elected officials), appointed to administer public housing created by the two senior governments in cooperation with the local municipality. The administrative regulations were laid down in a manual developed by the provincial Housing Branch. The rent scale was established by the federal housing agency, Central Mortgage and Housing Corporation, and applied coast to coast.

A FEDERAL-PROVINCIAL AUTHORITY FOR METRO

A new seven-member federal-provincial authority, entitled the Metropolitan Toronto Housing Authority, was appointed on December 1, 1955. It was charged with developing a metropolitan-wide program in the Toronto area.* The new authority had no housing to administer, and the gravity of the situation was underlined by its appointment nearly two years before housing accommodations were actually built and available for occupancy. This requires some explanation of the nature of a Canadian federal-provincial housing

* The writer served as the Vice-Chairman of the Metropolitan Toronto Housing Authority from early in 1956 until its dissolution and incorporation in the Ontario Housing Corporation in November 1964. Since September 1964, he has served as a member of the Board of Directors of the corporation.

authority, including comparisons and contrasts with city housing activity in the United States.

Until 1964, and even to some extent today all the planning and architectural design in urban renewal in Canada was undertaken by the federal agency, Central Mortgage and Housing Corporation, in conjunction with some agency of the appropriate provincial government. The local housing authorities are not consulted. They have not been considered appropriate participants in the urban renewal process. Instead, their role has been seen as that of a management authority to operate the public housing or other aspects of the urban renewal programs when they are completed.

All this is in contrast to the American experience, where the local or municipal public housing authority has had substantial powers to raise its own funds and to plan and design the programs, as well as to call for bids and let contracts, and in a sense govern the entire process. The role of state and federal government in America has emphasized the financing of housing.

In Ontario until 1964, an application had to be made to the Housing Branch of the Ontario Department of Planning and Development, approved by the provincial authorities, and forwarded to Central Mortgage and Housing Corporation for federal approval. If the proposed plan involved an urban renewal scheme in which land was to be acquired and cleared, approval had also to be obtained from the Community Planning Branch of the Ontario Department of Municipal Affairs. When the required approvals—from the local government to the provincial government to the federal government and back down the line—were obtained, the Architectural Division of the federal agency would then begin to design what seemed to be the appropriate number of dwelling units on the best site suggested in the previous discussions. The latter probably occupied the better part of two years. The housing was designed, the programs were tendered, and the contracts were awarded, but in none of these matters was the local government or the local federal-provincial housing authority consulted (if one already existed).

The federal government paid 75 percent of the capital costs of constructing the housing, and the provincial government the remaining 25 percent. This was the general formula, but the local municipality might also be required to contribute, depending on circumstances. Thus in the case of subsidized rental projects in the Province of Ontario, the local government was not required to make any capital contribution, if municipal taxes on the project were reduced in proportion to the subsidy. If, however, the accommodation were to be of the "full recovery" type, that is, for lower middle-income groups, the local government was required to contribute 7.5 percent of the total capital. In both types of public housing the subsidies (to cover operating losses) were provided on the same basis, that is, 75 percent federal, 17.5 percent provincial, and 7.5 percent local. It is easy to see why in many smaller communities, and medium-sized cities and towns, the housing authority sought to reduce or even eliminate this subsidy, which was burdensome even at 7.5 percent. In short, local municipalities felt that their tax resources did not permit them to contribute to housing subsidies.

In the metropolis, however, all partners saw the Metropolitan Toronto Housing Authority as perhaps the most important organization of its kind within the entire nation. Its first chairman was, in fact, the retired first President of Central Mortgage and Housing Corporation, Mr. David Mansur, who had served as President during the years 1945 to 1954. The remaining members included the Commissioner of Finance for Metropolitan Toronto, distinguished members of the business community, the judiciary, the educational system, and citizens' organizations. Nevertheless, this apparently powerful group began its work with no authority to develop a program of public housing and urban renewal throughout Metropolitan Toronto. It was expected instead to undertake responsibilities for the occupancy, management, and administration of publicly provided housing, just as was the case in many small communities in Canada where fewer than 50 dwelling units had been provided. The authority soon found it extremely difficult to accept this stunted role, and its influence in the development of Metro during the next decade was commensurate with its refusal to "lie down and remain uncounted."

THE CASE OF LAWRENCE HEIGHTS

The new Metropolitan Toronto Housing Authority inherited one major housing program, Regent Park South, encompassing 732 dwelling units in east-central Toronto (as recommended by a special committee which reported in 1955).[2] But the real test of metropolitan-wide potential in this field lay in the Lawrence Heights Public Housing Project. For about a year most of Chairman Gardiner's major addresses had included references to a substantial public housing program to be developed on publicly owned land within the Township of North York. The federal-provincial partnership had, as we have already noted, purchased several large sites in undeveloped areas outside the City. The first of these to be developed lay in North York, little more than a mile to the northwest of the City boundaries. By 1955 one of the largest shopping plazas of the time had been built on this land at the juncture of two major arteries, and a privately developed subdivision (tract), Lawrence Manor, was under construction with the assistance of National Housing Act mortgages.

A THREAT TO A WAY OF LIFE

As the new authority began to explore the potentialities of a public housing development on a site with an area of approximately 100 acres, all the political and social implications of providing public housing outside the central city in a modern metropolis came sharply into focus.* In the mid-1950's the Township of North York continued to cling to the rather realistic notion that its people, a small number of old-time rural residents and a much larger number of new suburban dwellers, were quite different in both political and social composition from the residents of the City.

The proposed introduction of several hundred low-income families as occupants of the Lawrence Heights housing project was thus seen as a potential threat to a traditional way of life—as described by local politicians and long-term residents. The project seemed to presage a social revolution in the township. For these reasons, as well as the almost instinctive dislike for public housing found throughout North America, Lawrence Heights was strongly opposed during the years 1956–1960. As we shall see, the soul-searching by township officials and the opposition by suburban residents to large public housing programs in the suburbs has continued to the present day, when 1,081 families now occupy Lawrence Heights.

---

* Frank Smallwood, *Metro Toronto: A Decade Later* (Toronto: Bureau of Municipal Research, 1963), p. 33. Professor Smallwood, who reviewed the first 10 years of Metro in substantial detail, wrote: "The Toronto public housing program represents a tangled web of overlapping governmental jurisdictions and its current woes are certainly not due to any problems of local financial inequities alone. Yet it is just as obvious that these local inequities have contributed additional complications to an already complex situation."

ANTICIPATED IMPACT OF SERVICE NEEDS

These were not wholly irrational prejudices and fears, as there was ample evidence that the movement of low-income families to the suburbs would bring quantifiable and substantive changes that would be reflected in service needs and demands made on local government. Thus only a nominal number of welfare cases or welfare expenditures had previously confronted North York. Consequently the local government had no social welfare administration, and few social services were available to township residents, or to other Metro residents outside the City itself.

Given such a situation, there was a good deal of apprehension about the impact of Lawrence Heights. Although the project's density was extremely low, as public housing projects go—only 12 families per acre—North York's legislators feared that it would precipitate extensive future educational and recreational service needs, as well as demands for social and health services. In projecting these responsibilities they were, in effect, pioneers who believed that the new metropolitan administration was overwhelming them with a show of political strength, rather than offering logical proposals with adequate financing to meet future needs.

These service-demand arguments were apparently based less on snobbishness than on hard facts such as the knowledge that the new host township would—within a year—become responsible for 50 percent (the proportion at that time) of public assistance payments to all such families requiring welfare assistance. During the first year of residence, the City of Toronto or another local municipality within Metro would be responsible for such payments. After that, the suburban township would take over that share.

For all these reasons, a protracted and bitter dispute was waged over Lawrence Heights, its location and its nature. Many citizens and elected officials threatened court action to block the development. Although the threats were not carried out, Metro Chairman Gardiner had to use all of his considerable powers of persuasion to get a reluctant North York Council to accept what has since become Canada's largest public housing project, in both numbers and area.

THE CHAIRMAN'S SUPPORT

Chairman Gardiner became involved in the controversy for several reasons. For one thing, he in effect "adopted" Lawrence Heights as his personal project. Presumably he did this in part to provide proof that Metro could do more than build water mains, sewers, and roadways. Moreover, he was under great pressure from various voluntary associations, as well as the Metropolitan Toronto Housing Authority, to decentralize the public housing program into the municipalities outside the central city. Finally, as we have noted, getting North York's assent, which was required by law, took his personal intervention.

Even Mr. Gardiner, however, could not entirely overcome the strong opposition and was forced to seek a compromise. The compromise, worked out with federal and provincial housing officials, took the form of a "blended project," in which a substantial proportion of the dwelling units would be rented on a "full recovery" basis. Presumably these dwelling units would be attractive to middle or lower middle-income groups. Hopefully the blending of inexpensive and subsidized housing would provide a form of social integration, instead of producing a monolithic collection of very poor families, bringing multiple problems with them.

COMPLETION AND SUBSEQUENT EXPERIENCE

Lawrence Heights was completed between 1959 and 1962. For the most part, it consists of row houses and maisonettes, with a number of small apartment dwellings of not more than 30 units each. A buffer strip of single detached homes for very large families was constructed between the public housing area and the privately sponsored subdivision to the east. Nevertheless, social tension has continued throughout the entire period. In summary, and depending upon one's point of view, it can be argued that the 6,000 residents of Lawrence Heights were for some years rejected by the larger community of North York.

By the mid-1960's it was evident that Lawrence Heights was in urgent need of a community center program, particularly for the development of day-care and day nursery facilities, and recreational facilities for the elderly. The center was constructed when the Township of North York agreed to divide the estimated $100,000 cost equally with Metro Council. The federal housing agency, Central Mortgage and Housing Corporation, had flatly refused to make a capital contribution and the province had followed suit.

The demand upon educational facilities soon proved to be enormous. An elementary school was built within Lawrence Heights, but was soon completely occupied. Thereupon senior elementary school pupils had to be sent to an adjacent neighborhood junior high school. The need for recreational facilities for teenagers led to an unpleasant controversy—having segregationist overtones—with the administration of a nearby secondary school. It was suggested that the school's swimming pool be used exclusively by the children from the public housing project on one or two evenings each week. In another development, the project's elementary school became a "community school" by 1968. The township Board of Education had awakened to the realization that the community was in need of a building, and of a recreational program that could be offered on an around-the-clock basis (early morning to midnight), seven days a week.

With respect to social services, the township first appointed a social worker exclusively for the Lawrence Heights area. Later, North York cooperated with the Metro Toronto Children's Aid Society and the Family Service Association of Metropolitan Toronto in the creation of an experimental program designed exclusively for families in the project. These programs continue in the early 1970's with reasonable success.

But unemployment among young people is a major overriding concern, and one that makes it extremely difficult to demonstrate substantial social progress. Moreover, the awareness that older teenagers, including those who have completed high school, suffer high unemployment is judged to have a devastating effect on their younger brothers and sisters. All is far from well in Lawrence Heights.

LESSONS OF LAWRENCE HEIGHTS, AND MOVES TOWARD A METROPOLITAN PROGRAM

The lessons of Lawrence Heights were not lost on the major governmental parties at interest. The Chairman of Metro Toronto saw that his emphasis on one huge project within a single municipality could not produce an adequate housing program for an expanding metropolis. Moreover, Lawrence Heights' unitary qualities, its location within one of the rapidly expanding suburban municipalities, its failure in the planning stage to deal adequately with social needs and social services—especially schooling and counseling services—produced a monstrous headache for Mr. Gardiner.

STAFF INADEQUACIES AND APPOINTED ADVISORS

At the same time, the Metro administration was seen as unable to cope with the provincial and federal agencies, or to adminster such programs during construction and occupancy. Although Metro was well staffed in the traditional fields of local government, it was not adequately equipped for the development and implementation of a metropolitan housing policy.

Thus there was need for some form of advisory body to help the Metropolitan Chairman keep abreast of a difficult area in program development, and also to enable the Metropolitan Executive Committee and Council to deal appropriately with the strong views and reservations of the Area Municipalities. The solution devised by the Chairman—after a series of meetings in late 1957 and early 1958— took the form of an Interim Housing Committee composed of the Metro Commissioner of Planning as Chairman, the Metro Commissioner of Welfare and Housing, and the Chairman of the Metro Housing Authority. The first two persons were senior civil servants, and the third, although a layman, was extremely knowledgeable in housing matters. As far as the writer has been able to learn, no formal status was provided for the Interim Housing Committee, formed early in 1958, either by the passage of a metropolitan by-law or any other legislative device. The Metropolitan Chairman was free to seek advice on these matters as he wished, and there could be little question that he had selected appropriate advisors.

HOUSING POLICY: A MULTILEVEL PROGRAM

The controversy over Lawrence Heights exposed a further weakness. The Metro Toronto Housing Authority appeared to have almost no role in the development of a metropolitan housing policy, or for that matter in the progress of any specific metropolitan proposal. The members of the Board of the Housing Authority were restive under the strictures governing the roles of federal-provincial housing authorities throughout Canada. First they urged that a full-time executive director, a senior person with appropriate experience, be hired to direct the activities of what promised to be the largest authority of its kind in the nation. By 1959 an executive director had been located and engaged; he became the secretary of the Interim Housing Committee. It was then but a small step to an important role for the authority in the development of a housing and urban renewal program for the metropolitan area.

Within a short time the Interim Housing Committee reported to Chairman Gardiner. The Chairman recommended to the Metropolitan Council, which approved, acceptance of studies conducted by the Metropolitan Toronto Planning Board. These studies pointed to a serious deficiency in public housing for low-income families and for elderly persons. The Metropolitan Council approved the recommendation that the three levels of government, together with the appropriate Area Municipalities within Metro, work diligently toward the construction of at least 1,000 public housing dwellings for families and 500 dwelling units for "senior citizens," during each of the five years between 1959 and 1963. This combined enunciation of policy and a quantitative program was widely hailed throughout Ontario and, indeed, throughout the nation. At least it seemed that Metropolitan Toronto was on its way toward accepting, as real policy targets, some of the major housing goals underlying its creation, and referred to in the Ontario Municipal Board's report of January 20, 1953.

SUBURBAN OPPOSITION

Meanwhile however, the Area Municipalities that were likely to provide sites for publicly provided housing had also learned the lessons of Lawrence Heights. This applied particularly to the three largest Townships, Etobicoke, North York, and Scarborough, but it did not exclude the Townships of York and East York. Throughout North America, these were years of growing opposition to public housing, based in substantial measure on the reports and studies of social and economic conditions in the large projects built just before and just after World War II. The limited Canadian evidence related particularly to downtown slum clearance and rehousing operations. Prior to the 1960's, this experience appeared to be favorable.[3] Metro legislators from outside the City concluded that publicly provided housing was much more appropriate in the urban core than in the suburban areas. In any event, the multiple dwellings, which were apparently typical of publicly provided housing, were viewed simply as blots upon a suburban landscape where, until 1960 few residential structures had stood, except for single-family, one- and two-story dwellings.

Not surprisingly, the opposition within the Area Municipalities mounted in geometric proportions when the Metropolitan Toronto Housing Authority and Mr. Gardiner recommended to the Metro Council that substantial public housing communities be constructed in both the Townships of Scarborough and Etobicoke. In Scarborough, the Warden Woods project was first discussed publicly about 1960 when a substantial block of land became available, and the Interim Housing Committee recommended its purchase to the metropolitan administration.* In Etobicoke, for a decade or more the senior levels of government had owned a site known as Thistletown, which contained enough land for 1,200 public housing dwelling units and many hundreds of additional homes. The proposal for Thistletown—to be developed by a mixture of public and private enterprise—envisioned a huge satellite community in the northern portion of the relatively vacant township. Both Warden Woods and Thistletown were strongly fought through the first three or four years of the 1960's. Both brought to the fore issues of considerable importance to the future of metropolitan government in Toronto.

The Township of Scarborough placed particular emphasis upon the additional costs for schooling and public welfare assistance that would be entailed by a large number of new families occupying public housing. During 1961 and 1962 officials of the Metro Planning Board worked diligently on a formula for special financial assistance —from the consolidated revenues of Metro—to municipalities in which substantial public housing would be located. At the western end of Metropolitan Toronto, the Township of Etobicoke fought almost viciously to head off the long projected Thistletown housing project. This occurred although Thistletown was a sincere and well-designed attempt by the three senior levels of government to create "an integrated community," blending public housing and privately produced housing, rental accommodation and home ownership, and low-income and middle-income families.

* The Interim Housing Committee, with the assistance of the Metropolitan Toronto Planning Board, undertook a broad examination of available public housing sites within Metro Toronto. Their recommendations concerning Warden Woods, O'Connor Drive and Scarlett Road, among others, led to intergovernmental land acquisitions that ultimately increased the public housing stock by nearly 1,000 dwelling units. Some of their proposed housing projects, however, were not constructed until the late 1960's, under the auspices of the Ontario Housing Corporation.

Etobicoke took a somewhat different line of opposition from that of Scarborough and North York. Its officials expressed the attitude of "noblesse oblige," stating that each of the major developing area municipalities "must take its share of poor families" or "public housing families" or "welfare families." Nevertheless, the difficulties anticipated from placing low-income families in a relatively well-to-do municipality like Etobicoke were viewed by them as more serious than in the case of a working-class community like Scarborough. Thus they argued that the people in Etobicoke were not in the habit of using public facilities. It was also pointed out that Etobicoke lacked an adequate public library system as well as an adequate system of parks and recreation. Moreover, it was alleged that it did not provide various social and recreational services of a kind commonly expected within the central city, as well as Area Municipalities composed of lower-middle, working-class, and lower-income families.

The resident of Etobicoke apparently provided his own social and recreational facilities within his home, his clubs and privately purchased recreational facilities, or his summer home. In a nutshell, Etobicoke was arguing that it really had not provided for "its own residents" the facilities that would be required to assist the "intruders," who would be applicants for public housing from the deteriorated areas of the central city or other older sections of the metropolitan area.

A DISMAL RECORD AND ITS CAUSES

Regent Park South (732 dwelling units) and the greater part of Lawrence Heights (ultimately 1,081 dwelling units) were completed and occupied from September 1957 through 1960. Unfortunately, the announced metropolitan housing program of 1,500 dwelling units per year for five years was a complete failure. Severe opposition by the Area Municipalities coincided with the onset of a serious economic recession that developed in the United States and Canada during the second half of 1957, deepened during 1958–1960, and continued through 1962. This five-year period roughly coincided with the time span for achieving the goal of an additional 7,500 public housing units for families and elderly people within Metropolitan Toronto, yet only 38 new houses for families were completed, the last portion of the Lawrence Heights project.

This dismal record was severely criticized in the press, and by citizens' groups, planners, and social scientists throughout Metropolitan Toronto and the Province of Ontario. During these years both the Government of Ontario and the Central Mortgage and Housing Corporation drastically curtailed their planned commitments to new public housing and urban renewal programs throughout Canada. At the time, however, these explanatory facts were not generally known. Certainly no public announcement of such curtailment was made by either of these senior partners in housing and urban renewal. Instead, criticism was focused on the administration of Metropolitan Toronto. The Metropolitan Chairman was hard put to explain the incapacity of the new government to make more than token progress. The politician's favored phrase in the late 1950's and early 1960's was to the effect that man is capable of sending satellites and astronauts into space and successfully recovering them but seems unable to solve his housing problems. The writer pointed out on many occasions that it was far simpler to send a man into space than to solve the human problems of providing decent housing to the lowest third of the population in our Western urbanized societies. But this rejoinder had no profound impact.

TOWARD A SINGLE HOUSING AUTHORITY

After 1960, efforts to break through obstructions to progress in housing and urban renewal focused on the possibility of creating a *single* housing authority for all of Metropolitan Toronto, an authority with sufficient power to overcome the frustrations implicit in the federal-provincial partnership that had been inaugurated in 1950. During the years 1961–1963 the pressure grew for a single administrative agency in the Metropolitan Toronto Housing Authority, and in such prominent citizens' organizations as the Community Planning Association (Metropolitan Toronto Branch), the Women Electors' Association, and, finally, within the Metropolitan Council itself.

In the first instance, this appeared to require a merger between the Housing Authority of Toronto and the Metropolitan Toronto Housing Authority. A committee was created in cooperation with the City of Toronto to discuss this possibility. Although the committee met several times between the fall of 1961 and the summer of 1962, its success was largely limited to identifying the difficult problems needing solution before such a merger could occur. In particular, the assets of the Housing Authority of Toronto, in the neighborhood of $15 to $20 million, would have to be purchased by a "higher level of government," or the City of Toronto would have to require appropriate financial compensation in some other way. City officials pointed out that they had turned over to Metro, without compensation, tremendously valuable capital assets in the form of waterworks and sewage disposal facilities, and they were in no mood to act similarly with respect to their public housing stock, which at that time was as large as that under administration by the Metropolitan Authority.

Political support for a single metropolitan-wide housing authority came from the newly elected second Chairman of the Metropolitan Council, William R. Allen, Q.C., who assumed office in January 1962. He appeared convinced that the principal factor in Metro Toronto's dilemma in public housing and urban renewal was the impotence of its two housing authorities, neither of which could take effective action to produce the vast quantity of public housing needed. On several occasions the new Metro Chairman voiced his support for the new conception of a metropolitan authority with real capabilities, including the power to plan and design housing, to call for tenders (bids) and award contracts, and to acquire sites well in advance of anticipated requirements. In short, he called for a much more powerful instrument than had previously existed in Canada. Moreover in 1963 it was well known that changes were contemplated in the National Housing Act to permit the creation of regional or metropolitan authorities capable of making an appreciable impact on the growing housing shortage. Thus there were grounds for optimism as Canada began to emerge from the severe economic recession of 1958–1962.

CHAPTER VI

METROPOLITAN GOVERNMENT IN TORONTO: THE SECOND SIX YEARS, 1960–1965

THE UNEASY RELATIONSHIPS among the City of Toronto, the Area Municipalities, and the new Metropolitan Council, despite the numerical balance between the City and the suburbs in the Council, were clearly evident throughout the first six years of metropolitan government (1954–1959). The distrust, which in part led to the imposition of a form of metropolitan government by the Province of Ontario in 1953, remained strong during the entire period. After all, neither the City, which had applied for an amalgamation of the 13 municipalities, nor the Area Municipalities, which with only one exception had fought hard against the City's application, had succeeded in making their point. The unfortunate review of the Metropolitan Toronto Commission of Inquiry in 1957, which resulted in an abortive interim report, did nothing to lessen the mutual distrust. By 1960, the beginning of the second six years of metropolitan government, the tensions had reached an intensity that produced many new efforts at political reorganization.*

---

* Examples of City-suburban tensions would include not only the public housing program, previously described, but also the application of a uniform wholesale rate for water throughout the metropolitan area; the question of the appropriate balance between the construction of arterial roadways, including expressways, and the expansion of the public transit system; the matter of representation on the Metropolitan Toronto Police Commission, which until the late 1960's always included a seat for the Mayor of the City of Toronto; and a

The City of Toronto had never formally given up the belief that Metropolitan Toronto should be governed by a unitary form of government. The concept of "one big city," dear to the hearts of all but one or two City politicians, was firmly rooted in the minds of most senior administrative officials, and in fact it was not considered unreasonable by a large majority of the City's residents.* Many observers pointed to New York, Chicago, Philadelphia, Detroit, Cleveland, and other American cities where a mayor elected from a constituency of more than a million voters appeared to govern reasonably well. It was not clear to these advocates why it would not be possible to create a City of Toronto encompassing the entire metropolitan area, with an electorate of some one-and-a-half to two million persons.

Most officials of the Area Municipalities considered the case of the City of Toronto, originally put forward in an application of 1950, to be even less supportable 10 years later in 1960.† During the intervening decade the large suburban municipalities had increased enormously in population and in strength of identity, if not in financial resources. By 1960 the question of inequality of representation in the Metropolitan Council, not only between the Area Municipalities taken together and the City of Toronto, but also among the 12 sub-

---

variety of tensions involved in further consolidation of municipal functions across the metropolitan area, notably fire protection services and public health facilities.

* The announcement by the Government of Manitoba on December 23, 1970, that it would amalgamate the Winnipeg Metropolitan Area is certain to revive the concept in Toronto. But the two situations are vastly different. In Toronto, the Metropolitan Council has always been composed of representatives of the constituent municipalities. Moreover, the powers of the Metropolitan Council have been important from its very beginning and have increased in scope and significance. In Winnipeg, however, metropolitan councillors were elected from entirely new constituencies, drawn so that each included a portion of the central City of Winnipeg and a portion of one or more adjacent municipalities. The original municipalities, including the City of Winnipeg, have thus consistently argued that they were not appropriately represented in the Metropolitan Council. The City of Winnipeg, led by an aggressive Mayor who has occupied that post for more than a decade, has carried on a continuous struggle with the metropolitan administration. For that reason, in part, the powers of the Metropolitan Council have not developed or expanded substantially since 1962.

† Some observers believe that the City of Toronto's continued espousal of a unitary concept of amalgamation of the 13 municipalities provided the rallying point necessary to bring the 12 traditional suburban municipalities into full participation and support of Metro.

urban municipalities themselves, was an extremely live issue. As already noted, this question occupied an important part of the presentation by the Metropolitan Chairman to the Review Committee in 1957. Many schemes were put forward in the Council, in the newspapers, and by other interested parties, but none seemed to commend themselves to the Metro Council or to the Ontario Department of Municipal Affairs at a time when both the population and assessment within the City of Toronto were still approximately 50 percent of the population and assessed property valuation within the metropolitan area.

As Chairman Gardiner indicated on many occasions, there were comparatively few outright City-suburban clashes within the Metropolitan Council. He stated that only once during the first six years had he been forced to vote, as Chairman of the Metropolitan Council, in a situation when all 12 City representatives and all 12 suburban representatives were on opposite sides of a question. In the late 1950's, however, on the matter of a uniform wholesale rate for water from the Metropolitan department to the 13 municipalities—a situation in which the City of Toronto had enjoyed a substantial advantage based on the pre-metropolitan experience—only the "defection" of one member of the City of Toronto Board of Control made it possible to initiate a uniform wholesale rate. The member in question later offered herself as a candidate for the mayoralty and was soundly defeated. This result was sometimes attributed to her sex and her own personal rigidities, but also her successful opponent emphasized throughout the campaign the fact that she had "broken ranks."

The three Toronto newspapers continued their barrage of stories and editorials throughout Metro's first years, in an effort to demonstrate its alleged lack of success in many fields. The newspapers were solidly behind the rather uninspired efforts of the Mayor of Toronto (one man occupied that post from 1954 to 1962) to initiate continued discussion on an amalgamation of the 13 municipalities into one City of Toronto. From time to time in the Metropolitan Council there was full-scale debate on this issue, but more often efforts to get the Council to seek changes in the legislation were either "talked out" or defeated.

In January 1961 the first Chairman of Metropolitan Toronto, Mr. Gardiner, dropped a veritable bombshell at the close of his inaugural address. He had just been reelected to his eighth term as Chairman, and on only one occasion had he ever been opposed by another candidate. At the end of his inaugural address and acceptance speech he indicated that 1961 would be his last year in the office of Chairman.[1]

NEW STUDIES OF METROPOLITAN REORGANIZATION

Mr. Gardiner's "lame duck" status was clearly not to be accompanied by a year of inactivity. In his address of January 10, 1961, he concluded by noting the controversy concerning the need for major reforms in the metropolitan system, and in effect asked the question, "Who are better qualified than we, the members of Metropolitan Council, to study the issues involved and the pros and cons of proposed solutions to these dilemmas?" His actual words were:

It is my view that there is no body better calculated to have the knowledge and experience to determine what is the best form of government for this area than this Council constituted as it is—with representation from all of the constituent municipalities.

There is a reservoir of knowledge and experience in this Council with respect to what should be the best form of government for this area which cannot be matched by any other governmental institution or by any consultants who might be engaged to investigate the subject and make a report upon what should be done. . . . My recommendation is that this Council should constitute itself into a special committee of the whole Council under the chairmanship of the Chairman of the Council to give consideration to what would be the form of governmental institution best calculated to provide the best municipal government for this area in the most efficient and economical manner.[2]

Early in 1961, therefore, the Metropolitan Council created a Special Committee on Metropolitan Affairs, which in fact was a committee of the whole. The Special Committee met early in the year and commissioned two major studies to assist it in proposing the fundamental changes that the Metropolitan Chairman had concluded were inevitable. The first study was requested of a committee of Metro department heads, with municipal department heads also being asked to supply information. The second was requested of the Ontario Department of Economics.

On hearing of Chairman Gardiner's proposed resignation, the Prime Minister of Ontario volunteered to make available to the Special Committee on Metropolitan Affairs whatever appropriate facilities were available in the Ontario Department of Economics and the Ontario Department of Municipal Affairs. The Metropolitan Council was quick to request a study to be directed by Mr. George E. Gathercole, then Deputy Minister of Economics of the Province of Ontario. Mr. Gathercole was one of the principal advisors to the Prime Minister, and it was hoped that a report from that source would reflect the views of the provincial government on the future political organization of the Metropolitan Area of Toronto.

REPORT BY THE METROPOLITAN COMMITTEE OF HEADS OF DEPARTMENTS

In his final inaugural address Chairman Gardiner stated:

There is one thing that all should remember and that is that there is financial amalgamation already in existence. On January 1, 1954, Metro assumed all the debenture debt of all the constituent municipalities with the exception of $70,585,000. That unassumed debt has now been reduced to $35,150,000 and will disappear entirely at a relatively early date.

All of the assumed debt and all new debt created since January 1st, 1954, now amounts to a total of $628,176,000 as of January 1st, 1961 and that debt is the joint and several liability of the Metropolitan Corporation and each of the thirteen municipalities.

Whether any individual municipality likes it or not what it can now finance can be no longer determined by itself. That decision must be determined by the Metropolitan Council. . . . The members of this Council should be calculated to know in an objective, practical, and realistic way the extent to which there is or is not duplication of administrative services and duplication of costs.[3]

The detailed study of the internal administrative operations of Metro and the local governments was assigned to the Metropolitan Committee of Heads of Departments. Its terms of reference, passed by the Metropolitan Council on February 21, 1961, asked the new committee to report to the Special Committee of the Metropolitan Council on Metropolitan Affairs by late spring. Included in the information to be obtained was: "a statement by the Head of each Department indicating the functions and work load (or volume of work) of his Department as of December 31, 1960; and to what extent he considers there is overlapping of services in relation to the thirteen local municipalities and the Metropolitan organization." [4]

An extensive questionnaire was sent to the heads of departments in all of the operative municipalities within Metro Toronto. The response to the questionnaire required more time than had been anticipated, and the Metropolitan Committee of Heads of Departments did not report to the Special Committee until October 18, 1961. The report was a substantial document of 283 legal-sized pages.[5] It contained an enormous mass of data, including a breakdown of information for the various departments, which were classified as follows: departments having metropolitan and local counterparts; local departments having no metropolitan counterparts; and metropolitan departments having no local counterparts.[6]

In addition to the administrative departments throughout the municipalities, the questionnaire was also completed by each local board, commission, and authority being supported in whole or in part by the municipal tax levy. The focus of the entire study was the consideration by each respondent—whether the clerk of the municipality, a department head, or the secretary of a board or commission—of the possible effects of an amalgamation of the 13 municipalities into one unitary form of government upon the administrative services and their cost. It should be noted, however, that a number of extremely important boards and commissions were excluded for a variety of reasons. For example, the metropolitan and local school boards and the library boards were excluded because they were the subject of another study. The Hydroelectric and Public Utilities Commissions and the Parking Authority of the City of Toronto were excluded because they were considered to be self-supporting.[7] The Toronto Transit Commission was excluded because it was also "generally regarded" as self-supporting.[8]

The Metropolitan Committee of Heads of Departments affirmed that the purpose of the report was not to provide all the information necessary to decide for or against amalgamation. Instead it had the much more limited objective of providing a picture of the total existing governmental and administrative structure in the metropolitan area. The committee felt that its submission supplied a considerable part of the data necessary to construct models of amalgamated structures. The authors made it perfectly clear that further investigations might be required, particularly in the absence of data from the boards of education, but even if further studies were undertaken, the ultimate decisions were political. Despite this disclaimer, the report was a noteworthy achievement: for the first time it gave a fairly comprehensive picture of the overall requirements of governmental organization in the metropolitan area.

In financial terms the study revealed that a total of approximately $133 million had been spent during the calendar year 1960. Throughout the 13 local governments and the Metropolitan Municipality, nearly 19,500 staff persons were employed. Seventy-two percent of total expenditures (nearly $95 million) was disbursed by departments at both the metropolitan and local levels.[9] Departments found only at the local level accounted for about 13 percent of the total (about $18 million). Departments found only at the Metro level accounted for approximately $20 million, the remaining 15 percent of total expenditures.

Six of the departmental categories each spent more than $5 million in the year under study, and among them accounted for over 80 percent of total expenditures. These departmental categories were: public works, roads, welfare, police, fire, and parks and recreation. Notably, among these six functional categories only one (police) was already amalgamated as a regional responsibility of metropolitan government; only one (fire) was purely a local responsibility; the remaining four were both local and Metro responsibilities.

REPORT ON THE METROPOLITAN TORONTO SYSTEM OF GOVERNMENT

By November 1961 Mr. Gathercole and his senior officials, in cooperation with the Ontario Department of Municipal Affairs, were ready to present a submission to the Special Committee of the Metropolitan Council on Metropolitan Affairs.[10] The report used 1959 and 1960 data for population and assessed valuation in the 13 municipalities to provide projections concerning the impact of various proposed solutions. It was a carefully developed, closely reasoned, and well-documented research report, giving no preference to the three major solutions explained in detail: amalgamation, a five-city (borough) system of metropolitan government, and a four-city (borough) system.[11] In this sense, therefore, those who hoped that Mr. Gathercole's report would be a clear enunciation of provincial government policy on the future political organization of Metropolitan Toronto were sorely disappointed. But the report was a tremendously important contribution to the analysis of alternatives. Accordingly it played a very significant role in the ultimate reorganization of Metropolitan Toronto into a new system embracing one City and five boroughs, which began to operate on January 1, 1967.

The Gathercole Report, as it was named, was basically concerned with "disparities in representation and economic balance." [12] The question of an equitable system of representation for the municipalities occupied much of the first quarter of the report. The several possibilities were soon dismissed, however, in favor of an analysis of proposed solutions to the problems of representation and economic balance. The terms "city" and "borough" were used alternatively throughout the report, which, at this stage, began with a description of the consolidation of the current 13 Area Municipalities under a "four-city or borough plan." The four boroughs would be composed as follows:

1. The Borough of Toronto would consist of the City of Toronto and five additional municipalities described as an "inner group of six municipalities" which would in 1960 have included 58 percent of the total population of Metro and 60.3 percent of the total assessed valuation.
2. The Borough of North York, which would include North York and one additional small municipality, which in 1960 would have included 16.8 percent of the total population and 16.5 percent of the total assessed valuation.
3. The Borough of Scarborough, composed of the Township of Scarborough only, which would have had in 1960, 13 percent of the total population but 10 percent of the total assessed valuation.
4. The Borough of Etobicoke, which would be composed of the Township of Etobicoke and three additional small area municipalities, would have had in 1960, 12.2 percent of the total population and 13.2 percent of the total assessed valuation.

The report states at this point: "It will be noted that under this suggested consolidation of area municipalities, representation by population could be made fairly consistent with representation by financial interest. The Borough of Toronto's proportion of total population and assessment would exceed the combined population and assessment of the other three Boroughs, but would steadily decline, reaching parity with them in 1970." [13]

This report was based on the fundamental assumption that the size of the Metropolitan Council could be readily controlled, and that the new Borough of Toronto would receive exactly half of the total representation. The other half of the Metropolitan Council would be divided among the three new boroughs in proportion to population, with five, four, and four members respectively, making a total Council of 26 members excluding the Chairman. The report argued that by the year 1970 the Borough of Toronto would have 48 percent of the population, and the three suburban boroughs (North York, Scarborough, and Etobicoke) 52 percent. Representation would remain on the 50–50 basis, at least until 1970, since approximately half of the total assessed valuation would remain within the Borough of Toronto. The number of persons represented by each member of the Metropolitan Council in 1970 would vary from 64,000 to 88,000, whereas under the existing system representation was grossly unbalanced. For example, the smallest municipality provided one Council member, representing 11,000 persons, while North York, also with only one member, had approximately 250,000 persons in 1960.[14]

Although it can be argued that assessed valuation is not the only measure of "economic balance" in considering the provision of physical and social services to a metropolitan population, the Gathercole Report focused careful attention on variations in local area expenditures and assessments. It is extremely important to emphasize that the three suburban boroughs projected by the Deputy Minister of Economics in his report of 1961 were ultimately created exactly as projected in the provincial government's legislation of 1966, which reorganized Metropolitan Toronto as of January 1, 1967. But the proposed composition of the Borough of Toronto was not accepted. Rather, the City of Toronto remained as a city, with the addition of two small Area Municipalities, while two moderately large existing townships, York and East York, were made boroughs in their own right. The influence of the Gathercole Report can hardly be overestimated, because it largely determined the shape of the restructuring.

MAJOR POLITICAL DEVELOPMENTS IN METRO, 1962–1965

Throughout 1961 there were almost as many projected schemes for the reorganization of Metropolitan Toronto as there were officials sitting in the Metropolitan Council and the Area Municipalities. The projection of new schemes, however, was not monopolized by officials. Editorial writers and many representatives of community organizations also proposed programs of political reform. Within the Metropolitan Council itself the reorganization issue was discussed largely in terms of inadequate and inappropriate representation.

After Chairman Gardiner had indicated that he would step down on December 31, 1961, a major suburban candidate emerged in the person of Norman Goodhead, the Reeve of North York—an articulate, self-made man who had gained a reputation as a powerful vote-getter and a good administrator in the rapidly expanding large northern township. Mr. Goodhead became the leading spokesman for the 12 suburban Area Municipalities during the year 1961. Eventually he forced the Metropolitan Council into several full-scale debates on the question of a four- or five-city proposal versus the amalgamation being demanded by the Mayor and Council of the City of Toronto.

The discussions were vigorous. On one historic occasion the council began a debate in the early afternoon and did not conclude until the following morning. It became obvious to the Metropolitan Chairman that his council was split 12–12 on the question of an application to the government of the province for a complete revamping of Metropolitan Toronto. Chairman Gardiner faced a dilemma. In his final inaugural address he had recommended that the Metropolitan Council, as a committee of the whole, constitute itself a Special Committee on Metropolitan Affairs.[15] It has never been revealed whether Mr. Gardiner had communicated with provincial officials on the question, but when the predicted 12–12 vote was recorded, the Chairman voted against the recommendation that the provincial government be asked for a complete reorganization. He stated publicly that with a vote so evenly split, he did not consider it appropriate to come down on the side of drastic reform. Rather, he felt that the council should continue—under a new Chairman in 1962 and thereafter—to debate its future organization and to ascertain the views of the government of Ontario.

January 1962 saw the first important electoral confrontation between two candidates for the position of Metropolitan Chairman, one a Controller of the City of Toronto and the other the Reeve of North York. The 24 members of the Metropolitan Council voted 14–10 in favor of William R. Allen, Q.C., a lawyer, an experienced former alderman, and a Controller of the City of Toronto. Mr. Allen continued to serve in this capacity during the next seven years, and was reelected without opposition through the entire period.

The election of Mr. Allen as successor to Frederick G. Gardiner did not, however, solve any of the major issues, nor did it please either the "city block" or the "suburban block" within the council. The representatives of the City of Toronto on the Metro Council, and in particular on the Metro Executive Committee, may have assumed that the new Chairman would be "more sympathetic" to the City's position on amalgamation of the entire area. But in fact Mr. Allen was not more sympathetic. He saw his position as that of an appointed administrator, and he began to function in the pattern that one would expect of a competent city manager.

On the other hand, the representatives of the Area Municipalities outside the City may have assumed that an aspirant to the office of Metropolitan Chairman would resist further dilution of local responsibilities and the expansion of metropolitan administrative responsibilities. They appeared to reason that amalgamation would not come about in the way the City officials suggested, i.e., by government fiat annexing everything to an enlarged City of Toronto. Instead the Area Municipalities seemed to anticipate a slow, gradual consolidation of functions as Metro assumed more and more tasks on a regional basis, so that eventually there would be no further need for the traditional local governments. If such gradualism was their expectation, they were also disappointed, because under Mr. Allen's chairmanship the Municipality of Metropolitan Toronto moved vigorously to take on far greater responsibility than might have been expected, and assumed functions that few officials would have predicted even at the time of his election in January 1962. In fact, during the second Chairman's tenure there was a substantial reorganization of metropolitan and local government within the Toronto area.*

* In the spring of 1969 Mr. Allen announced that he would resign as Chairman of the Metropolitan Council on September 1, 1969.

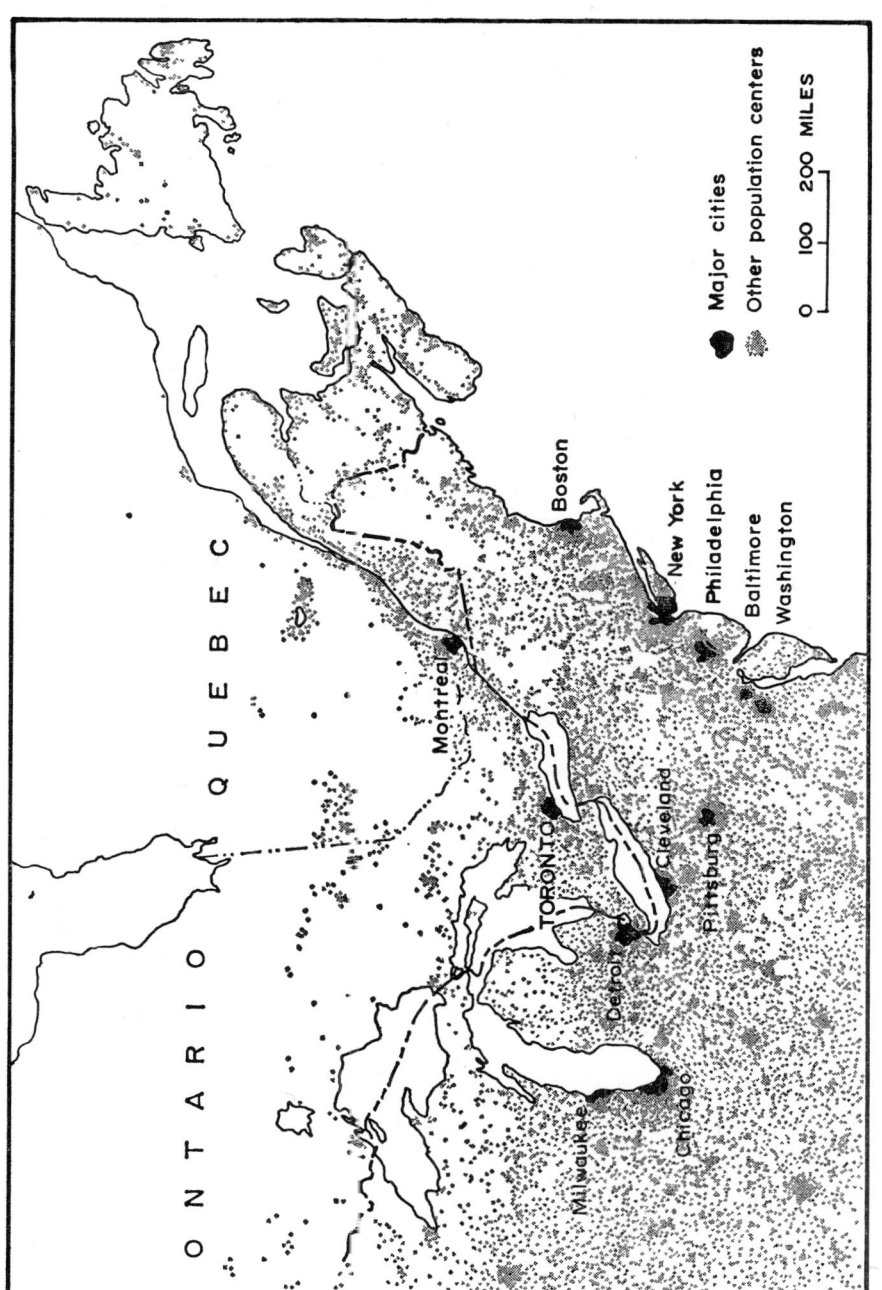

Map 1—TORONTO'S PLACE ON THE CONTINENT

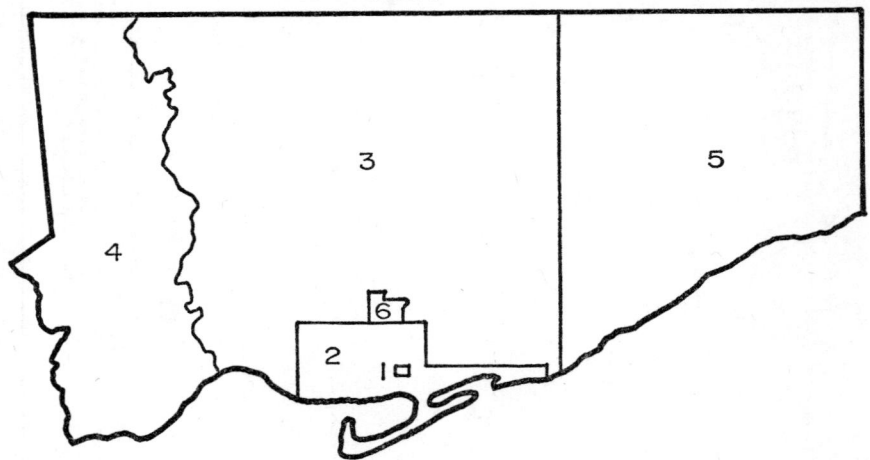

1 Original Townsite (1793)
2 City of Toronto (1834)
3 Township of York (1850)
4 Township of Etobicoke (1850)
5 Township of Scarborough (1850)
6 Village of Yorkville (1853)

MAP 2—A CENTURY AGO: 1867

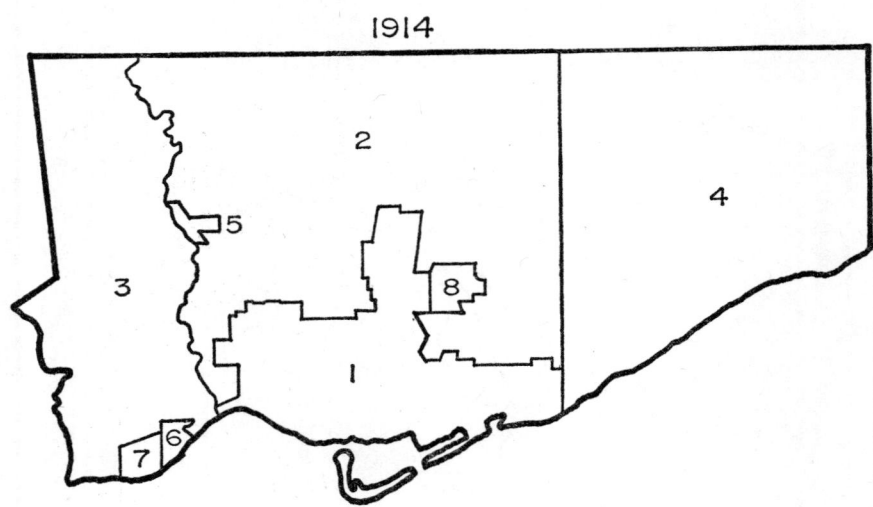

1 City of Toronto
2 Township of York
3 Township of Etobicoke
4 Township of Scarborough
5 Village of Weston (1881)
6 Village of Mimico (1911)
7 Village of New Toronto (1913)
8 Town of Leaside (1913)

MAP 3—THE END OF ANNEXATION: 1914

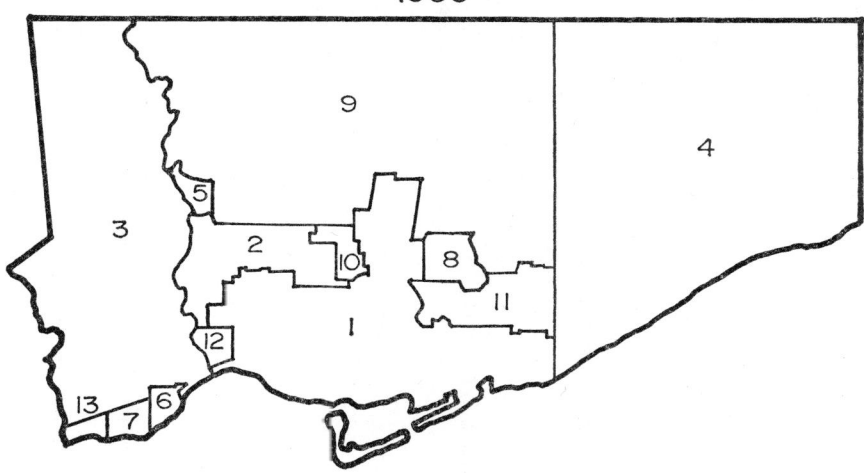

1 City of Toronto
2 Township of York
3 Township of Etobicoke
4 Township of Scarborough
5 Town of Weston
6 Town of Mimico
7 Town of New Toronto
8 Town of Leaside
9 Township of North York (1922)
10 Village of Forest Hill (1923)
11 Township of East York (1924)
12 Village of Swansea (1925)
13 Village of Long Branch (1930)

Map 4—THE FIRST REORGANIZATION: 1953

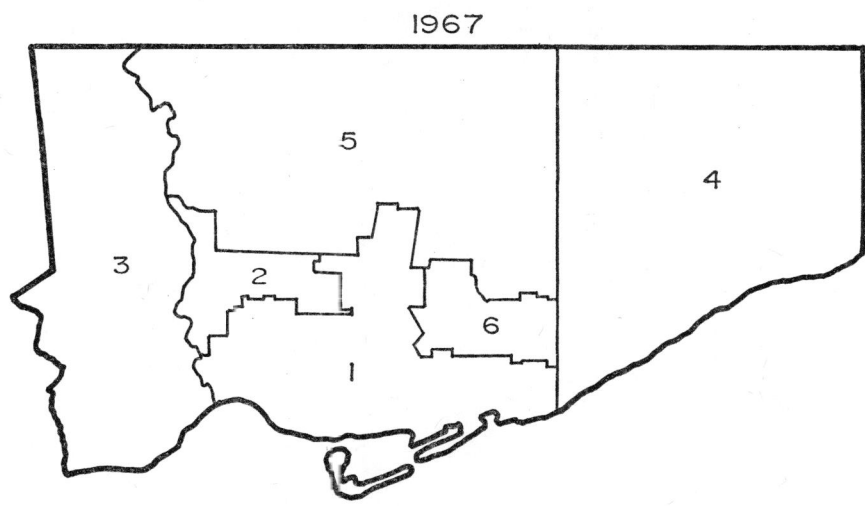

1 City of Toronto
2 Borough of York
3 Borough of Etobicoke
4 Borough of Scarborough
5 Borough of North York
6 Borough of East York

Map 5—THE SECOND REORGANIZATION: 1967

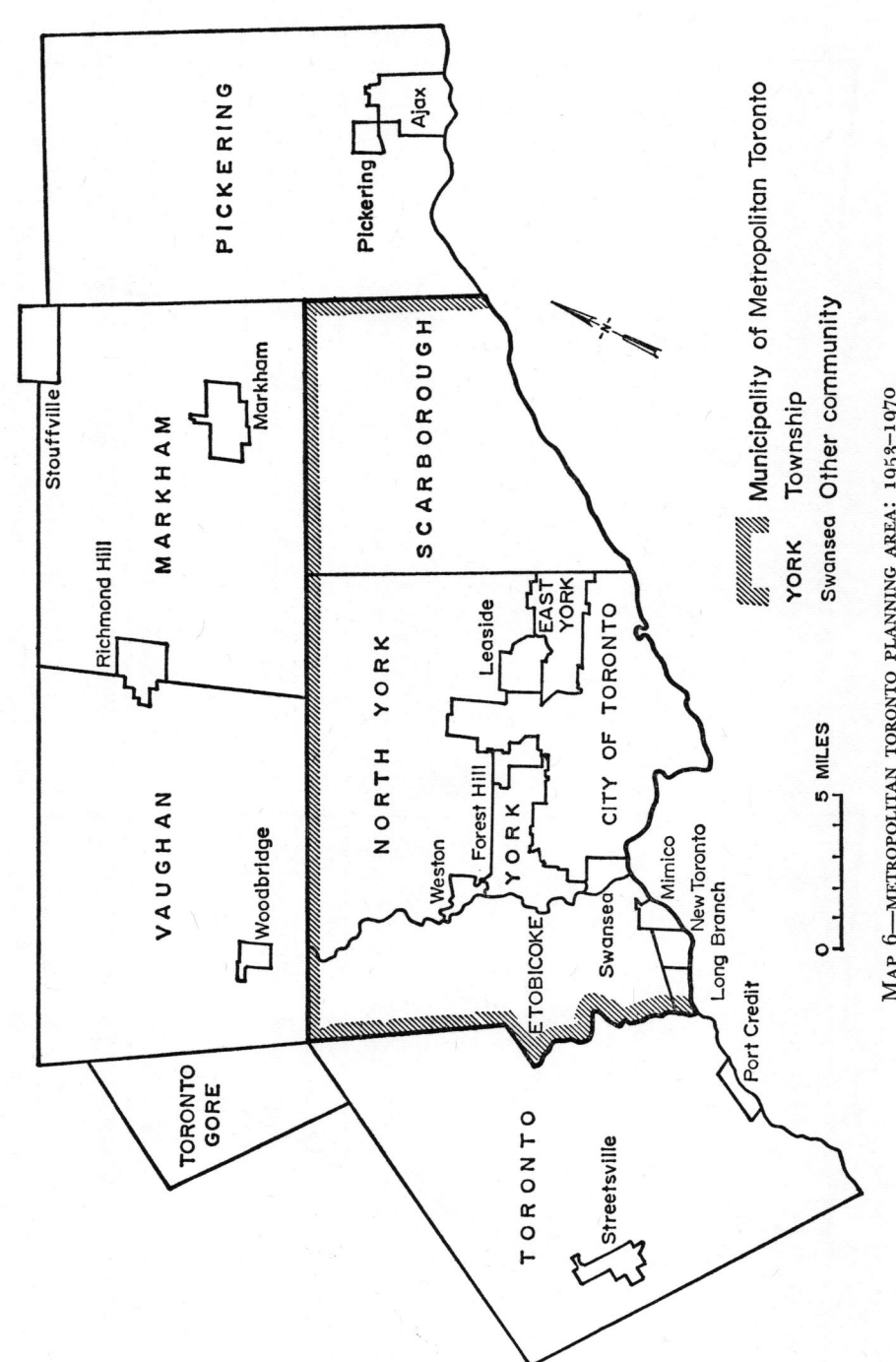

MAP 6—METROPOLITAN TORONTO PLANNING AREA: 1953–1970

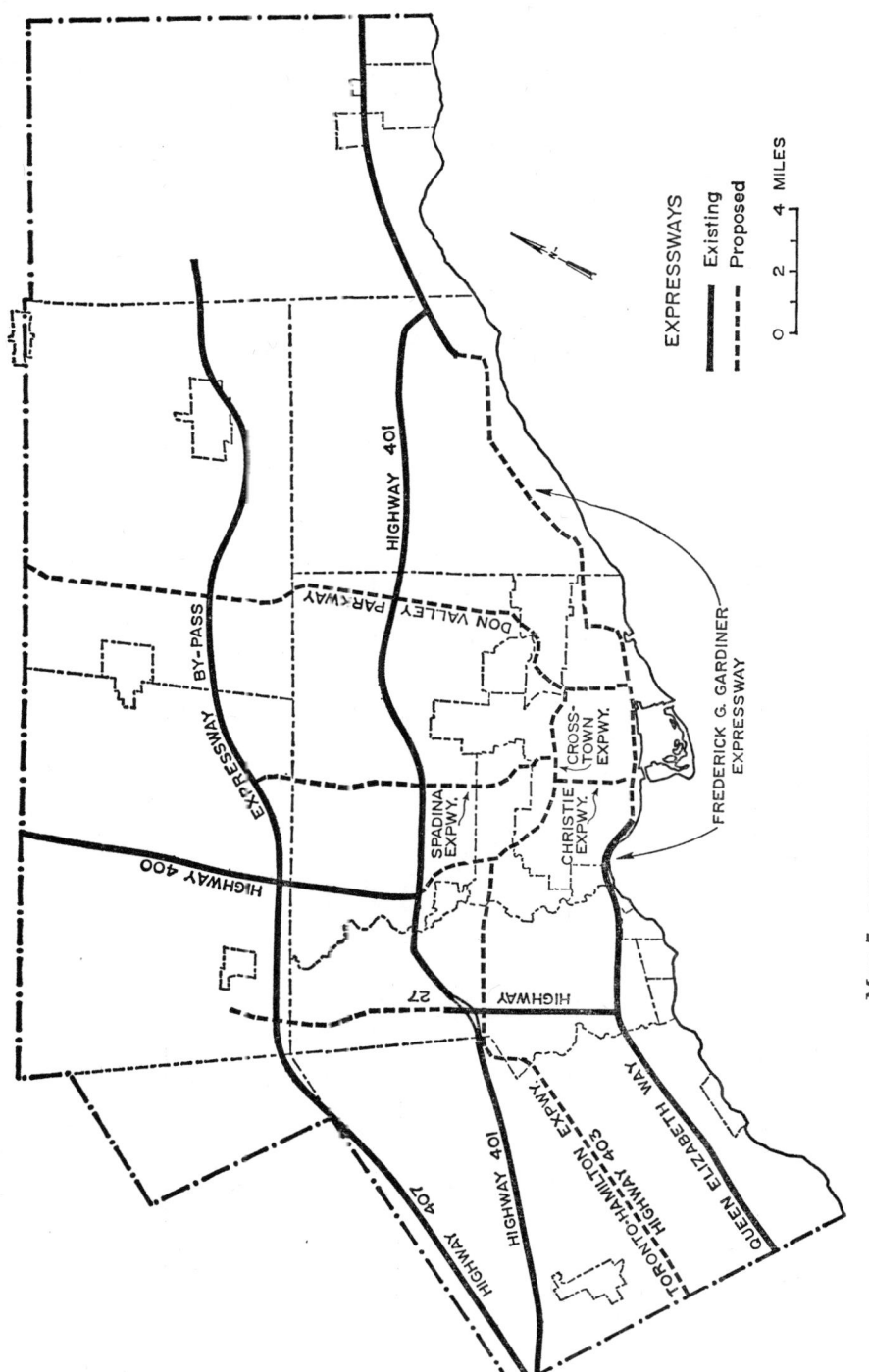

MAP 7—METRO EXPRESSWAYS EXISTING AND PROPOSED: 1959

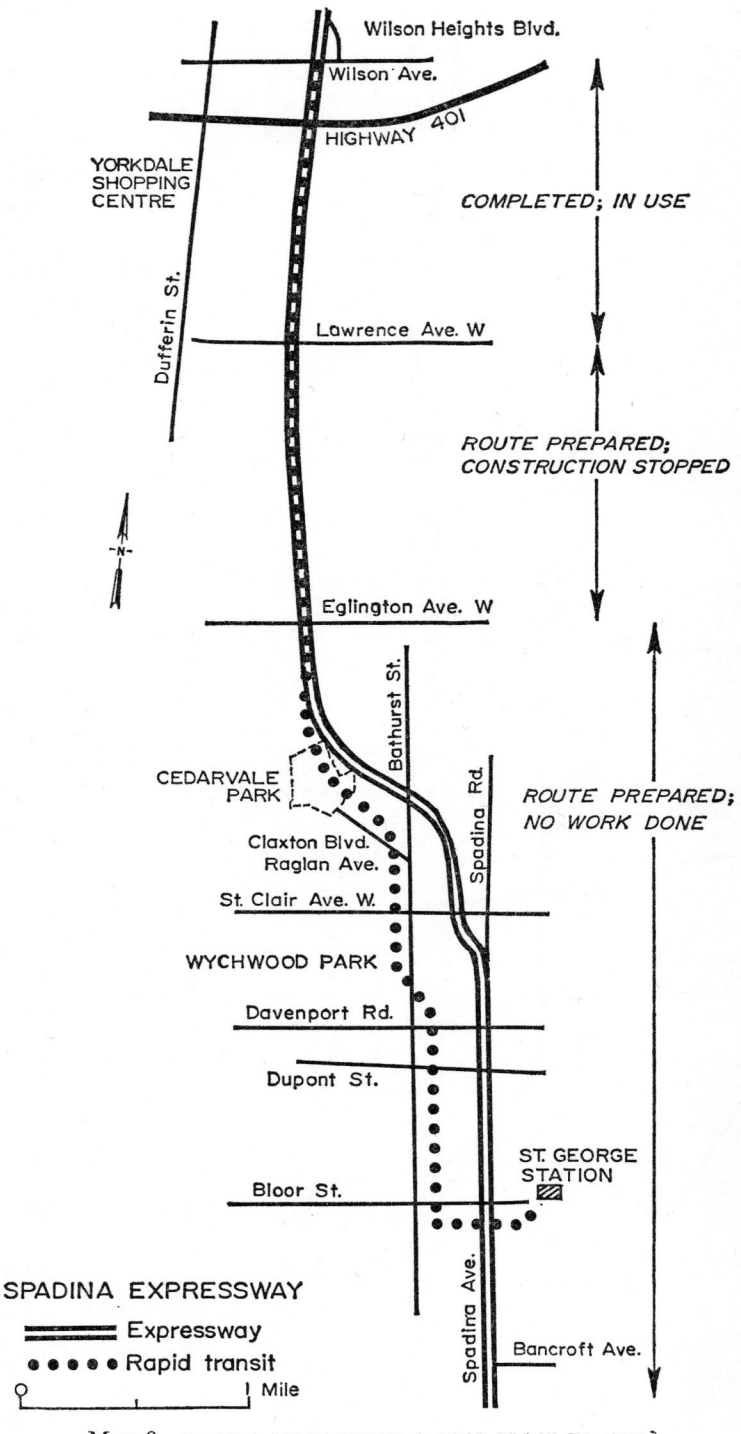

MAP 8—SPADINA EXPRESSWAY: A GOOD PLACE TO STOP?

CHAPTER VII

THE REORGANIZATION OF METROPOLITAN TORONTO, 1963–1967

THE METROPOLITAN COUNCIL's political tensions of 1959–1961 were caused by the City's renewed drive toward a unitary form of government, and the equally determined suburban resistance to that and several other forms of change. But 1962 was a year of respite. The new Metropolitan Council awaited its experience with the new Chairman, to see how he would perform and to learn his position on the major issues.

Few people, indeed, believed Chairman Allen would follow closely in the footsteps of Chairman Gardiner. The two men were very different in many respects. Frederick Goldwin Gardiner—he sometimes referred to himself publicly as "Metro Goldwin Mayor"—affectionately known as "Big Daddy," has been aptly compared with the late Fiorello La Guardia of New York. Both men were skilled in law, administration, and the science of politics. In stature both were stocky, with an appearance that properly conveyed a sense of bulldog determination. Both were accustomed to getting their own way, and each achieved distinction as the top official in a major metropolitan area.

William R. Allen, on the other hand, has always been an efficient administrator, but possesses none of the political flamboyance of his predecessor. In 1953 Mr. Gardiner was in his mid-50's; in 1962 Mr. Allen was in his mid-40's. Mr. Gardiner was a prominent Conservative; Mr. Allen was a well-known Liberal, though a less prominent figure than Mr. Gardiner. Mr. Gardiner was a member of the Protestant establishment in Toronto, although he was not a descendant of one of the founding families. Mr. Allen was the son of a trade unionist and a Roman Catholic. Thus the Metropolitan Council broke with many traditions in selecting him as its second Chairman.

THE MAJOR ISSUES IN METROPOLITAN REORGANIZATION

For the most part, the major issues in metropolitan reorganization under the new administration were those of the previous three of four years. But to these were added a host of new dilemmas.

THE NATURE OF THE REFORM

The most important issue, of course, was the nature of the metropolitan government's reform, if it were to meet some of the urgent pressures mounting in the vast expansion of the metropolis. Would the metropolitan system disappear as a result of the pressures for unification? Or could some new system of government be devised to perpetuate local responsibility and participation in municipal government at least to some degree?

This issue had been hotly argued in previous years, but the new Chairman had the great advantage of having been in the midst of some of these debates. Alternatively, he had been in the wings as a senior elected official of the City of Toronto, even though he did not always sit on the Metropolitan Council or on the Metropolitan Executive Committee. Nevertheless, he had once been a member of the Council and the Executive Committee, as a Controller of the City of Toronto. He was known as a man who "did his homework" and was well prepared to debate these issues.

INEQUITIES IN REPRESENTATION AND ADDITIONAL NEW PROBLEMS

The main issue was compounded, of course, by the inequities in representation described earlier. The real question was whether the problem of representation would be solved by some form of change, without major revisions in the political system itself. Would it be possible to introduce multiple voting? Could one or two of the smaller municipalities be combined with some of the larger ones, without radical reorganization? Would it be possible to create a Metropolitan Council without providing the City of Toronto with exactly half of the representatives? And if none of these possible solutions should prove acceptable, would a more radical solution have to be considered?

By 1963 a host of new problems confronted the new metropolitan administration. These might be described as social rather than physical. As the first decade of metropolitan government neared its end, there was almost complete accord on the part of officials, visiting observers from North America and elsewhere, students of government, members of the press, and the general public: The physical expansion of municipal services within the boundaries of Metropolitan Toronto had been accomplished with reasonable speed, economy, and flair.

The first Chairman of the Metropolitan Council often argued that the provision of water and sewer mains, arterial roadways, public transportation facilities, and the like was much more than simply a physical accomplishment, because the presence of these facilities was absolutely essential to permit an increase in the stock of housing—a social objective. There is much truth in this argument. Nevertheless, by the early 1960's praise for the accomplishments of the metropolitan system of government was often accompanied by criticism of Metro's apparent failure to meet the social or human requirements in the development of a metropolitan society.[1]

In his analysis of Toronto's first decade, Professor Smallwood wrote:

There is little doubt that Metro's great leadership strength to date has been in its response to the more dramatic physical service crises that have exerted the loudest demands for immediate and sustained attention. Metro has realized its greatest accomplishments in tackling such drastic situations as those that were to be found in the water supply, sewage disposal, school construction, and transportation services. Although this effort has required a massive organizational and financial capability, it has not placed too many subtle, or even controversial, demands on the Metro Council members because both the nature of these problems and the nature of the actions necessary to realize their solution have been relatively obvious. . . . Faced with a staggering backlog of previous neglect in a variety of public areas, the Metropolitan Council has had little choice but to emphasize the "steam-shovel approach" to its job in order to build the miles of new sewers and the myriad of new schools necessary to preserve metropolitan Toronto as a going, and growing, concern.[2]

INADEQUACIES IN WELFARE ADMINISTRATION

The new issues that began to emerge in the early 1960's were influenced by mounting interest in the families who were apparently subject to chronic dependency, extending often for two or more generations, and who were most likely to live in the heart of the urban core. Increasing attention was given to the inadequacies of the social welfare system, particularly the public welfare sector, in alleviating the problems of chronic dependency of families with dependent children—very often headed by a deserted or widowed mother—the needs of the elderly, the handicapped, the chronically ill, and so on.

Increasing awareness of these gaps in the social welfare system, plus Metro's failure to expand the stock of public housing to any meaningful extent between 1959 and 1963, supported the criticism that Metro had been successful in providing "physical services" but most unsuccessful in providing "social services." On this point Smallwood wrote: "Ten years' cumulative experience indicates that the Metropolitan Council has been consistently aggressive in tackling the so-called 'hard-core' problems where results are concrete and obvious, and considerably less assertive in meeting some of the 'softer', more socially oriented issue areas where results are usually less tangible and more controversial."

By 1962, it was obvious that Metro's role in the administration of public welfare assistance was seriously deficient on at least two counts. In the first place, since 1954 responsibility in the field of public assistance had been left with the Area Municipalities. Many of these local governments faced little or no demand for service, by virtue of the original socioeconomic composition of their residential populations, and because of the nature of their urban growth during the 1950's. There were modest pockets of poverty here and there outside the City, and they constituted an important problem in York Township, one of the oldest municipalities in the area; but for the most part the basic problems of dependency were found within the population of the City of Toronto itself.

The central city included many neighborhoods 70 or 80 years old, with an old and often deteriorating stock of housing; it was also the Mecca for much of the immigration to Ontario, and especially to Metropolitan Toronto. Certainly the majority of the increased immigration from Italy, Poland, Greece, Malta, and more recently Portugal and the West Indies, has been composed of persons whose first port of entry was downtown Toronto, where the neighborhoods appeared to have a sponge-like absorptive capacity. Moreover this was where the newcomers found their ethnic counterparts, their relatives who had preceded them, and their churches and ethnic associations, which had recently sprung up or been revived.

The budget of the Department of Public Welfare of the City of Toronto grew very rapidly during the years of the recession (1958–1963). During the years 1950–1958 the cost of direct welfare assistance had been divided evenly, under the provisions of the Unemployment Relief Act, between the government of a municipality and the government of the province. However, in 1958, with the passage of the General Welfare Assistance Act (Ontario) and the Unemployment Assistance Act by the government of Canada, the distribution of costs became 50 percent federal, 30 percent provincial, and 20 percent municipal. Thus, while the total costs were increased by the heavier welfare load, the proportionate expenses of the City of Toronto went down.

On a second count, Metro's involvement in the field of welfare was still more inadequate, and might even be described as reprehensible. In an effort to relieve municipal governments of some of the additional welfare burdens during the years of economic recession, the Province of Ontario had undertaken to provide unconditional grants to local governments presumably to meet the additional social obligation as well as to defray certain other growing municipal expenditures such as in the provision of public health and fire protection services. The provincial government decided that its unconditional grant (based upon population) would be transferred in the first instance to the Metropolitan Council for reallocation to the Area Municipalities.

The metropolitan administration made the colossal blunder—perhaps under political pressure, but there is no record of any extensive debate on the matter—of dividing the total sum among the Area Municipalities on the basis of population. This allocation provided certain Area Municipalities with a "profit," because their receipts far exceeded their expenditures on welfare assistance and other social services. In contrast, the City of Toronto's allocation was inadequate and unfair because the sum fell far short of the City's actual expenditures. This mismanagement led directly to the consolidation of welfare services in Metropolitan Toronto, and the creation by the provincial government of a single metropolitan welfare department by January 1, 1967—a result that was certainly not intended by the suburban Area Municipalities.

A RENEWED DRIVE FOR AMALGAMATION

Meanwhile the representatives of the City in the Metropolitan Council emphasized the inequities, and used both the failures in public housing, and the inequities in the distribution of burdens of welfare expenditures, to support a renewed drive for "an amalgamated Toronto." In the first instance, however, the government of Ontario took a partial step toward the consolidation of public welfare services in 1963 by removing from all the Area Municipalities the requirement that they must meet 20 percent of total assistance payments (the other 80 percent was provided in the ratio of 50 percent federal and 30 percent provincial grants). The Metropolitan Council was instructed by the Department of Municipal Affairs that it must assume responsibility for the 20 percent municipal share of public welfare expenditures as of January 1, 1964. The *administration* of welfare services continued to remain with the 13 Area Municipalities.

Early in 1963 the Council of the City of Toronto passed a resolution reiterating its 1950 request to the Ontario Municipal Board for consideration of its application that the 13 municipalities within Metropolitan Toronto be amalgamated into one unified City of Toronto. This application followed several years of debate, arguments about metropolitan reorganization, and proposals for the reform of representation on the Metropolitan Council. In the City's view the time had come for one last drive toward a unitary form of government. Were Toronto's officials unable to see the handwriting on the wall? The City's population had dropped below 50 percent by the federal Census of 1961, and the proportion of assessed valuation of property within the City would soon drop below 50 percent. Surely, officials of the City must have realized that within a very few years it would no longer be possible to resist the demands of the other 12 municipalities for a thorough reorganization of metropolitan government.

A ROYAL COMMISSION

The Government of Ontario did not, however, refer Toronto's new application to the Ontario Municipal Board, as it had done in

1950. Rather, the Prime Minister announced early in 1963 that the government had suspended the powers of the Ontario Municipal Board to hear the application of the City, and favored the establishment of a Royal Commission to explore the whole question of the strengths and weaknesses of the metropolitan system of government.

A one-man Royal Commission on Metropolitan Toronto was finally created late in 1963, in the person of Carl H. Goldenberg, Q.C. Mr. Goldenberg was and still is one of the most respected troubleshooters in the field of labor-management relations in Canada. He was well known throughout Ontario, despite the fact that he was a native of Montreal and maintained his law practice there. A few editorials in the Toronto newspapers insisted that there was no need for an "outsider," particularly from the Province of Quebec, to tell Torontonians how their system of government should work. Nevertheless, Mr. Goldenberg had explored the systems of local government in St. John (New Brunswick) and in Winnipeg before the development of a system of metropolitan government in the latter city in 1962. Within the Province of Ontario during the previous two years he had settled some of the most serious labor disputes, particularly in the public service, that had ever confronted the people of Ontario. His integrity was unquestioned and his experience almost unparalleled in Canada.

SUBMISSIONS TO THE ROYAL COMMISSION
ON METROPOLITAN TORONTO

Public hearings began on April 21, 1964, and 75 different submissions were received in the next two months. The first person to appear was the Metropolitan Council Chairman, Mr. William R. Allen. He was followed by presentations on behalf of each of the 13 Area Municipalities. These were followed by briefs by the Metropolitan School Board, by each of the 11 boards of education, by the County of York, and by many municipalities surrounding Metro. Briefs were presented by many professional and citizens' organizations, including the Town Planning Institute of Canada, the Social Planning Council of Metropolitan Toronto, the Toronto and District Labor Council, the Metropolitan Toronto Board of Trade, the Association of Women Electors of Toronto, and similar organizations. Finally, a number of individuals, scholars and officials with special points of view made appearances. The Royal Commissioner heard presentations by half a dozen citizens who wrote, in response to newspaper advertisements, asking to present their own points of view.* The final presentation was made by the Bureau of Municipal Research of Toronto on June 11, 1964. A year later, on June 10, 1965, Mr. Goldenberg presented his report, a few days short of two years following the passage of an Order-in-Council appointing him to conduct the enquiry.[3]

There is no need to comment here on the nature and content of the majority of the presentations. Clearly, the views that were most influential in assisting the commissioner and his staff to formulate their recommendations were those of the Metro administration; those of the most populous municipalities, particularly the City of Toronto; and those of the Metropolitan Toronto School Board and the City of Toronto Board of Education.

The formal Order-in-Council (OC-1864/63, dated June 20, 1963) creating the Royal Commission stated the terms of reference as follows:

(1) To inquire into and report upon: (a) the structure and organization of the Municipality of Metropolitan Toronto and, more particularly, of the Metropolitan Council and the Metropolitan School Board, their functions and responsibilities and the relations with the area municipalities and the local school boards respectively and with municipalities and planning boards within the Metropolitan Toronto planning area; (b) the purposes and objectives of the establishment of the Metropolitan Corporation and the Metropolitan School Board, the extent of the accomplishment of such objectives and whether such objectives can be better achieved under a new or revised system of local government, having regard to the past and future development and needs; (c) the boundaries of the metropolitan area and of the area municipalities and their suitability in the light of the experience gained through the operations of the metropolitan government, with due regard to probable future urban growth within or beyond the present metropolitan limits and future service requirements; (d) any related matters affecting the government of the Toronto metropolitan region.

(2) After due study and consideration to make such recommendations with respect to the matters inquired into under the terms set out herein as the Commissioner sees fit to the Prime Minister and the Executive Council of Ontario.[4]

---

* The writer presented a personal brief to the Royal Commission on May 20, 1964.

RECOMMENDATIONS OF THE ROYAL COMMISSION

As noted, Mr. Goldenberg submitted his report to the Government of Ontario in June 1965. As was anticipated, he recommended a fundamental reorganization of Metropolitan Toronto. In fact, the "Summary of Recommendations" begins with a capitalized subheading, "Reorganization of Metropolitan Toronto," which is herewtih presented in full:*

REORGANIZATION OF METROPOLITAN TORONTO

(i) The system of metropolitan government should be maintained, with a consolidation of the thirteen area municipalities into four cities, as follows:

The City of Toronto, consolidating the City of Toronto, the Township of York, the Village of Forest Hill, the Town of Leaside, the Township of East York, and the Village of Swansea.

The City of North York, consolidating the Township of North York and the Town of Weston.

The City of Scarborough.

The City of Etobicoke, consolidating the Township of Etobicoke, the Village of Long Branch, the Town of New Toronto, and the Town of Mimico.

(ii) The transfer of assets from the amalgamating municipalities to the amalgamated cities should be effected without compensation to any area municipality but subject only to the assumption and payment by the amalgamated cities of the relative outstanding capital indebtedness.

(iii) The cities of North York, Scarborough, and Etobicoke should continue to be considered townships for the purposes of provincial road grants.

(iv) With the introduction of the four-city system, the partial graded exemptions in Toronto and New Toronto should be abolished in stages over a five-year period by reducing the percentage of exempted assessment by ten percentage points in each year, with provision for assistance in the case of affected owners and tenants who show need.

(v) In integrating municipal staffs, the new authorities should offer employment to all employees who had permanent status on the first day of April in the year preceding the effective date of the reorganization. Existing wage and employment standards should, as far as possible, be protected.[5]

Following these recommendations the report of the Royal Commission considered the composition of the Metropolitan Council and

* The Royal Commission recommendations followed rather closely those of the Gathercole Report of 1961.

of the councils of the four proposed cities. This consideration meant that the whole matter of representation had to be dealt with, and the recommendations of Mr. Goldenberg are summarized as follows:[6]

THE METROPOLITAN COUNCIL AND PROPOSED CITY COUNCILS

(i) Representation on the Metropolitan Council should combine direct election of metropolitan councillors with representation of the area municipalities.

(ii) The Metropolitan Council should be composed of 26 members, with the following representation for each of the four cities: Toronto, 13; North York, 5; Scarborough, 4; Etobicoke, 4.

(iii) Each city should be represented on the Metropolitan Council by the mayor and by metropolitan councillors elected directly by each ward or by a combination of wards, the councillors to serve on both the Metropolitan Council and the respective city councils.

(iv) The existing provisions of The Municipality of Metropolitan Toronto Act governing the election of the chairman of the Metropolitan Council should not be changed, except to provide that on the election of the mayor of a city to the office of chairman, the office of mayor of the city shall become vacant.

(v) Representation on the Metropolitan Council should be reviewed every ten years on the basis of the last Census of Canada.

(vi) The four cities should be divided into the following number of wards: Toronto, 12; North York, 8; Scarborough, 6; Etobicoke, 6.

(vii) The division into wards should be made by the Ontario Municipal Board, by virtue of its authority under section 13 of The Municipal Act. The Board should aim at a reasonably approximate equality of population per ward and should also endeavour, as far as possible, to retain the whole of an amalgamating municipality within a single ward or within contiguous wards.

(viii) Each of the city councils should be composed of the mayor, to be elected at large and to be ex officio a representative on Metropolitan Council; metropolitan councillors, to serve on both Metropolitan Council and city council; and aldermen, to serve only on city council.

(ix) Aldermen and metropolitan councillors should be elected on the following basis:

Toronto: one alderman and one metropolitan councillor from each of the 12 wards.

North York: two aldermen from each of the 8 wards and one metropolitan councillor from each combination of two contiguous wards.

Scarborough: two aldermen from each of the 6 wards and one metropolitan councillor from each combination of two contiguous wards.

Etobicoke: two aldermen from each of the 6 wards and one metropolitan councillor from each combination of two contiguous wards.

(x) Each city council should have an Executive Committee composed of the mayor, who should also be the chairman, and four members elected by the council from among its members. The Executive Committee should exercise the powers conferred by The Municipal Act on a Board of Control.

(xi) The municipal franchise in the four cities should be uniform.

(xii) The term of office of members of the four city councils and of the Metropolitan Council should be increased to three years.

METRO'S BOUNDARIES AND THE FRINGE AREAS

(i) Before considering extension of Metro's boundaries, the Province should give consideration to the position and function of the counties and to municipal reorganization in the fringe areas, including the possible creation of a smaller "Metro" on the western fringe.

(ii) Failing satisfactory arrangements by Metro and the Ontario Water Resources Commission to provide the required water and sewage facilities on the northern fringe, the appropriate built-up area north of Steeles Avenue in Vaughan and Markham Townships should be annexed to North York without undue delay, with compensation for loss of assessment to the townships and the County of York.

(iii) The Provincial Government should formally recognize the special situation of dormitory municipalities adjacent to Metro by appropriate adjustments in grants for municipal and school purposes.

A number of presentations had suggested that the boundaries of Metro be extended, both to the north within York County and to the west within Peel County. The commissioner recommended that the two large townships immediately to the north of Metro Toronto, within the County of York, should be included within the boundaries of Metropolitan Toronto. His recommendation specified that they should be annexed to the Township of North York without undue delay, and that compensation should be paid to the county for its loss of assessment.

METROPOLITAN PLANNING

The recommendations of the Royal Commission in the fields of urban and regional planning were intended to enhance the physical planning function in the metropolis. Following a bow toward the adoption of a Metropolitan Official Plan, the report specifically recommended as follows:

The Municipality of Metropolitan Toronto Act should be amended to declare more explicitly the responsibility of the Metropolitan Corporation, as the designated municipality, for the general direction of the physical development of the Metropolitan Planning Area, with powers:

(a) to establish basic zoning standards and categories;

(b) to participate with an area municipality in redevelopment and urban renewal;

(c) to enact a uniform building by-law and to establish uniform engineering design standards;

(d) to review development applications and proposals and to make recommendations thereon to the provincial agency;

(e) to secure the conformity of local official plans and zoning by-laws in the Metropolitan Planning Area with the Metro Official Plan, reserving to the municipalities a right of appeal to the Ontario Municipal Board. The procedures to ensure conformity of plans should be prescribed by regulations under the legislation.

Moreover, the commissioner recommended that the Planning Act of Ontario be amended to permit municipalities to transfer the functions currently in the hands of local planning boards to a planning committee of the council. Acceptance of the British committee-of-the-council system was contrary to all the practice within the province since the passage of the Planning Act in 1946. Nevertheless, it had been recommended by the Ontario Division of the Community Planning Association of Canada many years before, and by other organizations from time to time. The argument in favor of the change is based largely on the fact that local planning boards in Ontario function outside the main stream of local government. This is intended by the legislation, which to some degree also restricts the number of elected representatives who may sit on such boards. A clear disadvantage to such autonomy or remoteness has been the frequent dismissal of planning board recommendations and programs by the councils on the ground that they are politically unrealistic, and also because they emanate from a staff of professionals who are somewhat removed from the regular civil service.

In any event, the planning board is intended to be advisory to the council, and its advice need not be accepted. The frustrations inherent in this set of procedures must be evident to all concerned: planning staff, planning board members, and local politicians. Accordingly the commissioner recommended that the planning staffs in the Area Municipalities within Metro be constituted as civic planning departments of the local governments. These two changes—eliminating independent local planning boards in favor of planning committees of councils, and creating local civic planning departments—would have constituted major changes in governmental organization to manage urban growth during the late 1960's and the early 1970's.

METROPOLITAN AND LOCAL SERVICES

Throughout the work of the Royal Commission, modifications in the development and delivery of municipal services were strongly urged. Many groups were concerned about specific services, but particular emphasis was placed on urban transit and public housing. A number of briefs suggested that the Toronto Transit Commission become an ordinary department of the Metropolitan administration, and thus lose its special status as a quasi-independent administrative commission. On this point the commissioner contented himself with the recommendation that there be a more formal coordination in overall transportation planning between staffs of the Transit Commission, the Metropolitan Planning Board, and other agencies.* A further recommendation also suggested, however, that the traffic engineering services within the metropolitan area be unified under Metro, and that Metro establish an area-wide parking authority.

In the field of public housing, the Royal Commission report was both disappointing and realistic. The commissioner did not face up to the question of metropolitan responsibility versus that of the Area Municipalities, but his report recommended that the Ontario Housing Corporation, created by the province in September 1964, act as a single agency on behalf of the federal and provincial governments in dealing with the Metropolitan Corporation on all further low rental housing developments in the metropolitan area. In addition, he suggested that Metro assume the local municipal financial respon-

---

* Ontario, *Report of the Royal Commission on Metropolitan Toronto* (Toronto, 1965), pp. 202–203. Some planners believe that the Municipality of Metropolitan Toronto Act of 1953, as amended, did not make it clear which body was responsible for transportation planning. Authority was divided between the Toronto Transit Commission and the Metropolitan Toronto Planning Board. As a result some serious difficulties arose, and severe differences of opinion had to be resolved. In particular, the problems associated with the expansion of the rapid transit (subway) system in 1958 epitomized these difficulties. The differences between the two formal organizations included the whole question of whether the Bloor Street subway should be built at all, as well as its location, its timing, and its position with respect to other rapid transit lines. The whole field of transportation planning was a matter of controversy, and continues so.

sibility, if any, for the intergovernmental housing arrangements. This meant that no Area Municipality would be responsible for either a capital contribution or a contribution toward the rental subsidies required in public housing.

In a number of other municipal services it had been expected that the Royal Commission report would recommend a consolidation of divided responsibilities. This happened, however, only in the case of waste disposal, where it was recommended that the Metropolitan Corporation assume responsibility for all waste disposal in the metropolitan area. In the more important fields of public health and fire protection, the Royal Commission assumed that these services would best be provided by the local governments, namely, the four cities recommended in its proposal for reorganization. The report stated: "It should be the aim of the four cities to make health and welfare services equally available to individuals and families with the same needs, no matter where they live in Metropolitan Toronto." [7] To this end the commissioner proposed that the health officers of the four cities form a Metropolitan Board of Health Officers to coordinate public health policies of the several municipalities. Similarly, the fire chiefs of the four cities were urged to form an area committee to advise on matters of mutual concern affecting fire fighting services.

EDUCATION

The Royal Commission made its most controversial recommendations in the field of education. Consequently, during the remainder of 1965 much of the discussion about the report centered around major educational matters. These questions were of extraordinary importance in view of the fact that about 35 percent of the total tax levy in the City of Toronto, and as much as 55 percent in the Township of North York, was devoted to educational purposes. The remaining area municipalities fell within these limits.

The Royal Commission recommended an entirely new educational structure. The metropolitan area would be divided into 11 school districts, with boundaries "fixed on the basis of criteria for determining the viability of school districts." The proposed boundaries were set out in detail. The following statements are a verbatim summary of the additional recommendations, which amount to a fundamental reorganization of the educational system:

(i) The Metropolitan Area should be divided into 11 school districts, with boundaries fixed on the basis of criteria for determining the viability of school districts.

(ii) An elected central board, to be called the Metropolitan Toronto Board of Education, should have overall responsibility for school finance and for the development of an acceptable and uniformly high metropolitan standard of education. The administrative responsibilities of the central board should be limited to matters relating to area-wide policies, including teachers' salary scales, to coordination of mutual services, and to the provision of services which can best be provided on a metropolitan basis.

(iii) Local elected boards, to be called District Education Councils, should operate the schools and administer the school program.

(iv) The central board should be composed of two trustees elected at large in each school district at elections held on the same day as the regular municipal elections, and two representatives of the Metropolitan Separate School Board.* The chairman should be elected from among the members. The term of office should be three years.

(v) The remuneration for members of the central board to be raised to a figure more commensurate with their responsibilities and the additional responsibilities of the chairman should be recognized by higher remuneration.

(vi) Each District Education Council should be composed of the two trustees elected to represent the district on the central board, one trustee appointed by the Separate School Board, and eight district trustees elected at large in the district. The chairman should be elected from among the members. The term of office should be three years.

(vii) A Director of Education should be the chief executive officer of the Metropolitan Toronto Board of Education and a District Superintendent should be the principal officer in each school district, reporting directly to the former.

(viii) Educational finance should be coordinated by the central board and a uniform tax for education established throughout Metro. The central board should secure all tax revenue for educational purposes from the Metropolitan Council through the uniform levy.

(ix) District education councils should be allocated a fixed percentage of their total budgets to enable them to add to their program if they desire to provide special equipment or a special service or to undertake educational experiments which are not included in the area-wide budget.

(x) The Metropolitan Corporation should assume the local school debt of the area municipalities outstanding on December 31, 1963.[8]

This detailed description of a reorganization of the educational structure became the focus of discontent with the report as a whole.

* See Glossary for definition of "Separate School Board."

The specific recommendations quoted above provided opportunities for all the groups involved in the educational process to raise sharp questions. The public never clearly understood for example, why the report chose to recommend 11 school districts, when it had previously recommended a four-city system of local government. The commissioner never satisfactorily explained why he did not recommend four city boards of education.

The powers and responsibilities of the Metropolitan Toronto Board of Education appeared to be substantially enlarged, and this caused much concern. The suggestion that the central board negotiate teachers' salary scales on a metropolitan-wide basis caused the various teaching associations great anxiety. The fact that the central District Education Council would be elected separately from the members of the local boards required a double form of election for boards of education, whereas the Royal Commission had rejected the possibility of separate electoral districts for the Metropolitan Council.

In other words, on the political level of Metro, a number of local councillors would be elected to represent the various wards into which the four cities were to be divided. In all likelihood, the person who also served as metropolitan councillor would be the person who had received the largest number of votes in each of these wards. Thus no new political constituencies solely for metropolitan purposes were suggested for Metro. But in the case of education, special elections were to be held for the Metropolitan Board of Education and the District Education Councils.

The recommendation that education be financed through a uniform education tax established throughout Metro was most favorably received. This proposal had been made by a number of groups, and in the view of many it was the only way to ensure equality of educational opportunity throughout the metropolitan area. Nevertheless, the proponents of decentralized school administration felt threatened by the recommendations, and the fear of additional interference by the central board in the affairs of all local boards was widespread. It appears to be no accident that the Government of Ontario rejected Mr. Goldenberg's two main recommendations in the field of education. Perhaps the statement by the Prime Minister on January 10, 1966, which clearly set forth the position of his government on the reorganization of Metropolitan Toronto, was strongly influenced by the furor concerning the educational recommendations. It may also be that some recommendations of the Goldenberg Report were rejected because the controversy in education spilled over into other areas.*

THE STATEMENT BY THE PRIME MINISTER OF ONTARIO

During the remainder of 1965, following the presentation of the Report of the Royal Commission on Metropolitan Toronto, no formal announcement was made by the provincial government either accepting or rejecting the recommendations of the Goldenberg Report, in whole or in part. The newspapers grew impatient, much speculation ensued, and many unwarranted assumptions were made about the probable course of action.

Not until January 10, 1966, did the Prime Minister of Ontario, The Honorable John Robarts, issue a "Statement Re Report of the Royal Commission on Metropolitan Toronto."[9] The statement began with an assertion that from the very receipt of the report the government had given "the full attention and exhaustive study which such an important, far-reaching, imaginative, and constructive document must receive." The Prime Minister stated firmly that although the position of the government might not coincide with the recommendations of the Royal Commissioner on all points, "we accept and endorse the main principles which he advocates: the continuation of the two-level federated system of metropolitan government; the consolidation of constituent municipalities rather than total amalgamation; an increase in the authority and responsibilities of the government of Metropolitan Toronto; a Metro-wide uniform school tax levy to provide a basic education programme for the metropolitan area; and a reform of the system of representation."[10] The Prime Minister also indicated that he had deliberately chosen to state the position of his government early in 1966 so that full dis-

---

* Some scholars and professional consultants who analyzed the report came to the view that Mr. Goldenberg's experience in labor relations was crucial to his later position in the reorganization of metropolitan government. In their view he attempted to achieve the maximum possible compromise—a political settlement with a minimum of political controversy. If this view is substantially correct, it goes a long way toward explaining the peculiar recommendations in the field of education, which some have interpreted as the consequence of too much compromise.

cussion could take place before the necessary amendments to The Municipality of Metropolitan Toronto Act were enacted. He might have added that a statement early in 1966 would also enable the new local governments to be created and to organize their administrative structure in time to assume responsibility on January 1, 1967. This timing was absolutely essential, and in due course the first three-year term of the reorganized Metropolitan Council, and of the councils of the five boroughs and an enlarged City of Toronto, began operations on that date.

ONE CITY AND FIVE BOROUGHS

The full statement by the Prime Minister of Ontario occupied some 27 double-spaced pages, 16 of which were devoted to the formal statement of changes, beginning with the very form of government itself. The two-level form of metropolitan government would be continued but the 13 municipalities would be consolidated to form 6 municipalities: the City of Toronto and the 5 boroughs.

The City of Toronto would consist of the current City, together with the Villages of Forest Hill and Swansea, forming a consolidation with a combined population of approximately 682,000. The Borough of Etobicoke would consist of the current Township of Etobicoke, together with the existing Village of Long Branch and the Towns of New Toronto and Mimico; this new consolidation would approximate a population of 240,000. The Borough of York would consist of the current Township of York, with the addition of the existing Town of Weston; this new consolidation would approximate a population of 139,000. The Borough of East York would consist of the current Township of East York together with the existing Town of Leaside; this consolidation would approximate a population of about 91,000. In addition to these four enlarged municipalities, two of the largest existing townships were simply converted into new municipalities designated as boroughs. Thus the existing Township of North York became the Borough of North York, with a population of 342,000. The Township of Scarborough became the Borough of Scarborough, with a population exceeding 253,000.[11] (See Table 3.)

COMPOSITION OF THE METRO COUNCIL

The creation of a reorganized metropolitan form of government consisting of a Metropolitan Council, one City, and five boroughs

Table 3
Population Distribution by Municipal Units, 1941–1971

	1941	1951	1961	1967	1971 (est.)
City of Toronto	667,457	675,754	672,407	682,000	750,000
Towns[a]					
Leaside (East York)	6,183	16,233	18,579		
Mimico (Etobicoke)	8,070	11,342	18,212		
New Toronto (Etobicoke)	9,504	11,194	13,384		
Weston (York)	5,740	8,677	9,715		
Villages[a]					
Forest Hill (Toronto)	11,575	15,305	20,489		
Long Branch (Etobicoke)	5,172	8,727	11,039		
Swansea (Toronto)	6,988	8,072	9,628		
Townships (Boroughs)[a]					
East York	41,821	64,616	72,409	91,000	100,000
Etobicoke	18,973	53,779	156,035	240,000	300,000
North York	22,908	85,897	269,959	342,000	500,000
Scarborough	24,303	56,292	217,286	253,000	310,000
York	81,052	101,582	129,645	139,000	150,000
Grand Total	909,746	1,117,470	1,618,787	1,747,000	2,110,000

[a] In the reorganization of January 1st, 1967 the townships became boroughs, and incorporated the towns and villages.
SOURCE: Census of Canada.

necessitated a radical change in the composition of the Metropolitan Council. The Prime Minister announced that the new council would be composed of 33 members: 32 members of the elected local councils, plus a Chairman to be elected by the Metropolitan Council. The City of Toronto would continue to be represented on the Metropolitan Council by 12 members, including the Mayor. The representation of each of the boroughs, however, was to be based upon the 1964 assessed population (estimated from the assessment rolls) of the City of Toronto divided by 12. On the basis of this formula, each Metropolitan Councillor would represent from 55,000 to 60,000 residents. Accordingly, commencing on January 1, 1967, representation on the Metropolitan Council was distributed like this:[12]

City of Toronto	12
Borough of North York	6
Borough of Scarborough	5
Borough of Etobicoke	4
Borough of York	3
Borough of East York	2
	32
Chairman	1
	33

The new system retained the principle of choosing the members of the Metropolitan Council indirectly, through their election to the local councils. Also retained was the principle of electing the Chairman by the Metro Council members, and not directly by the citizens. The Prime Minister's statement further indicated that in the case of each municipality the members of the Metropolitan Council must include the mayor ex officio. Moreover, in the City of Toronto, and any other municipality with a board of control (see Glossary for definition), each member of the board would be an ex officio member of the Metropolitan Council.

Any additional members allocated to a municipality would be appointed by the municipal council prior to the inaugural meeting of that council following each election. In the case of the City of Toronto, this meant that its 12 members would be composed of the Mayor, 4 members of the board of control, and 7 aldermen. This formula was an immediate cause of concern, since the City was subdivided into 9 wards, and the previous system of representation from the City had included one councillor from each ward. The Prime Minister made no statement on this matter, but the Council of the City of Toronto argued for months thereafter, and considered many formulas for solving this problem. The consolidation of the 9 wards into 7 was the most favored solution, but as the months passed the ultimate proposition to which the province agreed was to reduce the representation from the board of control to two members, retaining the previous system of representation as far as the City was concerned.[13]

The Royal Commissioner had referred to certain advantages in the replacement of municipal boards of control by executive committees, but this suggestion was not accepted.* Instead, the Prime

---

* Within the City of Toronto Council the question of ward boundaries, the number of wards and thus the manner of individual representation on the

Minister stated that in the view of his government, local municipalities would continue to have discretionary powers to decide whether they should operate with boards of control or executive committees.

Nevertheless the government did agree with the commissioner that the Metropolitan Council's executive committee should be retained. At that time the Metro executive committee was composed of the Chairman of the Metropolitan Council, three representatives from the City of Toronto, and three representatives from the Area Municipalities. The government felt that an enlarged committee would facilitate a more equitable distribution of representation. Consequently, the appointment of a Metro executive committee with the powers of a board of control would be made mandatory, and its membership increased to 11, as follows: the Chairman of the Metropolitan Council; the Mayor of the City; the Mayor of each borough; and the four members of the Toronto Board of Control (later, the City executive committee).[14]

This arrangement maintained equality of representation between the City and the other municipalities on the powerful executive committee, while in the Metropolitan Council the City's share of representation was fixed at 40 percent. The formula was obviously an attempt by the provincial government to walk a tightrope between the contending positions. Those urging substantial suburban representation pointed to the population growth in the Area Municipali-

---

Metropolitan Council became a live issue during the years 1968–1969. After much discussion the Toronto council voted to abolish the Board of Control in favor of an executive committee that would not be elected at large. New ward boundaries were drawn by the city clerk, and the number of wards was increased to 11. The council rejected this design, however, although not the number of wards, and asked the Ontario Municipal Board to consider a set of ward boundaries in which the traditional north-south "strip system" would be replaced by a "block plan." The strip approach gave most wards a cross-section of social and economic groups, whereas those who advocated the block plan stressed greater representation from the lower-income and social groups. In July 1969 the OMB handed down its decision favoring the block plan. With the election of December 1, 1969, therefore, the Mayor was the only member of Toronto's city council who was elected at large. Each of the 11 wards elects two councillors. The councillor who gains the largest number of votes automatically becomes a member of the Metropolitan Council. The four members of the executive committee of the City of Toronto are elected by the City Council from among its 11 Metro councillors. Curiously enough, while the City was doing away with its elected-at-large board of control, the major boroughs in the Toronto area were creating boards of control for the first time.

ties, whereas those pressing for a stronger City voice emphasized the undeniable fact that Toronto was, in the first Chairman's words, "the financial anchor of the Metropolitan Area."

Despite this redress in the balance, the new formula did not satisfy the more militant members of Toronto's City Council. They could see no reason for the five representatives of the executive committee to consist of their Mayor and all members of the board of control. They argued that the board members in particular could not carry both responsibilities satisfactorily. During the balance of 1966 this argument was an important part of the larger debate concerning the City's representation in the new metropolitan government. Eventually, the Mayor and two senior controllers were to be appointed, and the council was to select the two additional representatives. The same argument was carried on in the various boroughs.

THE NEXT REVIEW

A further statement by the Prime Minister covered the question of future reviews of representation on the Metropolitan Council. He said that "to maintain the principle of 'representation by population,' there must be reviews of representation in the light of population changes within Metropolitan Toronto. However, stability must be maintained if the proposed reorganization is to be successful. Therefore, the first review of population and representation will take place after the third, but before the fourth triennial election." [15]

The first election would take place on or about December 1, 1966. Since the statement had previously accepted the Royal Commissioner's recommendation that the terms of office throughout the entire metropolitan system (including the boards of education) should be increased to three years, it is quite clear that Mr. Roberts promised a review after the election of December 1972. To put the matter another way, he promised that a review of representation would take place sometime during the seventh, eighth and ninth years of the newly reorganized metropolitan government. It is incredible that this clear statement was often misinterpreted during the first three-year term, the most common misconception being that the promised review would take place whenever sufficient pressure for it could be exerted. Almost from the beginning of the first three-year term, on January 1, 1967, both the newspapers and some elected officials in the new boroughs were demanding another review.

METROPOLITAN AND LOCAL SERVICES

The Prime Minister's endorsement of an increase in the authority and responsibilities of the government of Metropolitan Toronto was implemented by transferring several services to the Metropolitan Council. The most important transfer involved public welfare, including both mandatory and optional services under the General Welfare Assistance Act and related legislation. Consequently, in the remaining months of 1966 it was necessary to establish a Metropolitan Department of Welfare, which took over the staff of all local welfare departments. In addition, responsibility for an area-wide public emergency ambulance service was assigned to Metro.

Waste disposal was also made a Metro responsibility, the council being given power to establish disposal facilities anywhere in the Metropolitan Toronto area, or within a reasonable distance beyond its limits, subject to protection of local residents.

The government of the province viewed Mr. Goldenberg's recommendations on the administration of justice—with special reference to the Metropolitan Juvenile and Family Court and other court facilities—as an appropriate subject for negotiation between the province and the Metropolitan Corporation. Subsequently, by 1968, the province had assumed far more responsibility in these areas.

The government accepted the recommendation of the commissioner that fire protection should remain the responsibility of the Area Municipalities. Moreover, the Prime Minister was convinced that the reduction in the number of municipalities from 13 to 6 through unification and consolidation would appreciably improve fire protection services, thus helping justify their remaining a local responsibility.

Finally, the government accepted the recommendation of Commissioner Goldenberg that a Metropolitan Toronto Library Board be established. This new board would have as its major function the development of central and regional reference resources and the coordination of local library facilities.

EDUCATION

Prime Minister Robarts insisted that particularly careful study had been given to those sections of the Goldenberg Report dealing with education, not merely because that function involved "some of the most complex and vexing problems of government" but also because the commissioner's suggestion involved a frontal attack upon the principle of local control of education.¹⁶ The Prime Minister insisted that a successful solution to the educational problems of Metropolitan Toronto required adherence—as far as practicable—to a principle that had guided education in Ontario from 1867: the principle of local control.

Accordingly, the government proposed: "(1) to continue the local control of education as far as practicable with a local board of education in the City of Toronto and one in each of the new Boroughs; (2) to continue the existing two-level structure with a Metropolitan School Board endowed with broad powers of control and coordination of finance." ¹⁷ Membership on the Metropolitan School Board would be based on representation by population. The Prime Minister announced that the new board would be composed of 18 members as follows: 6 members from the Board of Education of the City of Toronto, 3 members from the Board of the Borough of North York, 2 each from the Boards of the Boroughs of Scarborough and Etobicoke, one each from the Boards of the Boroughs of York and East York, and 3 representatives from the Metropolitan Separate School Board. All of these persons would be appointed by their respective local boards.*

Perhaps the most important aspect of the Prime Minister's statement on educational reorganization appeared in the following paragraph: "We accept the recommendation of the Goldenberg Report that to equalize educational opportunities to a greater extent through the use of the total resources of Metropolitan Toronto, the Metropolitan School Board will have the responsibility of reviewing and coordinating all local school board budgets and providing, through Metro-wide taxation, the funds required by the local school boards for their basic educational requirements." ¹⁸ The statement did not, however, expand upon the meaning or interpretation of the phrase "basic educational requirements."

* Ontario, *Statement by the Hon. John Robarts, Prime Minister of Ontario, Re Report of the Royal Commission on Metropolitan Toronto* (Toronto: Government of Ontario, January 10, 1966). The significance of the government's decision with respect to education lay in the fact that educational services would be coterminous with the province's realignment into a "six-city" rather than a "four-city" arrangement, as recommended by Mr. Goldenberg. Once this decision became clear, the composition of the new Metropolitan School Board was relatively easy to arrange and avoided the difficulties which the Royal Commission's recommendations on education would have involved.

In the future, the Metropolitan School Board would examine the current expenditures of the local boards and allocate funds in accordance with variations in local requirements and, of course, with the Metropolitan Board's capacity to provide funds. Henceforth, the local boards would be given a limited opportunity to supplement the major metropolitan tax by a local levy. The Prime Minister noted that coordination of capital financing had already been in effect for a decade, and no immediate change was planned in this aspect of the program. The Metropolitan School Board would continue to be responsible for financing the cost of capital improvements —including construction of new schools, additions, renovations, and sites—under a formula with a uniform ceiling. Local school boards wishing to exceed this ceiling could continue to do so, within limits, through a local tax levy.[19]

Finally, the Metropolitan Corporation would assume all the municipalities' local school debts outstanding as of December 31, 1966. There was, however, one additional point of interest, namely that the legislation would be amended to provide for an appeal to the Ontario Municipal Board to settle disputes between local municipalities and Metro with respect to financial aid for both capital and current costs.[20] Before 1967 an appeal was available only with respect to proposed capital expenditures.

1966: YEAR OF TRANSITION

Prime Minister Robarts' statement made it clear that the government saw no reason why the proposed reorganization of the Area Municipalities, the Metropolitan Toronto Council, and the school boards should not come into effect on January 1, 1967. It was expected that the normal elections for the new consolidated municipal councils and school boards could take place in December 1966. The new councils and school boards would be organized in the normal way to hold office for a uniform three-year term commencing January 1, 1967. The political reorganization, however, required changes in certain sections of the Municipality of Metropolitan Toronto Act dealing with the division of local municipalities into wards, the preparation of new voter lists, and similar matters, so that the necessary approval of the Ontario Municipal Board could be obtained for the creation of new wards.

Meanwhile the Prime Minister expected that the municipalities concerned could begin studying the necessary reorganization of municipal staffs and services through joint committees of elected and appointed officials. Mr. Robarts emphasized that the experience gained in 1953–1954, with the creation of the Metropolitan Corporation, and in 1957, with the unification of the police forces, should be of great assistance in effecting a smooth transition.[21] Staff reorganizations resulting from the transfer of local functions to the Metropolitan Corporation started during the early months of 1966.

BILL 81: THE NEW MUNICIPALITY OF METROPOLITAN TORONTO ACT

The announcement of the provincial government's intentions paved the way for an amending bill that was submitted to the legislature of the Province of Ontario at its spring session in 1966. In his statement the Prime Minister noted that the new bill would necessarily be more extensive than any previous amendment to The Municipality of Metropolitan Toronto Act. Officially, Bill 81 was simply named "An Act to Amend The Municipality of Metropolitan Toronto Act," and was given its first reading in the House on March 31, 1966. After substantial debate and deliberations in committee, the bill was formally passed on April 26 and became law on May 18.

The original Municipality of Metropolitan Toronto Act had been a new and startling piece of legislation, particularly since it differed in many important aspects from the proposals outlined in the report of the Ontario Municipal Board (the Cumming Report, 1953). In contrast, the major amending legislation of 1966 contained no surprises, because the Prime Minister had already described the major changes to be implemented. As a consequence, the new bill merely translated into law all of the government's proposals, and in many respects reads like a basic document in municipal housekeeping.

The remarkable thing about the Prime Minister's statement and the consequent passage of the new legislation was the virtual absence of public dissent. Perhaps the experience of the previous 15 years had instilled an attitude of resignation. In any event, there was a curious difference between the excitement of 1964 and 1965, when the hearings of the Royal Commission were in progress and the public was anticipating the report of the commissioner, and the almost apathetic acceptance in 1966 of the position of the Government of Ontario. This may simply have been a sensible acceptance of reality.

The newspapers made it clear that the provincial government had spoken. The members of the councils of the 13 Area Municipalities seemed to accept the fact that the decisions had been made, and that for the next three, six, or even nine years the ground rules for governing Metropolitan Toronto had been determined. Those who were charged with administrative responsibility simply got down to the business of political and administrative reorganization, and the Municipality of Metropolitan Toronto and its constituent Area Municipalities entered a new phase.

CHAPTER VIII

REGIONAL PLANNING AND PROVINCIAL POLICY ON REGIONAL GOVERNMENT

THE CONCLUSION of Metro's first decade was widely celebrated. It officially ended on December 31, 1963. The annual brochure, published by the Metropolitan Toronto Planning Board since 1954, appeared in the late summer of 1963 and was entitled *Metropolitan Toronto 1953–1963: 10 years of Progress.* It began with the following paragraph:

Ten years ago, the Toronto area was the first community in the Western hemisphere to give official political recognition to the metropolitan area as the newest form of urban settlement created by the modern industrial society. Incorporated on April 15, 1953, the Municipality of Metropolitan Toronto is a federation of thirteen separate municipalities which retain their local autonomy and responsibilities while passing over to the Metropolitan Government the responsibility for major regional services. The legislation which established metropolitan government gave the new level of government many responsibilities. While the local municipalities retained their individual identity, the central authority took into its jurisdiction the wholesale supply and purification of water, provision of major storm and sanitary sewers and the control of water pollution, responsibility for basic education costs, public transportation and the major road network, regional planning, administration of the county jail and the lower courts, public housing, regional parks, homes for the aged and the care of indigent hospital patients and neglected children.[1]

THE FUTURE: SOCIAL PROBLEMS LOOM

This was followed by a relatively brief but detailed history of the origins of metropolitan government in Toronto, and was concluded with a section on "The Future" with these two long paragraphs:

While much has been achieved, many problems remain to be solved. The changing nature of the metropolitan problem is perhaps best reflected in the shifting focus of metropolitan concern. Where the emphasis in the first 10 years has of necessity been largely on the basic and essential physical services, that of the next 10 years will be increasingly on social and community welfare. In the first 10-year capital works program adopted by Metro in 1955, the projected expenditure of $585 million (exclusive of area municipality expenditures) was allocated on the basis of 76% to roads, sewers and water supply; 21% to education; and only 3% to all of the other services and facilities, such as housing, welfare, conservation and parks, and the administration of justice. The 10-year capital program adopted in 1963, totalling more than $1 billion (again exclusive of local projects) presents a far different picture: 36% on roads, sewers, and water; 28% on education; 30% on public transit; and 6% on the other Metropolitan services.

The form of Metropolitan government is itself subject to change. One of the great advantages of the principle of federation is that it is flexible and may be adjusted to changing conditions when required. The sharp changes in the physical development of the area over the past 10 years have led to increasing concern over the form of political representation and the detail of municipal structure within the federation. Just as Metro was born out of a Provincial Commission of Inquiry, so it enters its second decade with the establishment of a new Provincial study which will review the accomplishments of the past 10 years and assess the problems of the future. On April 18, 1963, the Hon. John P. Robarts, Prime Minister of Ontario, announced that a commission would be established to provide an independent assessment and evaluation of all aspects of the metropolitan federation, and stated: "In the consideration of the entire subject of the government of Metropolitan Toronto it must never be forgotten that, although the present metropolitan government is new, it has, nevertheless, been eminently successful and it greatly affects the lives of one-quarter of the people of this province. The government must, therefore, proceed with care and with full recognition of its responsibility to encourage the evolution of a form of government that will meet the immediate and foreseeable future needs of the people of the area and will, at the same time, fit within the framework of the traditional governmental patterns of our province." [2]

These extracts constitute the first formal admission that, despite the outstanding success of Metro's efforts to improve and develop the physical services required for urbanization, the effort was undertaken at the neglect of social services.* Nevertheless, the breakdown of the

---

* It should not be assumed that these declarations of policy were simply offered by those responsible for compiling the annual report. The statements quoted would not have been published without the approval of the Chairman

ten-year capital program adopted in 1963 does not clearly substantiate the argument that "the emphasis . . . of the next ten years will be increasingly on social and community welfare."

Thus a 25 percent increase in the capital expenditures devoted to education was inevitable, considering the extremely high birthrate of the years 1944–1959. Moreover the development of public transit and additional money spent on roads, sewers, and water supply obviously did not represent strong new support for "social and community welfare." But at least there was public recognition by the close of Metro's first decade that the social services had been bypassed beyond reason.

THE PAST: A DECADE OF PHYSICAL DEVELOPMENT

The lack of attention to social services was troubling and unfortunate, if not deplorable. Nevertheless a heavy emphasis on physical services during Metro's first decade was probably inevitable and certainly essential, given the basic facts of population growth. In the decade 1953–1962 the population of Metropolitan Toronto increased by some 450,000 persons—from 1,175,000 to 1,625,000—an increase of about 40 percent. The Metropolitan Toronto Planning Board judged that about 45 percent of this growth was due to natural increase. The remaining 55 percent represented immigration, with a majority of the migrants coming from abroad.[3] The average annual population increase during Metro's first decade was about 50,000 persons.

Metro's long strides toward the status of an urban metropolis—accommodating about one in every 11 Canadians, and one in every 9 jobs in the nation—more than doubled the urbanized area during the decade. In 1953, about 45 of Metro's 240 square miles were urbanized; by 1963 this figure had reached 92 square miles. In brief, the rate of urban development averaged about five square miles per year. As much urbanization took place in Metro's first decade as had occurred in the previous 100 years! Moreover, since 1963 there has been no diminution in this voracious consumption of available land. In the words of the 1963 Metro report:

To accommodate growth on this scale, the stock of housing has increased by more than 50 percent since 1953, with the addition of 160,000 new

of the Metropolitan Council, and perhaps they were the product of a consultation with the executive committee as a whole.

dwellings to the 1953 housing stock of 285,000 dwellings. From a community of single-family, owner-occupied homes—the traditional picture of Toronto in past decades—the metropolis is now the scene of much rental activity. About 45 percent of the new units are in single-family detached houses, and about 55 percent in multiple-family dwellings.[4]

The pace of the trend toward the construction of multiple dwellings has accelerated, producing a sharp visual contrast between the metropolis of the late 1950's and that of the early 1970's.

It is worth noting that the 1963 report also points to the sociophysical concerns of the social planners as they examine the results of a decade of metropolitan physical expansion: "While this new development [the rate of urbanization] is expected to continue, the renewal of the older parts of the area is assuming increasing importance; public and private efforts are directed more and more toward replacing and rehabilitating buildings in the central core and the inner residential areas." [5] Physical and social planners both see a substantial contrast between the idealism of these words and the facts of life in the urban core.

The interrelated processes of population growth, urban development, and a substantial increase in housing stock, made it inevitable that the basic physical facilities of the modern metropolis would have to be expanded commensurately, or chaos would result. It has already been emphasized that Metropolitan Toronto's record in the areas of water supply, sewage disposal, and the development of private and public transportation facilities was almost unexcelled within North American metropolitan areas. Thus a brief description of the progress that achieved these results during Metro's first decade is warranted.

WATER SUPPLY

In ten years the water treatment capacity within Metro was increased 45 percent, from 235 million to 345 million gallons per day. Much of this was achieved by doubling the capacity of the main plant within the City of Toronto from 100 million to 200 million gallons per day. In all, Metro spent about $60 million during the decade. About two-thirds of the expenditure represented capital investment in the enlargement of water treatment capacity, and the balance financed distribution and storage facilities. The Metro report states: "It is noteworthy that all of this debt is self-liquidating and is paid for through the sale of water to the area municipalities rather than through taxes." [6]

The storage capacity of the water supply system taken over by Metropolitan Toronto in 1953 amounted to 93 million gallons. A decade later capacity had increased to 132 million gallons, and an additional reservoir was under construction to add another 30 million gallons. Similarly, from the 85 miles of trunk water distribution mains that Metro assumed in 1954, the system grew within ten years to 207 miles of mains, most of which were of 36-inch diameter or greater.

Annual water consumption increased from 51 billion gallons in 1954 to 69 billion gallons in 1962. Members of the Metropolitan Council rarely failed to emphasize that all of the earlier summer restrictions on the use of water for any purpose, including lawn watering, had vanished by the end of the 1950's. Nevertheless, the continued development of the urban area and its increasing consumption of water indicated that there could be no respite in the growth of the metropolitan water system. In 1963 construction began on a new purification plant with a first-stage capacity of 100 million gallons per day, and an ultimate capacity of 300 million gallons per day. Finally, by 1963 the Metro report foresaw that construction of an additional purification plant would be necessary within the second decade, as well as new storage reservoirs in the two largest rural townships north of the metropolitan boundaries.

WATER POLLUTION CONTROL (SEWAGE DISPOSAL)

Ten Years of Progress indicates that Metro's "overall plan for water pollution control . . . required that all sewage be fed into large trunk mains leading to a few major disposal plants along Lake Ontario, where adequate treatment could be given and a safe effluent discharged in the Lake." [7] During the first decade capital expenditures within this area of service amounted to about $69 million, of which $38 million was spent on the sewage treatment plants and an additional $31 million for approximately 88 new miles of trunk sewer. In addition, roughly 1,700 miles of local mains were constructed in the Area Municipalities.

By 1963 the main sewage treatment plant taken over from the City of Toronto, and 16 minor plants in existence on January 1, 1954, had been completely remodeled into a new system. Moreover, the capacity of the main plant had been enlarged from 84 million to 120 million gallons per day and, equally important, secondary treatment facilities had been installed. New plants developed by the Metropolitan Council provided an additional treatment capacity of 62 million gallons per day. By 1963, total sewage treatment capacity reached 192 million gallons per day, an increase of 70 percent over the capacity 10 years earlier.

Metro's enthusiastic authors wrote: "The result has been an ample supply of adequately serviced land, in all parts of the metropolitan area, for residential, commercial, and industrial purposes, in quantities able to meet all anticipated demands." [8] This optimistic interpretation of Toronto's accomplishments can perhaps be forgiven in the light of the very real progress made in meeting basic physical needs of city dwellers.

TRANSPORTATION

The report states:

From the outset, the Metropolitan Council recognized that roadways and public transit are each required to perform the particular function for which they are best suited—public transit to handle the mass movement of persons in the areas of relative concentration, and private automobiles to handle the many diversified movements throughout the day which characterize a metropolitan area. This has led to the simultaneous development of a public transportation system which is generally acknowledged as being among the best in North America, and a road system which takes full advantage of the most advanced techniques of highway design.[9]

During the decade, approximately $120 million was spent by the Toronto Transit Commission on the development of the entire public transit system. Three-quarters of this sum ($92 million) was devoted to rapid transit facilities, while the remaining $30 million was invested in new buses, streetcars, and other equipment. Transit revenues produced about 60 percent of the total. By the late 1950's, following a request by the Toronto Transit Commission for subsidization, the Metropolitan Corporation became directly involved in transportation development, and provided 40 percent of total capital expenditures out of tax revenues.

In addition, the Metropolitan Corporation spent about $160 million on roadways, receiving a subsidy from the province approximating 50 percent of these expenditures. The report also predicted that the decade ending in 1973 would see vastly increased expenditures on transportation, with a total projected investment of $290 million in transit facilities and $190 million in the arterial road system. Provincial highways cutting through the metropolitan area were another matter, being the responsibility of the Province of Ontario. Expenditures amounted to $54 million during the decade ending in 1963, with a projection of twice that amount during Metro's second decade.

An analysis of peak-hour travel and of all movements during the day revealed that about 70 percent of the peak-hour travelers into the central business district came by public transit. Nevertheless, the suburbanization of population, employment, and housing reduced the public transit proportion of average daily—24-hour—movements to about one-third of the total. The end-of-decade Metro Report sums up the transportation picture:

> To produce a balanced transportation system it is necessary to pursue a unified transportation policy in which all aspects of the problem are carefully evaluated. Because the Metropolitan Corporation exercises jurisdiction over the entire network of expressways and arterial roads covering an area of 240 square miles and because it is ultimately responsible for the operations of the Toronto Transit Commission over this same area, it is able to produce integrated transportation policies which pay attention to the needs of both private vehicles and public transit passengers.[10]

The statement concludes by indicating that in 1963 the average journey to work in Metropolitan Toronto did not exceed a half hour, despite the tremendous growth. The quotation is accurate as far as it goes, but as Harold Kaplan points out, it is a great oversimplification to argue that Metro and the TTC had produced an integrated transportation system, that is, one satisfying the needs both of automobile drivers and of public transit riders.[11] This dilemma has persisted throughout Metro's second decade. In fact, the question of achieving an appropriate balance between public and private transportation facilities remains one of the major unresolved issues of the 1970's.

THE OFFICIAL PLAN OF THE
METROPOLITAN TORONTO PLANNING AREA

The long-awaited revision of the Official Plan was submitted to the Metropolitan Toronto Planning Board in December 1964. The board considered the proposed plan at three special meetings in the early months of 1965. Ultimately in April of that year 1,500 copies were distributed throughout the Metropolitan area. About one-third of these went to the local municipalities and about one-fifth to taxpayers' groups and businessmen's associations. The Chairman of the Metropolitan Toronto Planning Board reported in a letter to the Metropolitan Council on February 16, 1966:

> The document was displayed in 41 public offices and libraries in the Metropolitan Planning Area for a period of 3 to 4 weeks during May and June 1965, advertisements were placed in 32 daily and weekly newspapers, and 8 public meetings to discuss the Plan were held during June at various locations within the Planning Area, with a total attendance of about 2,230 persons.
> All of the municipalities and other parties receiving the document were requested to submit comments, and persons attending the public meetings were also requested to submit comments in writing. The Board received comments from all 26 municipalities in the Planning Area, and 60 written representations were received from private individuals, ratepayers' and businessmen's associations, Metropolitan Departments, and various organizations.
> Following receipt of these comments the Board held five more special meetings to consider the Plan. The Official Plan was adopted by the Board on December 15, 1965.[12]

The manner in which the council would study the proposed Official Plan was referred to the executive committee, which decided on May 3 of that year to form an "Official Plan Committee." The committee solicited comments from each of the 26 municipalities in the Metropolitan Toronto Planning Area, and from a selected group of voluntary organizations, such as the Urban Development Institute (an association of major apartment developers, small housebuilders, and professionals concerned with urban development) and the Social Planning Council of Metropolitan Toronto. The Official Plan Committee was constituted for the purpose of: "(a) hearing representations from the municipalities within the Metropolitan Toronto Planning Area with respect to the adoption of the proposed Official Plan recommended by the Metropolitan Toronto Planning Board and dated December 19, 1965, as the Official Plan of the Area; and (b) making recommendations to the Council with respect to the adoption of the proposed Plan."[13] The committee included the Metro Chairman (ex officio) and two members of the council's executive committee, plus the four chairmen of the council's standing committees: Transportation, Welfare and Housing, Works, and Parks and Recreation. The committee first met on May 17, 1966, and subsequently held six sessions from July to November. Ultimately, it submitted its report for consideration by the Metro Council on December 15, 1966.[14]

This sequence has been explained in some detail to illustrate the care with which consideration of the proposed Official Plan was undertaken. It will be recalled that the preparation of an Official Plan was one of the major requirements of Bill 80, the act creating the Municipality of Metropolitan Toronto in April 1953. Throughout the middle and late 1950's the newly constituted Metropolitan Toronto Planning Board labored to produce a draft Official Plan, which was brought forward for political and public consideration in 1959. It is a moot point whether the first submission was anything more than an exercise. Perhaps it would be more generous to insist that without the study, critical comments, and sometimes indifference with which the 1959 report was received, the refined document brought forward in 1965 would not have received the consideration that was essential if Metro Toronto were ever to have an "approved" Official Plan. As things stood in 1971, however, the Minister of Municipal Affairs of the Province of Ontario had not yet formally approved the Official Plan. Again, the Metropolitan Council did not in fact send its Official Plan forward to the minister for his approval. The tortuous process which engaged the council during 1966–1967 is explained below.

As noted, the Official Plan Committee undertook its assignments in May 1966. Subsequently 14 of the 26 municipalities within the Metropolitan Toronto Planning Area indicated that they would make no representations before the committee. Four others indicated that they would prepare written submissions, but would not send representatives to appear. Eight governments—including the City, four major traditional townships within Metro, and three townships outside Metro—submitted written comments and sent deputations to the Official Plan Committee's hearings. (The four townships became boroughs on January 1, 1967.)

The *Official Plan* of December 1965 was a modest document, in contrast to the *Official Plan of the Metropolitan Planning Area* of 1959, with its 272 pages and 58 maps. Although its format was similar, the entire 1965 publication consisted of 30 large pages. A second document, entitled *Official Plan of the Metropolitan Toronto Planning Area: Supplement,* also dated December 1965, consisted of 22 pages and five major maps. When the work of the Official Plan Committee was completed, both documents were reissued (dated December 7, 1966) in a more customary size and incorporated some but not all of the changes suggested by the various municipalities and nongovernmental bodies canvassed and interviewed in the intervening year. The final documents of late 1966 are entitled: the *Metropolitan Plan* per se and the *Supplement*. Finally, on June 6, 1969, the Commissioner of Planning for Metropolitan Toronto issued a *Consolidation of Amendments,* incorporating all the changes in the Metropolitan Plan accepted from December 1966 to December 1968. For the time being, this document completes the roster of major publications issued in Metro's long and often stormy progress towards the preparation of an "urban general plan."

Despite all the care taken to encourage widespread participation in the preparation and amendment of a Metropolitan Official Plan, the Metropolitan Council decided on December 15, 1966, not to adopt the revised plan but rather to accept it "as a statement of the policy of the Metropolitan Corporation for the planning of future works and services and as a guide for future development in the Metropolitan Toronto Planning Area." [15] There were two main reasons for this curious action, which some observers also considered craven. First, the report of the Official Plan Committee came to the Council of the Municipality of Metropolitan Toronto just before January 1, 1967, when the entire form and structure of Metropolitan Toronto was about to undergo fundamental change. The statement of Prime Minister Robarts of January 10, 1966, had led to new legislation. Elections had just been held (on December 1, 1966) to choose a Mayor and Council for the City of Toronto and for each of the five new boroughs. A new Metropolitan Council was scheduled to take office in the first ten days of January 1967, and a three-year term was about to commence for all elected officers, as well as the Metropolitan Council's Chairman.

Accordingly, on December 15, 1966, the Metropolitan Council recommended: "that the Plan be referred to the Legislation Planning Committee of the 1967 Council for continuous study and to recommend changes in provincial planning procedures to the 1967 Council." [16] This referral of the difficult question of formal adoption of the Metropolitan Plan to the newly elected council is quite understandable under the circumstances, but the significance of the odd final clause in the recommendation, referring to "changes in provincial planning procedures," remains unclear.

Perhaps the explanation lies in the second major reason why the Metropolitan Council of 1966 did not formally adopt or reject the Metropolitan Plan after seven years of effort. Apparently, the 1966 Council feared further important controversy within the Metropolitan Toronto Planning Area if it formally adopted the Metropolitan Plan. In the view of competent planners the real fear—which still exists—was that approval of an Official Plan by the minister would reduce the power of the council to make new policy decisions quickly. Any policy decision requiring an amendment to the Official Plan would involve a process similar to the adoption of the plan in the first place, and hence could be frustrating, controversial, and time consuming. In fact, this process could result in the minister failing to agree with the council on a particular amendment to the Official Plan. Perhaps that is the reason for urging that the 1967 Council "recommend changes in provincial planning procedures." It is small wonder that most citizens found the process at best difficult to understand, and at worst either futile or irrelevant.

TROUBLE IN TRANSPORTATION PLANNING: THE CASE OF THE SPADINA EXPRESSWAY

The Metropolitan Council's responsibility for transportation is clearly outlined by the Municipality of Metropolitan Toronto Act, particularly by Part V, Metropolitan Road System, Part VI, Metropolitan Transportation, and Part XIV, Planning. The last specifically includes "public transportation" within the scope of the Official Plan. Some indication of Metro's future design for public and private transportation appeared in the draft Official Plan of 1959, which devoted an entire chapter to the subject, and enunciated the transportation plan for the future in general terms.

INITIAL PLANS AND THE START OF CONSTRUCTION

As early as 1959 the Metropolitan Council had received a plan that included an analysis of both a road and public transportation system. In the midst of the first portion of its future plan, the authors presented a substantial analysis of the expressway system, including a specific reference to a future major arterial roadway known as the Spadina Expressway:*

> The Spadina Expressway will extend north from the Crosstown Expressway to Highway 401 and Wilson Avenue, providing access from the centre to the northern section of Metropolitan Toronto. Up to Wilson Avenue it will be an expressway with a rapid transit line in the centre median. . . . Although not strictly an expressway, Spadina Avenue south of the Crosstown Expressway will be developed to distribute heavy traffic volume onto the downtown city streets. Detailed plans for the improvement of Spadina Avenue are being studied in conjunction with the City of Toronto Planning Board.[17]

As noted, the authors of the draft Official Plan promised a series of major reports in the early 1960's to provide more detailed information on certain aspects of the material sketched in the 1959 draft. Thus on December 29, 1964 the Commissioner of Planning sent the Chairman of the Metropolitan Toronto Planning Board a report entitled *Metropolitan Toronto Transportation Plan*. Meanwhile, however, the Metropolitan Council had already approved several aspects of the projected expressway system, including the tentative route of the Spadina Expressway. Moreover, still earlier, in 1962, the Ontario Municipal Board had given approval to the Metropolitan Council for the expenditure of approximately $155 million, the estimated total cost of the roadway and transit line. The latter was to occupy the median strip along the northern half of the proposed route.

Construction began in 1963, and the first section, of about one and a half miles at the northern end of the route, was completed within two years. The new section provided access to Canada's first completely covered and air-conditioned shopping plaza, Yorkdale. The fact that the plaza represented a huge investment and housed substantial branches of Canada's two largest department stores, not only caused a certain amount of criticism of that particular section of roadway, but also drew public attention to the nature of the Spadina Expressway and the total transportation plan. When the plan appeared at the end of 1964, however, there was no indication that the expressway system was in any danger of strong public opposition, or that it did not have the approval of provincial officials.

* Spadina is pronounced Spa-DYE-na.

HINTS OF FUTURE PROBLEMS

The material on transportation that had appeared in the 1959 Official Plan was described in 1964 as "The Preliminary Transportation Plan." Studies in the intervening years were published in substantial detail, and went far toward providing a scientific basis for the recommendations of the staff of the Metropolitan Toronto Planning Board. Although the report on the Metropolitan Toronto Transportation Plan devotes only 30 lines to the Spadina Expressway, the suggestions and comments therein, when viewed in the light of the newly emerging concerns of the late 1960's, point directly toward the difficult problems and opposition that have beset the project since 1969. For example, the report indicates that the adequacy of the existing arterial roads to handle the expressway traffic at the terminal ends has been examined. Accordingly it was suggested that, at the southern end, the expressway would have to be extended below Bloor Street. Furthermore, the report stated flatly that Spadina Avenue to the south would be adequate, with certain intersection improvements, for the projected traffic movement.

Perhaps the most significant language in the 1964 report appeared in a brief paragraph that stated: "These projections are based on the assumption that the Crosstown and Christie Expressways will be constructed to complete the inner ring. A special study which was made to determine the likely effect of not constructing the Crosstown Expressway indicated that traffic on Spadina Avenue would increase up to 10 percent. However, no examination has been made of the situation which would arise if neither the Crosstown nor the Christie Expressways are built." [18] These statements implied that the Spadina Expressway was only one step in a continuous road-building program, threatening many neighborhoods in the central city.

"A PLATE OF SPAGHETTI" AND HOUSING DEMOLITIONS

During the years 1965–1967, work proceeded on the Spadina project within the authorized expenditure of $76 million, but also with the additional assistance of financial contributions from the provincial government for the construction of the most intricate highway interchange ever built in Ontario. In fact, two important components of the expressway were under simultaneous construction. In the first place, there was the northern interchange between the expressway and the provincial Highway 401, which runs from the eastern boundary of Ontario at the Quebec border to the western boundary at Windsor. The complex interchange can only be described as fantastic, and some observers have called it "a plate of spaghetti." This was an involved and costly project, particularly since Highway 401 was being expanded from six to 12 lanes.

Simultaneously, the Spadina Expressway was extended southward for a distance of about one and a quarter miles, to reach an important east-west arterial road known as Eglinton Avenue. In order to do this, a number of private homes were expropriated and demolished. It soon became clear that the Eglinton Avenue interchange would be a substantial construction project requiring many more housing demolitions. At this point, the expressway was extending from the Township of North York into the former Village of Forest Hill, and the Township of York, all areas of middle- and upper-middle class families. These developments fed fears that the expressway would eventually have a tremendous impact upon less well-endowed neighborhoods and their residents, as it proceeded farther south.

Things soon wound down to a standstill. The extension to Eglinton Avenue was completed in 1969, but was not paved. The route for the six-lane highway was fully prepared, the median for the transit line was "roughed in" and a number of bridges over the arterial space were built. But the road ended abruptly at Eglinton Avenue.

"STOP SPADINA, SAVE OUR CITY . . ."

Construction was stalled primarily by the rise of a determined opposition, not only to the expressway but also to the whole transportation plan. The Spadina Expressway became extremely important in itself by 1968–1969, primarily because its history and future development posed all the major issues that were the new concerns of citizens' groups, many elected officials, several departments of the Government of Ontario, as well as of urban society in general.

Air pollution was one of these major new concerns, and opposition to urban renewal was another. The movement of new people into old neighborhoods, and rehabilitation of the latter, was a third factor of substantial importance. Many forces thus provided support for a strong citizens' organization that emerged in 1968, calling itself the "Stop Spadina, Save Our City Co-ordinating Committee"

(SSSOCCC). The very title of this organization implied a determined effort to save the entire city. In 1969 the committee prepared a map of Metropolitan Toronto, entitled "This is the Spadina Expressway," upon which all projected expressways for the future were drawn. Spadina was described as "one tentacle in the two-hundred mile, two-billion dollar expressway octopus projected in the 1964 Transportation Plan."

METRO HALTS CONSTRUCTION

By 1969 opposition was so strong that the Metro Council decided to halt further construction and reassess its position. All but $10 million of the approved $76 million was found to have been spent by the beginning of 1970. During 1969 and 1970 the Metropolitan Council met on a number of occasions to discuss its transportation plan and its future course, and continued to support completion of the Spadina Expressway. But the council soon learned that the total estimated cost of the combined expressway and transit line had increased to $237 million. Not only was it necessary to return to the Ontario Municipal Board for approval of additional capital borrowing, but it became essential to indicate, both to the board and to the general public, that the overall estimates had soared by $82 million. The Metropolitan Council heard several proposals that the project be further deferred until a complete review of the transportation plan was carried out, perhaps by Metro officials and additional consultants, perhaps by so-called "independent consultants."

THE MUNICIPAL BOARD SUPPORTS THE PROJECT

Ultimately, the council voted to ask the Chairman of the Ontario Municipal Board, Mr. J. A. Kennedy, to conduct a public hearing late in 1970. The citizens' organizations opposed to the project asked for further time to prepare their case. The Chairman scheduled hearings to begin January 4, 1971, and suggested that they might continue from four to six weeks.

At this point a number of citizens' organizations combined, adopted a new name, "The Spadina Review Corporation," engaged the services of one of Canada's leading trial lawyers, Mr. J. J. Robinette, and set out to raise $50,000 to meet his fees and other expenses. As the hearings began early in January 1971, these opponents had raised more than $10,000 and were ready to confront the expert testimony of Metro officials and their consultants.

The Municipal Board, composed of the Chairman and two members, held hearings over a period of 16 days in January and then reserved judgment. The board transmitted a split decision on February 17, 1971, voting two-to-one in favor of Metro's application for additional funds to continue construction of the Spadina Expressway. Mr. J. A. Kennedy, the Chairman, dissented.

"A GOOD PLACE TO STOP"

Within a few days the Spadina Review Corporation appealed directly to the provincial cabinet. On June 3, 1971 the $237 million Spadina Expressway was scrapped by the Ontario government. In a statement to the legislature the Prime Minister, William G. Davis, stated that no further work would be permitted on the expressway, but that increased aid would be forthcoming for completion of a rapid transit system into the heart of the City. Mr. Davis's presentation incorporated statements that became the watchword of citizens' groups and a major theme of his party's campaign for the next provincial election:

In the final analysis, in determining how best to serve the future needs of Metropolitan Toronto, we must make a decision as to whether we are trying to build a transportation system to serve the automobile or one which will best serve the people.

If we are building a transportation system to serve the automobile, the Spadina Expressway would be a good place to start.

But if we are building a transportation system to serve people, the Spadina Expressway is a good place to stop.

A PROFOUND SHOCK

This analysis will not explore the pros and cons of the Spadina Expressway—which was renamed the William R. Allen Expressway, following the retirement of the second Chairman of the Metropolitan Council in 1969. Nor will the writer pass judgment on the conduct of the Metropolitan Toronto Planning Board or the citizens' organizations opposing the expressway. It is important, however, to emphasize the issues that the Spadina Expressway problem has posed for the Metropolitan Council and the provincial government, and for their future programs of regional and transportation planning.

The strength of the expressway opposition, and its effects on the entire program of transportation planning to the year 2000 have been a profound shock to the Metropolitan Council.

It will be argued later that the council was inexperienced in dealing with citizens' organizations, and had had very little contact with them during the early 1960's because such groups were busy opposing the urban renewal programs being considered by the City of Toronto. Moreover, the Metropolitan Council appeared demoralized or at least inept in the face of citizen opposition. The citizens' groups were led by architects, planners, engineers, and scholars in the social sciences from various universities, and were reasonably well financed. Consequently this was no ordinary confrontation with a local neighborhood group concerned with such relatively minor matters as overnight parking on streets.

FOUR MAIN ISSUES

The Spadina Expressway controversy posed four main issues:

1. First, the expressway sharply raised the question, "Who plans?" This matter had been discussed by Harold Kaplan, who pointed out that in the period 1953–1965 over two-thirds of the policy issues coming before the Metro Council were defined and initiated by key Metro department heads.[19] This theme was picked up by groups opposed to the expressway, not directly because of Kaplan but because the leaders of these groups were astute enough to identify what the Bureau of Municipal Research has called "the politics of expertise."[20]

In the case of transportation, the bureau affirmed that two factors encouraged the concentration of expert policy-making, and its isolation from the Metropolitan Council. First, the council had failed to provide its senior officials with a clear and explicit policy direction on the basis of which to formulate transportation plans. Second, experts at the operating level and in the planning board were dealing with highly specialized technical data that were extremely difficult to explain clearly to citizens and their elected representatives. In the view of the bureau, as this information became available by the mid-1960's, the experts came to control the direction and limits of policy:

Transportation planning methodology has created an aura of impartiality and expertise around transportation planners and technicians, and has lent credibility to potentially unpopular policies. No transportation decision is either exclusively technical or exclusively political. Technical and political decisions each have their own language and each is justified by appeals to quite distinct authorities. While not political in substance, most major technical decisions are political in consequence; and the technical expert has become an effective political force in deciding transportation policy.[21]

2. Second, the Spadina Expressway has raised the whole question of the role of the Ontario Municipal Board in determining metropolitan policy through its control over capital borrowing. The Ontario Municipal Board was originally created in the 1930's because many municipalities in Ontario were technically bankrupt, and it set out to control their borrowing and debt. In dealing with Metropolitan Toronto, the board controls significant areas of public policy by virtue of its concern with borrowing capacity, the ratio of debt to assessed valuation and tax rates. The board has a strong influence not merely in transportation planning, but in all aspects of planning, as most plans require capital expenditures for their implementation.

The case of the Spadina Expressway is perhaps the most significant illustration of these trends, because both sides had appealed to the board for a quasi-judicial decision. The Metropolitan Council had the board's earlier approval of the expressway and substantial expenditures on it. The Chairman of the board, however, expressed shock at finding that only a small portion of the expressway had been constructed by the end of 1970 although most of the authorized funds had been spent. He was asked to provide a large additional sum, and would later be asked for the remainder. However, there was great uncertainty as to the total cost of a project that might not be completed before 1977 or 1978, even if work were resumed at once.

The Ontario Municipal Board was in a difficult position. If it turned down future construction of the expressway at this point, a "white elephant" would be left on the landscape to remind the public of the way resources had been squandered. On the other hand, if the board approved the total concept, even with further additional costly design modifications to limit the disruption at the interchanges and reduce the flow of traffic into adjacent neighborhoods, the board would be accused of destroying communities and sound residential areas, and of introducing vast amounts of air pollution into the downtown areas.

3. Third, the Spadina Expressway has raised the question of

whether the Ontario Municipal Board is an ombudsman-like agency, a protagonist of citizens' organizations opposed to the activities of local government in any sphere. Citizens' groups opposed to the expressway have reason to expect a great deal of sympathy from the Municipal Board. During the past three or four years the Chairman and other members of the board have spoken out sharply against alleged examples of poor planning in many municipalities, including Metropolitan Toronto. They have demonstrated sympathy and understanding for residents of single-family homes threatened by demolition and replacement with high-rise apartment buildings. They have spoken out against inadequate planning procedures that tend to disrupt residential neighborhoods, albeit on a smaller scale than poorly conceived transportation plans. They have decried the loss of open space, parks and recreation facilities in many municipalities.

It is doubtful, however, that the Government of Ontario ever intended the Ontario Municipal Board to take up the causes of citizens' groups. Some politicians have complained that the Chairman of the board is in a very fortunate position because he gains tremendous publicity, has freedom to speak out against either side in any controversy, has a great deal of power, and does not need to stand for election. Nevertheless, there has been no indication by the Prime Minister or by the province's other political leaders that they would do anything in the near future to restrict the role of the Ontario Municipal Board. It has served the province well, after all, as a controlling force over potentially unbridled local expenditures.

4. Finally, the Spadina Expressway issue has also brought into question the role of the Metro Chairman and the Metropolitan Council in the handling of such controversies. The Metropolitan presentation was managed entirely by the Metropolitan Solicitor, who called as witnesses the Metropolitan Commissioners (of Roads and Traffic, Planning) and the City Commissioner of Works. Witnesses for Metro have also included such distinguished consultants as the American transportation planner Alan Voorhees. Legal counsel for the opposition groups presented testimony from citizens residing in neighborhoods affected by the expressway, and from their own group of consultants who included urban planners, economists, and architects.

It is significant that neither the Metro Chairman nor any member of the council appeared for either side, although it was known that the councillors were split on the issue. Perhaps the central question relates to the role of the Metro Chairman. It may be argued that since this project had been approved on a number of occasions by the Metropolitan Council, he had a major responsibility to defend it before the Ontario Municipal Board. But he appears to have rejected that responsibility in favor of a neutral position.

WIDE RAMIFICATIONS

In sum, the Spadina Expressway has tremendous significance for the future of metropolitan government because of the wide-ranging issues it raises concerning Metro policy and decisionmaking. It is no longer a case of "good" or "bad" transportation planning. Neither is it a question of deciding the expressway's future. Instead, the controversy has ramifications that extend to all areas of metropolitan administration.

Prime Minister Davis was both strongly supported and attacked on his decision to halt the Spadina Expressway. For several weeks the press speculated on the impact of this decision with respect to the future of Mr. Davis and his party. When a provincial election was called in September for October 21, 1971, the prospects were openly debated by politicians from all parties. The Prime Minister's advisors and 'image-makers' pursued vigorously their campaign, based upon the argument that the 'Davis Party' was different from the Conservative Party of the past and the Spadina decision was strong supporting evidence. In any event, he and his followers were not only swept back into office, but also his strength within Metro increased sharply.

The overriding immediate concern has inevitably turned to the question of a rapid transit line to replace the expressway. By January 1972 a technical committee composed of provincial and Metro officials brought forward five possible routes for public consideration. One must be selected during 1972, if the vast population in northwest Metro is to receive the alternative access to downtown Toronto that the Prime Minister promised when he dismissed the expressway. But the Metro Council has not by any means abandoned hope that the notorious Spadina decision of June 1971 will be reversed. In council debates, informal speeches by the Chairman, and in approaches to the provincial government, they are maintaining a significant degree of pressure. It is too soon to write off the prospect of building additional expressways within Metro.*

In other ways it is difficult to predict the longer-term outcome. Even if the Spadina Expressway were again approved, the reverberations of the earlier rejection will inevitably influence other major programs developed by the Metropolitan Council, programs that must be completed during the balance of this century in order to meet the needs of a population expected to double its present size.

PROVINCIAL POLICY ON REGIONAL GOVERNMENT

The Municipality of Metropolitan Toronto was the first regional government to emerge in the burgeoning Province of Ontario following World War II. Its design, political structure, two-tier system, and distribution of functions, as well as its successes and failures, all played their part in influencing the Prime Minister and his Cabinet in their subsequent policy on regional government.

A SERIES OF REGIONAL STUDIES

The policy began to emerge in the early 1960's. The Department of Municipal Affairs commissioned a series of regional studies centered upon several expanding and politically divided urban areas in various parts of the province. The studies began in the Ottawa region (the national capital), insofar as that portion of the urban area within the Province of Ontario could be separated from the contiguous urbanization in the adjacent Province of Quebec.

Other studies related to the Lakehead region, including the twin cities of Fort William and Port Arthur and adjacent municipalities at the head of Lake Superior; the area to the west of Metropolitan Toronto, later known as the Peel-Halton Local Government Area Review; the Niagara District, including the major cities of St. Catherines and Niagara Falls; the Hamilton Metropolitan area, known as the Hamilton-Wentworth Regional Area Study; and the Muskoka region, a vast recreation and playground area for Metropolitan Toronto, about 130–160 miles north of the metropolis. Fi-

---

* In fact, the province announced early in 1972 that it will build an expressway from the proposed new international airport northeast of Metro, to provide access to downtown Toronto.

nally, a local government review was made in the Kitchener-Waterloo region, a rapidly growing urban area about 70 miles west and north of Metro Toronto, whose population had grown from less than 50,000 in 1951 to a projected excess of 100,000 in the Census of 1971. By 1970 reports on all these studies had been issued, the last to appear being the Kitchener-Waterloo Local Government Review in March 1970. The Government of Ontario has acted on many of the major recommendations in the studies.

ONTARIO'S POLICY AND METRO'S FUTURE

The evolution of provincial policy in the field of regional government merits detailed review, not merely because of the impact of Metro Toronto's experience upon the studies and the future policies of the provincial government, but also because of the impact of governmental policy on the future of Metropolitan Toronto itself.

In April 1966 the Prime Minister of Ontario introduced the policy of his government on regional development with a statement labeled "Design for Development." [22] The province had already been divided into ten regions in which regional development councils had been created. From an administrative point of view, new divisions were set up in the Treasury Department (a regional development branch) and the Department of Municipal Affairs (a regional research section). The regional development councils were responsible for determining both short- and long-range development proposals, which were formally published in March 1969. They take the form of general master plans for large geographical sectors within the province, sectors with such names as "Eastern Ontario" embracing 11 counties, and "Lake Erie" embracing four counties.

In the view of the Government of Ontario, "Design for Development" was intended to encourage public acceptance of the importance of regional economic activities, regional social problems, and ultimately regional planning. The creation in June 1968 of a two-tier regional government in the Ottawa area, called the Regional Municipality of Ottawa-Carleton, was a firm indication that the government meant business, and that its ultimate intention was to create such regional governments, throughout the province wherever feasible. In 1969 legislation was passed to create such governments in the Niagara Region and in the Lakehead area (later renamed

Thunder Bay), and on January 1, 1970, new two-tier governments came into operation with high hopes for the solution of area-wide problems.

In 1968, however, the Metro Chairman and Executive Committee, and the Mayors of the City of Toronto and the five boroughs began to view the rapidly evolving provincial policy on regional governments as a danger that would forestall the growth and development of Metro Toronto. These fears were reinforced by statements by the Prime Minister on November 28, 1968, and by the Minister of Municipal Affairs on December 2, 1968, in introducing a policy statement in the provincial legislature, later published as *Design for Development: Phase Two*.[23] The Minister of Municipal Affairs made it clear that what he visualized was a series of regional governments to the west, north, and east of the current boundaries of Metropolitan Toronto. The consternation caused by these statements reopened not only the question of the ultimate boundaries of Metro Toronto but also the question of "amalgamation," the concept beloved of City politicians since the late 1940's.

During 1969, in one speech after another, the Metro Chairman and various elected officials decried the destructive consequences of a policy that would keep Metro's boundaries as they had been since 1953. At the same time, the Mayor of Toronto and his cohorts criticized the two-tier system and continued divided jurisdiction within the traditional boundaries of Metropolitan Toronto. Although it is difficult to distinguish between these two arguments, it can be done. The Metropolitan officials argue primarily for expanded Metro boundaries without amalgamation of the area into "one big City." On the other hand, City politicians argue first for amalgamation of the area and elimination of the local municipalities, and then for the expansion of Metro's boundaries to the north and east.

GUIDES FOR REGIONALIZATION

The provincial-level statements of late 1968 amounted to a program for the regionalization of municipal government in Ontario. They set forth provincial guidelines for the creation of regional government and outlined the general characteristics of such governments as they would emerge during the 1970's. Principal guidelines include the following: A region should exhibit a sense of community and have a balance of interests. There must be an adequate financial base. The region should be large enough to permit local responsibilities to be performed efficiently. Finally, regional boundaries should facilitate maximum cooperation between regions.[24]

The Prime Minister went on to state:

To these criteria put forward by the Smith Committee [the Ontario Committee on Taxation] the Government has added three others of immense importance. First, we shall seek community participation in the formation of regional governments and, where possible, we shall strive to achieve community acceptability of the proposal. Second, we shall seek to have the new regional boundaries, or combinations of them, usable by other institutions. And third, we propose that in cases where there are to be two tiers of government within a region, the smaller units would be designed using the same criteria used at the regional level.[25]

The vision of regional governments offered by the Minister of Municipal Affairs included the notion of a minimum population of some 150,000 to 200,000. Local municipalities under a two-tier system would have a minimum population of some 8,000 to 10,000 persons. In addition, regional governments would exhibit such other characteristics as the following: (1) a region would cover an urban and rural area; (2) a region would have either a one- or a two-tiered government, depending on local circumstances; (3) in a two-tiered system, the regional municipality would have jurisdiction over area-wide functions such as planning, fire and police protection, health and welfare, water supply and distribution, and sewage and garbage collection and disposal; (4) municipal councils would be strengthened by the transfer to them of some powers of special districts; (5) regional government representation would be based on population; and (6) in a two-tiered system, representatives would be elected either directly or indirectly.[26]

Significantly, the statement by the Minister of Municipal Affairs—in addition to concepts and comments on the distribution of functions between the two tiers of regional government—contained references to 14 possible regional governments in the province, including Metro Toronto, Ottawa-Carleton, the Niagara Region, and the Lakehead area, all of which are now in existence.

The situation is most unsatisfactory, so far as the elected and appointed officials within Metro Toronto are concerned. They tend to view the expansion of Metro to the north within York County, and to the east within Ontario County as absolutely essential if Metro is to grow and expand, particularly in view of the shortage of serviced land for single-family housing within the traditional boundaries. Matters are further complicated by the fact that early in 1969 several municipalities to the east of Toronto held meetings with Metro officials, in the hope that they might be annexed before they could be incorporated within a regional government extending east of Metro to the City of Oshawa. Metro Toronto officials have made no secret of the fact that they welcome these overtures and that they hope to put sufficient pressure upon the provincial government to permit formal annexations before new regional governments are created along their boundaries. Their bitter references to "iron curtains" and a "hemming-in" process have not been lost on the members of the legislature, and at the end of 1971 these major questions were still not settled.

DESIGN FOR DEVELOPMENT:
THE TORONTO-CENTERED REGION

Another phase of the province's consideration of regional planning and regional development was presented in May 1970 at a formal gathering of federal, provincial, and municipal officials, planners, members of school boards and representatives of business, industry, and agriculture. The Prime Minister opened the proceedings with a statement indicating that this was the first of a number of major reports to be presented in the course of several years, each dealing with a region, as defined by his officials.

In the specific case of the Toronto-centered region, the planning area was a 90-mile arc centering on Toronto. This was clearly the most substantial area ever encompassed in the planning of the region around Toronto. The concept of a Toronto-centered region had now been greatly expanded from the administrative area of 240 square miles drawn in 1953, and from the 720 square miles mapped as the Metropolitan Toronto Planning Area, to a region encompassing 8,600 square miles "from prime impact, while the interaction area comes to about 15,000 square miles." [27] In the intermediate stages, a study, commenced in 1962 and published in 1968, known as the Metropolitan Toronto and Region Transportation Study (MTARTS), had conceived of a planning area of about 3,200 square miles. In short, the interrelated concepts of regional development, regional planning, and regional government produced a progressively expanding geographical scope, with the full approval of the Prime Minister and his senior cabinet colleagues.

In his introductory statement, Prime Minister Robarts stated:

> In "Design for Development: Toronto-Centred Region," there is presented the first broad brushstrokes of a regional development policy for the dynamic heart of Ontario. The Toronto-Centred Region contains approximately 50 percent of the population of Ontario and has a growth rate well in excess of the provincial average. . . . In our earlier statements of regional development policy, the Government of Ontario stated that regional development is distinct from and yet related to, regional government. For example, under our Regional Development Program we can examine and recommend on the use of all provincial expenditures having a regional impact. The program will also assist municipalities by supplying a provincial framework in which they can plan and grow. On the other hand, regional government proposals arise from the need of some municipalities to group themselves into larger administrative units which will enable them to identify and solve a wide variety of problems ranging from detailed planning to the supply of water, sewerage facilities, police, fire and other services.
>
> The creation of regional governments can make local involvement in the implementation of broad regional development policies much more effective.[28]

The report itself—an impressive document of 23 single-spaced pages, including several carefully drawn illustrative maps—outlined the main purposes of the Toronto-centered region development concept. These are (a) to shape the growth of the region's metropolitan core into a two-tiered urbanized area; (b) to encourage growth in selected communities beyond easy commuting range of Metropolitan Toronto, and thus help to decentralize the region and prevent a swollen growth within and near Metropolitan Toronto; and (c) to set basic guidelines for regional land use. "Of the Region's expected population of nearly 8 million people, 5.7 million or 71 per cent are targeted for the lakeshore urbanized area, 300,000 or 4 per cent for the adjacent commuting zone, and 2 million or 25 per cent for the peripheral belt." [29]

THREE ZONES

The three geographical portions of the concept were described as Zones One, Two and Three, respectively. Zone One, the lakeshore urbanized area, encompasses the Metropolitan core itself, plus nearby settlement. Zone Two is the commutershed, a belt beyond the lakeshore urbanized area, but within easy daily commuting range of employment in Toronto. Zone Three, the peripheral zone, is the area beyond the commutershed, but still well within the orbit of highly specialized influences of the metropolitan core. The economy of Zone Three is tied to the core of the region, and it serves as open space and recreation territory for the urban population.[30]

Design for Development: The Toronto-Centred Region was presented on the basis of five "Development Principles" and 12 "Goals for the Region." These are as follows:

DEVELOPMENT PRINCIPLES

"The development concept rests on five basic principles, each of which relates both to current and future conditions:

1. The principle of *linearity,* which seeks as far as possible to align urban places along a series of more or less straight paths to take maximum advantage of parallel routes for transportation and services.

2. The principle of *functional efficiency,* which seeks a best set of political, economic, and social relationships for all urban and rural places.

3. The principle of *decentralization,* which emphasizes (i) the importance of metropolitan centre influence, and (ii) a logical distribution of urban places within a metropolitan region, with special attention to the encouragement of smaller centres which functionally are related to the metropolitan region, but geographically are located beyond easy commuter range to the metropolitan centre.

4. The principle of *space conservation,* which stresses, on a per capita basis, adequate open space and recreational requirements.

5. The principle of *natural resource conservation,* which stresses the need for careful use of land, water, and air."

GOALS FOR THE REGION

"Each of the following 12 goals has social implications, although these are mentioned specifically only in Goal 11. In accordance with the recommendations of our internal committee working on the Report, the vital social implications are to be considered in conjunction with all twelve goals. The goals are:

1. To facilitate the achievement of the Region's economic potential, consistent with the overall provincial interest and development.

2. To preserve the unique attributes of the regional landscape.
3. To minimize the urban use of productive agricultural land.
4. To minimize the pollution of water and the atmosphere.
5. To facilitate and maintain a pattern of identifiable communities.
6. To provide best possible accessibility for the movement of people and goods.
7. To provide essential transportation, water, and sewer facilities at minimum cost consistent with overall benefit.
8. To maximize opportunities for using specialized services and facilities.
9. To develop in a manner consistent with the needs arising from long-term population trends, particularly in scale of growth and anticipated changes in household size and composition, and in age distribution.
10. To develop in a manner consistent with emerging and probable future technological innovations, i.e., to facilitate, adjust to, and receive the benefits of such possibilities.
11. To develop in a manner consistent with the needs arising from social changes resulting from future economic and technological developments, e.g., changing patterns of leisure.
12. To develop the Region in a manner that provides flexibility." [31]

It will be noted that the writers of the report, who were apparently members of the staff of the Regional Development Branch of the Department of Economics, were very sensitive to the possible criticism that their design ignored social considerations. The five lines preceding the numerical enumeration of "Goals for the Region" do not appear by accident. It must have been clear to the writers that the presentation of regional goals would inevitably be cast in language with a physical tone and an emphasis upon physical attributes of the environment. Hence the caveat that each of the goals must be considered with respect to "vital social implications," although only the eleventh goal appears specifically to encompass social considerations.

DECENTRALIZE, IF POSSIBLE

With the publication of this document, the residents of Metropolitan Toronto and of the Province of Ontario were given a clear interpretation of the government's resolve to influence the course of future growth, particularly urbanization, in the province's most heavily populated area. The import of this presentation, and especially the delineation of three interrelated zones, lay primarily in the determination of the province to influence residential, commercial, and industrial location, and thus the settlement of population over at least the next three decades, and probably well into the twenty-first century.

The provincial government intends, if possible, to decentralize future population away from the boundaries of Metropolitan Toronto. In order to do this, it must stimulate growth in Zone Three. Presumably in due course it will propose legislation that encourages industry to move to certain designated future growth areas or centers in the peripheral zone. In numerical terms the goal is to adjust the percentages of the population of the three zones by the year 2000, as follows:[32]

	1966	2000
Zone One: Lakeshore urbanized area	75.6%	71%
Zone Two: Commutershed	4.5	4
Zone Three: Peripheral area	19.9	25

In 1966 the residents of Zone One numbered approximately 3 million; by the year 2000 they will be about 5.6 million. If the goal of decentralization from Metropolitan Toronto is to be achieved, then clearly a number of growth centers to the east and north where growth has been slow, must be strongly stimulated. This, of course, is the government's intention.

HEMMING IN METRO? STIMULATING GROWTH ELSEWHERE?

A second major implication of the presentation was suggested by many Metro politicians and the press, who held that the report cast the final die in the process of hemming in Metro Toronto through a series of regional governments to the west, north, and east of the metropolis. But if this was the intention of the provincial government, it was certainly not spelled out in the report. Instead they were primarily interested in stimulating growth elsewhere.

Nevertheless, it can reasonably be concluded that substantial expansion of the area under Metro's administration is not seriously contemplated. The lakeshore urbanized area is to be developed in linear fashion from east to west, with Metro Toronto as its core.

Zone Two is conceived as a parkway belt within which the regional transportation system would operate.[33] Thus the traditional concept of a greenbelt to separate a major conurbation from a series of satellite communities or new growth centers at distances of approximately 60 to 90 miles from the metropolis is very much a part of the development idea.

Throughout 1971 the situation with respect to regional development in the Toronto-centered region remained relatively unchanged. The Minister of Municipal Affairs indicated on several occasions that he would bring out a further report, presumably the most comprehensive yet to be issued on the Toronto-centered region. But no such report was issued in 1971.

At the beginning of 1971, however, the Regional Municipality of York was incorporated to the north of Metro, with its southern boundary corresponding to the Metro's northern boundary. The York government's very creation and its stated boundaries appeared to be a re-affirmation of government policy limiting Metro's geographical growth. Still, the minister continued to insist that the northern boundary of Metro and the southern boundary of the new regional government were not definitely determined.

The Metropolitan Council continued strong efforts during 1971 to exert pressure on the provincial government to make specific decisions concerning the expansion of Metro's boundaries. Metro continued its flirtation with Pickering Township, a large relatively unpopulated semi-rural municipality immediately to the east. From time to time the Metro Council debated the desirability of incorporating Pickering Township into Metro. On one occasion the council of Pickering Township voted in favor of this move. If these "games" had any effect whatsoever on provincial policy or attitudes with respect to Metro's boundaries, there was no indication of it during 1971.*

This evidence of careful and cautious policy-making on the part of the provincial government may have been related to the fact that the ruling Conservative Party chose a new leader in April 1971 when John Robarts was replaced by William Davis. During the next sev-

* In March 1972, the federal and provincial governments announced the site for Toronto's new international airport, which will be located northeast of Metro in Pickering Township. This will effectively block any expansion of Metro to the east.

eral months Davis was deeply engrossed in the reorganization of his government, and in constructing a new image for his administration. He made a number of significant decisions, some of which will be considered subsequently. But he was careful not to commit himself on the issue of Metro's future growth.

He prepared diligently for the provincial election of October 1971, which resulted in an electoral sweep increasing the number of Conservative seats and seriously weakening the two major opposition parties. The vote within Metro did not seem to have any clear relationship to the boundary question or to provincial policies on regional development. Thus the Conservative Party did very much better within Metro Toronto than had been predicted. If the officials of Metro had anticipated a strong reaction from their constituents against presumed provincial policies on the future of the Toronto-centered region, they were surely disappointed.

REGIONALIZATION THROUGHOUT ONTARIO

With the presentation of the 1970 report, the Government of Ontario took another major step toward a comprehensive policy on regional development, regional planning, and regional government throughout the entire province. In the evolution of planning and policy, it is possible for some observers to discern an effort to dampen the expansionist spirit that on occasion appears to dominate the thinking of some elected and appointed officials in Metro. Their plaintive cries that Metro needs space in which to grow, needs room for expansion, and cannot ignore those who work within its boundaries but live beyond them, have not been accepted.

If such expansionist arguments were acceded to in full, there would be no end to the outward growth of Metro. It would be possible to conceive of a metropolitan administration with 12 to 15 boroughs in a huge Toronto-centered region, even one as large as that drawn in the report of May 1970. Conceivably, therefore, the provincial government is advising Metro's policy makers to forget their concern with continued outward growth, and to turn their attention to neglected aspects of growth and development still remaining within the current boundaries of Metropolitan Toronto. The neglected problems may continue to be ignored so long as Metro's boundary question remains unresolved.

CHAPTER IX

CONCLUSIONS: THE ISSUES OF 1970 AND AFTER

AFTER NEARLY two decades of regional government in the Metropolitan Area of Toronto, it is perhaps surprising that certain major problems confronted during the entire period remain unsolved. Still, there has been tremendous growth in social and economic terms, and many economic and political issues have been dealt with. In the early 1950's Metropolitan Toronto had just over one million population. By 1970 this had doubled. During the late 1940's and early 1950's the metropolitan area was faced with an absolute shortage of supplies of pure water and waste disposal facilities. These shortages have been eliminated. Today water supply and waste disposal facilities appear adequate to accommodate the population of 5 to 6 million expected by the year 2000. Moreover the water supply is fluoridated, as a consequence of a favorable vote recorded in the only metropolitan-wide plebiscite held during the eighteen-year period.

In retrospect, the array of major problems for which effective solutions have been developed since 1945 is so vast that it staggers the imagination. A transportation program—assiduously seeking balance between motor expressways and public transit facilities—has been under development throughout the entire period. Hundreds of millions of dollars have been invested in modern multilane controlled-access expressways. Moreover a thirty-mile network of rapid transit subway facilities, requiring an additional investment of hundreds of millions of dollars, has been created under the aegis of the Toronto Transit Commission.

The public has recognized the appropriateness, and indeed the inevitability, of area-wide service consolidation. Thus, by 1970 the Municipality of Metropolitan Toronto was responsible for an array of functions substantially increased beyond its initial assignment in 1954. The consolidation of the 13 police departments in 1957 was accomplished so successfully and with so little dissent or complaint that the shift to a Metropolitan Police Department was scarcely noticed by the general public. The same was true of the consolidation of public welfare services, effected on January 1, 1967.

In short, during the 17 years, 1954–1970, Toronto grew into a metropolis in the full meaning of the concept as understood in the major nations of the world. Simultaneously, the establishment of a metropolitan form of government made it possible for the administrative services of local government to change and expand to meet the requirements of the rapidly growing population. This two-fold development inevitably raises the ancient dilemma of the "chicken or the egg." Thus it can be argued that without the establishment of the Metropolitan Council, the vast urban development would not have been possible. But it can also be argued that without the rapid spread of urban development the metropolitan government would not have been necessary.

Despite Toronto's organizational progress, a number of major governmental and policy issues remain unresolved. Although these are not identical with those of the immediate pre-Metro period, many bear a close resemblance. A listing of the most important perennial concerns must include: (1) the role of the Metro Chairman; (2) the boundaries of Metro, and the geographic scope of the metropolitan planning area; (3) a unitary versus a two-tier concept of metropolitan government; (4) the growing interaction between neighborhood groups and municipal authorities; (5) the introduction of political parties into local and metropolitan politics; (6) the question of establishing future priorities; (7) the position of the City of Toronto within Metro.

All these major issues are interrelated. One cannot, for example, discuss the potential future role of the Metro Chairman without considering the form of metropolitan government over which he is expected to preside. If the Chairman is the appointed or elected head of a unitary, one-tier metropolis, the nature of his leadership and the roles he plays will clearly be very different from those to be anticipated if the present structure of metropolitan government continues into the late 1970's and beyond. Similarly, decisions on the geographical limits of Metropolitan Toronto will significantly influence the form of metropolitan government within the designated boundaries, as well as the nature of the Chairman's leadership role.

THE ROLE OF THE METRO CHAIRMANSHIP

The first two Chairmen of Metropolitan Toronto served approximately eight years each. The way each viewed his function and carried out his role was in large measure a matter of personal style, but this explanation in itself is insufficient to account for the differences.

THE FIRST CHAIRMAN: WHAT METRO NEEDED

The first Metro Chairman, Mr. Gardiner, was appointed by the Prime Minister of Ontario at a time when the physical and social troubles of Greater Toronto were immense. Mr. Gardiner saw his role as that of a dynamic political leader whose goal was the accomplishment of tangible physical improvements—arterial roads, trunk sewers, water mains, school buildings, and bridges over previously unbridgeable ravines connecting two or more uncooperative municipalities. His political style was implicit in his personality—aggressive, pugnacious, forthright.

In retrospect, there can be little doubt that the fortuitous combination of metropolitan requirements on the one hand, and the personality of the first Chairman on the other, gave Metro almost exactly what it needed. During the years 1953–1961 Mr. Gardiner was a superb politician, and although his annual election was held within the confines of the Metropolitan Council, his continuation in office was almost a foregone conclusion. On only one occasion in those years was he challenged by another candidate, who was easily defeated. For these reasons, the question of area-wide direct election of the Metro Chairman was not given serious consideration. Perhaps it was a question for political scientists to debate, but not for serious politicians.

THE SECOND CHAIRMAN: NEW FORCES IMPINGE

The election of the second Chairman in January 1962 was bitterly contested by two candidates, and it brought into office an entirely different personality at a time when, again in retrospect, it appears that a new set of forces demanded a new conception of the Chairman's role. Mr. William R. Allen proved to be a consummate administrator, far more a city manager than a politician. By the time of his election, still held within the Metropolitan Council, the Municipality of Metropolitan Toronto was well on the way to attaining a degree of maturity. The major physical concerns causing the government of Ontario to create a metropolitan form of government had largely been solved. The growth of Metropolitan Toronto seemed assured even in the midst of a serious economic recession.

The issues that were emerging by the early 1960's were the large social questions: Metro's role in a greatly expanded public housing program; the function of Metro in urban renewal; Metro's position in developing an adequate public welfare system; and its responsibility, if any, for providing a variety of new social services, ranging from day-care centers for the children of working mothers to social and community services for senior citizens and other moderate- or low-income family units.

By virtue of background, temperament, and conception of his role, Chairman Allen brought different attitudes and capabilities to the task. The assumption of new responsibilities by the Municipality of Metropolitan Toronto required a social dynamism equivalent to the political dynamism required in the 1950's. In the first year or two, Chairman Allen espoused the cause of an expanded regional public housing program, and argued convincingly for the establishment of a more independent Metropolitan Toronto Housing Authority. At a critical point in the deliberations, however, he appeared to lose interest, and by 1964 had apparently accepted the inevitability of defeat and the transfer of the existing metropolitan housing administration to a newly established provincial authority.

In a similar but less publicly evident style, Mr. Allen worked hard for the elimination of municipal inequities in the divided public welfare system within Metro Toronto. In this case, however, he was apparently unable to shift the social assistance program to the provincial department, and was compelled to accept a Metropolitan Department of Welfare.

In the Metropolitan Council and community organizations outside, including the press, it was argued that the major focus of Metro Toronto during the middle and late 1960's must be social, rather than an almost exclusive continuation of physical development. But the Metro Chairman apparently did not accept this view, or was unable to convince the council of its significance.

EMPHASIS STILL PHYSICAL AND FISCAL

The great issues debated in the middle and late 1960's related essentially to physical and fiscal needs: the expansion of public transit facilities versus the expansion of automotive freeways; the expansion of the boundaries of Metro Toronto in the hope of ensuring the continued development of privately financed housing programs; the vast expansion in educational spending on both operating budgets and capital requirements, and the impact of educational expenditures upon the metropolitan and borough tax rates; the question of the disposition of the former city hall of Toronto, sold to Metro as a possible police headquarters building, and ultimately as the focus of a vast privately proposed urban renewal scheme by the largest retail chain in Canada.

AREA-WIDE ELECTION OR CHOICE BY COUNCIL?

The nature and role of the chairmanship in the 1970's cannot be predicted, but one burning question has remained just below the surface of public interest: whether the Chairman should be elected on an area-wide basis or continue to be chosen by the members of the Metropolitan Council. It will be recalled that Chairman Gardiner first raised this issue publicly in a submission to the Commission of Inquiry set up by the government of Ontario in 1957.

But the issue could not be considered seriously while Mr. Gardiner remained in office. His tremendous prestige militated against a change in the legislation, and it was unrealistic to imagine that an opponent could defeat him in a Metro-wide election. In the 1960's, however, Mr. Allen's posture as an administrative rather than essentially political head of a regional government was one of the factors that encouraged public discussion of the issue. The three daily newspapers in Toronto brought up the question repeatedly after 1965, when it was clear that the second Chairman was not committed to an amalgamation of the 13 municipalities into one political unit. The newspapers obviously see an area-wide election of the Metropolitan Chairman as a major thrust in the direction of the "one big city" concept they have favored throughout Metro's history.

This argument is not made publicly, however, in the form of editorials or major analyses of metropolitan government in the daily press. Rather, the issue has been posed as a question of direct democratic participation by the electorate versus indirect non-democratic election by a council of 32 persons who each at best represent some 60,000 or 70,000 electors in their own constituencies. The opponents of these arguments, primarily elected politicians and candidates for public office, contend that a metropolitan election within an area of 240 square miles encompassing 2 million people would be very demanding on the candidates, physically and financially. Thus it is alleged that successful candidates would probably have to be very wealthy, and not necessarily best qualified to lead the growth and development of Metropolitan Toronto.

To counter these arguments the newspapers insist that area-wide elections have proved to be feasible in such cities as Chicago, Detroit, New York, and Philadelphia, and that, although vast resources are required in such electoral campaigns, the mayors elected in such cities have almost invariably proved to be competent and even outstanding leaders, whether or not they were endowed with vast financial resources through inheritance or business acumen.

THE THIRD CHAIRMAN

In the spring of 1969 the second Chairman of Metro Toronto announced his retirement, to take effect from September 30, 1969. Accordingly the third Chairman, Mr. Albert M. Campbell, was chosen by the Metropolitan Council over three other candidates on that date. Because this election took place near the close of a three-year term of office, a second election of the Metro Chairman was required at the first council meeting in January 1970. Mr. Campbell was re-elected by acclamation. The press agreed that the selection of Mr. Campbell was justified because of his long service in municipal government and his great knowledge and experience in metropolitan government in Toronto. They nevertheless deplored his "indirect" election, not merely on the usual grounds but also because, they argued, such elections would invariably choose "an insider."

In fact, the election of September 1969 was contested by four candidates, only two of whom were currently members of the Metropolitan Council, although the other two had been the elected heads of large municipalities in past years. Moreover if the term "insider" is meant to include persons whose records include long political service in local government and substantial experience within Metro, then it is difficult to see why such an "insider" should not be preferred to an "outsider" with little or no relevant experience.

Mr. Campbell is a former school teacher who holds a degree in agriculture. His style is rather quiet, rural and "folksy," and he continues to reside in the Borough of Scarborough on one of the few farms remaining within Metro's boundaries. His political career began when he was elected as a councillor in the Township of Scarborough in the early 1950's. In 1957 he was elected Reeve of Scarborough and became a member of Metro's executive committee.

Mr. Campbell is not a flamboyant politician like Frederick G. Gardiner; nor is he a consummate administrator like William R. Allen. Within a few months he received Metro Council's approval for the appointment of an executive assistant, whose task would be day-to-day administration, background research for decisionmaking and, presumably, the drafting of the Chairman's major speeches. There has been some criticism of the alleged concentration of power in the hands of Executive Assistant John Kruger, a man in his early forties, and a former local councillor and resident in the Township of Pickering on Metro's eastern boundary. For example, a major article in the Toronto *Daily Star* in September 1971 termed Kruger "the man they call the power behind the Metro Chairman."

Developments during the first two years of Mr. Campbell's Chairmanship suggest a very different interpretation of his leadership role. In fact, one may argue that the third Metro Chairman proved once again to be just the kind of person that Metro Toronto required at the time of his accession to office. In his first year, Mr. Campbell's approach appeared to blend cautious administration with political leadership. During 1970 his speeches and statement on Metro's future assumed increasing strength, and he emphasized the danger that Metro Toronto would be hemmed in and its growth arbitrarily restricted by provincial policy. First quietly and then more vigorously he urged the Government of Ontario to reverse its position on Metro's boundaries, and to reconsider Metro's ultimate growth potentials.

In 1971 his addresses became much more forceful and attracted wide attention throughout the province and the nation. He was extremely disturbed by the provincial government's decision on transportation policies within Metro. Again and again he warned that the Toronto metropolis was in danger of being stifled by its own uncontrolled growth.

The year 1971 saw increased respect for Mr. Campbell among local and provincial politicians, and in the press. In January 1972 he announced that he would stand for re-election to a third-year term at the first meeting of Metropolitan Council, following its election in December 1972.

THE BOUNDARIES OF METRO, AND GEOGRAPHIC SCOPE OF THE PLANNING AREA

The 1953 delineation of a metropolitan region of 240 square miles was described earlier as a bold stroke of statesmanship by the Government of Ontario. At that time and for perhaps a decade afterward this area appeared vast in geographical terms, particularly in contrast with the long established City of Toronto, which occupied a mere 35 square miles. In 1953 the boundaries of Metropolitan Toronto appeared adequate to accommodate 20 or 25 years of population growth as then projected from the experiences of the early postwar years. Recognition of the startling rise in the Canadian birthrate after 1944 was not yet widespread, nor was it possible to predict the magnitude of immigration into Canada from abroad after 1950. At least one-quarter of the more than 2 million newcomers to Canada who arrived between January 1, 1946 and January 1, 1961 settled in the metropolitan area of Toronto.

Although this increase was not anticipated, the new growth soon became a fact and pressed hard. In the early 1950's social scientists and members of the professions interested in urban development learned that most of the land within the traditional 12 suburban municipalities in Greater Toronto had been optioned by land developers, investors, or speculators. Although a preponderance of the territory outside the well-established residential, commercial, and industrial areas remained unserviced, the Metropolitan Toronto Planning Board, in conjunction with local planning boards, had long since developed programs calling for urban services to meet projected population increases and related land use demands. Such planning efforts have helped reduce some of the substantial unknowns in the equations of urban development: the availability of capital resources, the related matter of the rate of interest and other borrowing charges, strikes and other labor disputes, and political questions within specific municipalities, to name a few. But new governmental arrangements are now required.

Thus persistent high growth rates have made it clear that a decision must soon be forthcoming on the future boundaries and geographical scope of the Metropolitan Planning Area. As noted, the population of Metro Toronto expanded more rapidly in the 1950's and 1960's than had been expected. Moreover, Canada's general prosperity during 1950–1957, and again since 1963, has accumulated enormous demands within Metro for housing, social facilities (schools and universities, hospitals, libraries, recreation facilities, airports), and commercial and cultural facilities of every conceivable type, as well as for a continuation of the traditional emphasis upon light and moderate industry. Metro Toronto has followed the path outlined by Gottman in his study *Megalopolis*: It has become a vast network of service-producing and service-distributing activities, rather than a center of basic physical production.[1]

THE NEW TORONTO

The fundamental change, particularly in the central city, has been far more extensive than this analysis would suggest. Toronto has also become a modern metropolis in the cultural sense. Not only does it provide new cultural facilities for arts, music, and drama but also it has led in the development of a new metropolitan culture. All the "in" activities of modern living are available in profusion. Moreover, a preponderance of youth is combined with the persistence of the elderly in an urban center whose population doubled in approximately 15 years.

Significantly, these changes have made Metropolitan Toronto an interesting and more attractive place in which to live. Not the least of its appeal for many newcomers is the existence of the metropolitan form of government itself. Whatever the explanation, Metro Toronto has been transformed from a city in which the single-family detached house was the principal form of dwelling to one in which high-rise apartment buildings of 20 to 40 stories dominate the skyline. The city of "homeowners and churches" has become a metropolis of tenants and secular entertainment. The great dilemma, now is not to explain these phenomena but to determine when, if at all, the growth of the metropolitan area of Toronto should be brought to a halt.

METRO-ONTARIO CONFLICT?

In the 1960's newspaper reporters, social scientists, and politicians began to speculate on the potential conflict between Metro Toronto and the Province of Ontario, should the metropolis ever encompass as much as 40 to 50 percent of the total population of the province. In 1951 Greater Toronto's population represented 20 percent of the entire province; in 1961 the proportion had increased to 25 percent. In 1970 Metro Toronto had approximately 27 percent of the provincial population.

The primacy of the metropolitan area is far greater, however, than the mere population data would suggest. Toronto is not only the political capital of Ontario but its financial capital as well. Some observers also consider it the financial capital of Canada. Whatever the origin of its residents' income or the nature of their economic activities, the people of Metropolitan Toronto contribute a significant proportion of the income and corporation taxes collected in the whole of Canada and later distributed, in part, to the provinces.

Quite naturally, Ontario officials have been reticent on a subject as politically dangerous as the potential rivalry between a metropolitan government and the provincial government. Actions taken during the late 1960's to create a series of regional governments east and west of Metro were explained in detail in the previous chapter. The reality of this process was clearly demonstrated by the establishment of the Regional Municipality of York (to the north of Metro) on January 1, 1971. Moreover, in mid-1970 the Minister of Municipal Affairs enunciated the view that the Metropolitan Toronto Planning Area should be reduced, upon the establishment of other such regional governments, to the original boundaries of Metro (a diminution from 720 to 240 square miles).

These actions were seen by some officials of the City of Toronto and the five boroughs as a gigantic pincer movement that would hem in Metro and restrain its growth. Provincial officials rarely responded to these suggestions and provocations, remaining committed to the principles enunciated by the Prime Minister in 1966. As far as can be judged, the Government of Ontario moved into the 1970's unswayed by the arguments that Metro Toronto should be permitted to expand, and that it must be enlarged to the north, to the east, or in both directions simultaneously.*

AN EXPANDING METRO: F. G. GARDINER

The last words on this subject have not yet been uttered. It may be significant that in mid-October, 1969, Metro's first Chairman, Frederick G. Gardiner, published a substantial article in the most widely circulated evening newspaper in Toronto. The article was in two parts, entitled respectively "Metro Must Expand or Be Strangled" and "An Iron Curtain Must Not Stifle Metro." [2] Mr. Gardiner's exposition is summed up in the following excerpts:

> If Ontario's Municipal Affairs Minister Darcy McKeough persists in his plan to freeze the boundaries of Metropolitan Toronto, he will be making a tragic mistake.
>
> Right now, Metro has an unlimited potential for future development into one of the important cities on the continent. If Metro is surrounded by an iron curtain of municipalities preventing its natural growth, the development of the whole area would be thwarted. . . .
>
> While Metropolitan Toronto is not a regional government in the accepted use of the term, it is in many respects similar to one. It should be allowed to expand naturally without artificial boundaries. . . .
>
> The main difficulty at the moment is that practically all of the land in Metropolitan Toronto is developed and future development must either be on land which is far beyond an economical cost or the development must be a vertical one with multi-storey buildings for residential purposes, and in the case of industry it will go where single storey buildings can be built at an economic cost.

The pragmatic consequence of this basic argument would be an expansion of the boundaries of Metro Toronto, increasing its total area from approximately 240 square miles to approximately 700

---

* Ontario, *Design for Development: Toronto-Centred Region* (Ontario: Queen's Printer, May 5, 1970). When *Design* was published, the minister indicated that his government was considering an enlargement of Metro to the north, up to the route of a new major east-west highway, the exact position of which has not yet been determined. Thus, the southern boundaries of the new Regional Municipality of York have not been settled. It is believed that this expansion would add between 25 and 40 square miles to Metro. Expansion to the west does not appear to be one of the major objectives of the expansionists. However, some planners hold the view that it was primarily the presence of the Mayor of Mississauga on the Metropolitan Toronto Planning Board that forestalled a drive towards the west. Certainly, rapid growth on the western fringe of Metro might suggest incorporation of that area within Metro, instead of a move to the east.

square miles. The number of municipalities would not, however, be increased substantially, as Mr. Gardiner proposed three phases in his total plan: (1) The enlarged Boroughs of York and East York, created on January 1, 1967, would be incorporated within the boundaries of the City of Toronto, on the argument that these relatively old and well-established areas fall naturally within the City. This would reduce the number of municipalities within Metro Toronto from six to four. (2) Metro Toronto would be expanded to the north, incorporating and converting into boroughs two very large semi-rural townships—Vaughan and Markham—whose population growth during the past two decades has been slow, because of the lack of water and sewage facilities. These new boroughs would be somewhat larger than the present townships lying immediately north of Metro, on the ground that they should extend to the northern limit of the watershed that drains into Lake Ontario. This would involve a further expansion to the north. (3) The present large municipality known as Pickering Township, immediately to the east of Metro in Ontario County, would be renamed the Borough of Pickering and added to Metropolitan Toronto. It would also be expanded somewhat to the north to encompass the watershed.

Mr. Gardiner's adjustments would eliminate two of the present boroughs and add three new ones, so that the Municipality of Metropolitan Toronto would then consist of the City of Toronto and six boroughs. The argument did not, however, indicate the changes in representation that this plan would require, or consider the impact of the ultimate urban expansion upon the role of the City of Toronto. Mr. Gardiner commented "Nothing which I recommend is on the basis that the metropolitan area of Toronto has any designs for any territorial aggrandizement but simply that the metropolitan area will not be impeded in its development and will have the City of Toronto as the central point in that region."

Clearly, the last word on the subject of Metro's boundaries has not been said, nor the final decisions made. The comprehensive report of the Oshawa Area Planning and Development Study, which appeared in June 1971, strongly recommended that Pickering Township become part of a new two-tiered regional government to be created east of Metro. Although at the close of 1971 it appeared that the October provincial election had forestalled open intergovernmental discussion, the several municipalities that had received the report in mid-summer were still in the process of considering its recommendations.

A UNITARY VERSUS A TWO-TIER CONCEPT OF METROPOLITAN GOVERNMENT

The federal system of metropolitan government legislated by the government of Ontario for Metropolitan Toronto in 1953 has persisted in its fundamental form to the present. The two-tier concept has been challenged often, but the province has remained adamant in its opposition to amalgamation of Metropolitan Toronto. Amalgamation, of course, means "one big city" and thus a unitary form of government, presumably with a directly elected Chairman or Mayor for a population of 2 to 4 million.

The three major newspapers have not budged in their opposition to the federal, two-tier concept, but none of the opposition parties in the provincial legislature has formally adopted the unitary principle for Toronto as a firm plank in its policy platform. It is true that an occasional Liberal or New Democratic legislator will speak out in favor of amalgamation, but neither Ontario's Liberal Party, the official Opposition in the early 1970's, nor the New Democratic Party, with almost as many seats as the Liberals, has espoused unification as a legislative objective, should either of these parties achieve power.

The arguments in favor of a unitary versus a two-tier concept of metropolitan government have been explained fully in earlier chapters, but neither new nor convincing arguments have been made to alter the views of the Government of Ontario since the decisions of the early 1950's. Moreover, it is not evident to any social scientist or participant observer, or to the elected officials most concerned, that the general public is greatly concerned with the form of metropolitan government. Elected officials rightly assume that the residents of Metropolitan Toronto are primarily interested in the quantity and quality of municipal services available to them and their children, and that they have good reason to believe that in these respects Metro's efforts have been surprisingly successful.

GOVERNMENTAL INTERACTION WITH NEIGHBORHOOD GROUPS

In the mid-1960's, the world-wide phenomenon of protest and participation inspired by such forces as "the war on poverty," the war in Vietnam, and the increasing sense of involvement by citizens in the decision-making process, struck Metro Toronto with increasing force. The most notable activities were centered around issues that concerned the City of Toronto and its Planning Board, the Metropolitan Council, and the Metropolitan Toronto Planning Board.

URBAN RENEWAL

Within the central city the process of urban renewal under public auspices gained strength following a series of important amendments to the National Housing Act in 1964. Part III of the act, which had traditionally contained the provisions for slum clearance and urban redevelopment, was formally retitled "Urban Renewal." Thus for the first time the concept was incorporated in federal legislation. Many schemes put forward tentatively by the City's planning board in the late 1950's and early 1960's now appeared capable of implementation.

It soon became clear, however, that traditional neighborhoods housing a large proportion of low-income families stood squarely in the path of urban renewal. Moreover it became increasingly doubtful whether low-income families should be driven out of the downtown area, particularly when their relocation in public housing was not possible during these years. Finally it became obvious that relocation of most applicants for public housing was not socially or economically desirable, let alone humane, if their new housing was distant from places of employment, from social and community agencies, and from available professional services, particularly health care.

TRADITIONAL CITIZENS' ORGANIZATIONS

In the previous half-century, citizens' organizations in Greater Toronto have been primarily of two basic types. In the first, upper- and middle-class persons banded together to found "charitable agencies" or organizations designed to assist families and children or to provide services to newcomers. These were the traditional forms of citizen participation in community work in metropolitan areas of Canada and the United States during the late nineteenth and early twentieth centuries. In the second, associations of neighborhood property owners or taxpayers formed organizations, which in Toronto adopted British terminology and were often called "ratepayers' associations." In the first 15 years after World War II there were dozens of these associations in Metro Toronto constantly appearing and disappearing; they often sprang up to protest activities of a municipal council in a particular neighborhood and then dissolved when the immediate crisis passed.

A NEW FORCE: NEIGHBORHOOD GROUPS

Citizens' organizations participating effectively in local government were scarcely known in Metropolitan Toronto before 1965. Within the next two or three years, however, nearly every neighborhood formed a group, which was usually called a neighborhood or a tenants' association. The first of these groups to attract the attention of the public generally sprang up in neighborhoods that had been designated as urban renewal areas. Whether this designation was formal, in the sense that a local municipal by-law had been passed to ensure the application of federal and provincial laws aimed at renewal of the neighborhood, or whether urban renewal by the local government was merely rumored, an association was almost certain to spring up.

Those associations that survived were able to do so largely because of one or two crucial sources of leadership. First, in some neighborhoods the leadership of long-term residents was strong, persistent, and continuous. Where this was the case, the associations might survive for several years with little or no financial support, despite rebuffs by the planning board or the municipal council. Second, in other neighborhoods, citizens' organizations drew strength from the participation of highly educated, professionally trained residents who made opposition to urban renewal programs a hobby or even a career.

For example, as the old residential neighborhoods within a mile or two of the downtown core became fashionable and many homes were renovated to become "townhouses," these urban renewal neighborhoods attracted a share of residents with an artistic and intellectual bent. They paid great attention to preserving the old homes, or to modifying proposed urban renewal schemes that would affect them. This sort of leadership, based not upon older residents, who might be poor, uneducated, and inarticulate, was composed instead of scholars, lawyers, engineers, architects, and urban planners. By about 1967 such groups had become a formidable force.

Notable confrontations occurred from time to time, although violence was rare. There were marches and demonstrations, and occasionally groups occupied committee rooms in Toronto's new city hall (the site of City and Metro offices, and the location of both the City Council and the Metropolitan Council meetings). The continuing polemics and pamphleteering produced important contributions to the literature of housing rehabilitation and urban renewal planning.

FINANCING LOCAL ACTION

As the decade drew to a close, the problem of financing citizens' organizations in residential neighborhoods, or major protest movements on a wider scale, appeared capable of solution. In 1969 the federal government announced a grant of more than $80,000 to an organization known as the Community Improvement Association of Regent Park, an association of tenants in two contiguous public housing projects with a population of nearly 10,000 persons, occupying some 2100 dwelling units.

The grant was made available over a three-year period. This enabled the association to hire a community development worker and to organize the tenants in their concerns with the quality of their neighborhood, the quality of their housing and its maintenance, and their relationships with the Ontario Housing Corporation. The grant was made jointly by the federal Department of National Health and Welfare (Welfare Grants Division) and the Central Mortgage and Housing Corporation. It was probably the first grant of its kind in Canada, and it predictably aroused strong objections from some local and metropolitan councillors who saw it as a federally sponsored irritant, or goad, to further citizen opposition to local government activities, particularly in housing and planning.

In a second approach, the most prominent group opposed to a project of the Metropolitan Council campaigned to raise at least $50,000 from interested persons in the community who were against the expansion of the freeway system, and in particular the Spadina Expressway. This organization's fund raising was sufficiently successful to permit hiring one of Canada's most prominent lawyers to appear before the Ontario Municipal Board at a hearing beginning in January 1971. The objective was to defeat the project through an exploration of its pros and cons before the board could consider

Metro's application to expand its borrowing program and thus its right to proceed with the expressway.

FORMIDABLE FORCES

As the 1970's began, the Metropolitan Council came to realize that citizens' groups, in the form of neighborhood associations and protest movements founded around such concerns as public versus private transportation, were formidable forces influencing the determination of public policy. Before 1970 the council had had little experience with such groups, and beyond a few delegation visits and the presentation of a few briefs, there had been no major confrontation. But the attitude of the Chairman, most borough mayors, and the Mayor of the City was one of restrained suspicion and resentment.

Nevertheless, it is important to emphasize that the officials and City Council of Toronto have borne the brunt of public displeasure. Before 1967, dissatisfaction with the City's welfare programs, and particularly with its urban renewal schemes, led many delegations to visit City Hall. The heart of the matter is that the ailments of the central city of a modern Western metropolis become a prime focus for discontent and protest. It was not the residents of single-family homes in the suburbs who marched on local government offices; it was the residents of old and deteriorating renewal areas downtown, who saw their miserable housing threatened with demolition and their families threatened with relocation. Meanwhile the issues were extended beyond the core by a project like the Spadina Expressway—which would cross several Metro municipalities and have a great impact on industrial and commercial locations, on first-rate residential neighborhoods, and on traffic patterns. This brought into play the highly educated and highly organized protest movements of the 1970's, which began to press the Metropolitan Council with all their strength.

THE ENTRANCE OF POLITICAL PARTIES?

The idea of introducing political parties into local and metropolitan politics was not new in Toronto, but in the mid-1960's it appeared possible that, for the first time, the parties might actually be able to capture enough seats, including a number of mayoralties, to exert a real influence at both the borough and metropolitan levels. Those eager to see this happen received favorable though not overwhelming support from the three Toronto newspapers.

EARLY EFFORTS

About 1965 a group of interested citizens in Toronto formed a new association dedicated to electing candidates who were ready to accept a definite platform or set of policies. This organization soon became known as CIVAC (Civic Action). In election campaigns to inaugurate the new organizational arrangements taking effect in Metro Toronto on January 1, 1967, CIVAC was unable to offer candidates who were firmly committed to a set of policies; thus it was not clear what they hoped to achieve. There was no evidence that any Mayor or councillor elected on December 1, 1966, would serve the first three-year term, following the Report of the Royal Commission on Metropolitan Toronto, with any clear political commitment to any new or traditional party.

In the politics of the City of Toronto, the party affiliations of most candidates have always been clear. It was known that the Mayor of Toronto was either a Liberal or a Conservative, and there were one or two occasions in the early 1930's when the Mayor was said to be a "trade unionist" or a "labor man." This apparently meant that he was not a member of either the Liberal or Conservative parties, but perhaps leaned in the direction of the newly emerging CCF Party (later the New Democratic Party). Moreover, it was not clear that the particular party affiliations of the candidates from 1945 to 1965 were of any importance in their success or failure. No doubt such affiliations did play a role, however, in the sense that the party associations within the provincial and federal constituencies could come to the assistance of candidates who sought their support.

THE 1969 ELECTION

As noted, in the middle and late 1960's not only were traditional party labels invoked, but also new organizations like CIVAC attempted to introduce party politics into local government in Metro Toronto. By 1969, when the second election after the reorganization of Metro was scheduled, many candidates openly stated their party affiliations, and the electorate gained the impression that certain candidates were likely to join with others bearing the same party label to promote a set of agreed-upon policies.

In Toronto, one young university scholar, a member of the Liberal Party, stood for election to the mayoralty of the City. He ran last, and in the course of his defeat the vote was split three ways. The incumbent Mayor was reelected. It is paradoxical that the defeat of the second candidate, who was acknowledged as an advocate of "reform" in many of the policies of the City of Toronto, was largely caused by the introduction of alleged party politics into the election. The cry for reform defeated a reform candidate.

As far as the City Council of Toronto was concerned, however, two persons from each of the three so-called parties were elected in a council of 22. Two were said to be Liberals, 2 were members of the New Democratic Party, and 2 were members of CIVAC. Although the advocates of political parties in local politics were greatly encouraged by these results, the decision of the Ontario Municipal Board on Toronto's new ward boundaries may have been the deciding factor. In any event, at the beginning of 1970 it appeared that at least six elected councillors of the City were "reformers" or, at the very least, constituted "an opposition." It was argued that the City's so-called "one-party system" might be at an end.

By this line of reasoning, the absence of party politics during the previous 30 or 40 years represented nothing more than a "one-party system" in which there had been no opposition. Now there was to be an opposition, and for the first few months the newspapers delighted in printing stories about the united view of the six "oppositionists" toward certain policies put forward by the Mayor and his executive committee. By mid-1970, however, doubts were being expressed, especially in the daily press. One Liberal member of the council allegedly did not see eye-to-eye with a second member, and was actually considered to be closer to the CIVAC members on many issues. The two members who were allegedly of the New Democratic Party also disagreed. Thus the party labels did not seem particularly useful in the policy-making process. Moreover, members of the council who were more traditional in outlook had become wary of being caught off-guard by clever "oppositionists," and were attacking rather than retreating.

THE OUTCOME UNDECIDED

Whatever the ultimate outcome of this experience, it appears that in the early 1970's political parties have clearly not been introduced into local politics in Metropolitan Toronto. But the issue is by no means dead. Montreal's experience, where the Mayor established a party, and where he was opposed in a late 1970 election by another group calling itself a party, is not being ignored. Many members of the council are convinced that it is only a matter of time before Toronto sees the introduction of the British practice, or that which prevails in many American metropolitan areas. Thus they anticipate the identification of each candidate with a political party; the formation of a "government" party headed by the Mayor, with a number of followers who receive assignments akin to those of cabinet ministers; and determination of a party program which the Mayor and his followers would attempt to implement during their tenure.

Conceivably the present system in both the City Council and the Metropolitan Council has outlived its usefulness. This is more obvious in the case of the City Council, where the Mayor and members are elected directly, and where there is great dissatisfaction with the lack of stated policies and with the apparent non-aggressive stance of City members of Metro's executive committee.

The introduction of parties seems much less likely in the Metropolitan Council itself, where members are indirectly elected, and where it is much more difficult to conceive of the Metropolitan Chairman introducing a program with the support of a group of followers affiliated under the same party label. In fact, the Metropolitan Chairman does not yet appear to see himself as an enunciator of a program to be implemented during a specific time period.

DEFICIENT MACHINERY FOR SETTING FUTURE PRIORITIES

As Metro Toronto approaches the close of its second decade, one of its major weaknesses is the lack of a method for establishing future priorities. In the first decade the pressing priorities were obvious, and stemmed directly from the fundamental difficulties that had led to the creation of the Municipality of Metropolitan Toronto. Action was required to correct evident weaknesses in the availability of basic municipal services. At the same time, other competing priorities seemed too distant or dimly perceived, or were considered "controversial." Thus, the provision of vastly increased supplies of pure water was a definite priority, whereas the expansion of the stock of public housing, particularly on sites in the suburban municipalities, was not a matter of high priority, and was surely controversial.

POLICY AD HOC-ERY

Urging the need to establish future priorities is not simply a way of repeating that physical planning has been given pre-eminence over social planning. It would appear that the Metropolitan Council is in grave danger of degenerating into what could crudely be termed *"ad hoc-ery."* The primary symptoms are already apparent. The Metropolitan Toronto Planning Board has delivered an Official Plan to the Metropolitan Council, including a series of amendments bringing the plan up to date to the beginning of 1969. Major studies have been completed in the fields of transportation and urban renewal. Metro Council has commissioned a number of investigations to enable it to forecast capital requirements, but contradictory results and judgments—as between Metro staff members and consultants, for example—increase the difficulty of fixing future priorities.

Although the Metro Council has a great many studies available, and has the advice of competent officials and a highly trained staff serving the Metropolitan Toronto Planning Board, there is still no clear locus of responsibility for the setting of future priorities. In his analysis of Metro's first decade, Frank Smallwood devoted a good deal of attention to what he called the council's "lack of decisiveness." He illustrated this point in many ways, but in particular he described an organizational void in several crucial areas. He pointed to the assignment of the council's information responsibilities to "an already busy operating unit," the Metropolitan Toronto Planning Board.

In the same vein, Smallwood insisted that the council had relegated its research and central intelligence responsibilities to the Treasury Department "without any major staff commitment." [3] It is not clear whether these "by default" assignments of responsibility have placed the determination of future priorities in the hands of the planners and treasury officials, or whether *any* organization bears these responsibilities. In the author's view, there is simply no adequate machinery to determine or establish future priorities.

RAPID ROTATION AND LACK OF MUTUAL CONCERN

Moreover, the system of indirect election and rapid rotation has not helped bring priority questions into a clear focus. Thus in past elections, and certainly since the introduction of the two-year term in the 1950's and a three-year term in the late 1960's, the Metropolitan Council has seen considerable turnover. In addition, the three-year term has meant that within the boroughs one seat on the Metropolitan Council is rotated on an annual basis through an election within the borough council. Consequently few Metro councillors now serve long enough to learn much about Metro. They often seem unaware of both its history and its future needs.*

Moreover, the Metropolitan councillors elected from the five boroughs in 1969 do not seem particularly concerned with the disabilities of the central city. Since these difficulties are in part physical in nature (for example, the need to replace the City's sewer system) but substantially social as well, many members of the council find the question of priority determination painful, to say the least.

Perhaps the Metropolitan Council can continue to do without effective machinery to establish priorities only by continuing to ignore the critical problems of the central city. Toronto has only 40 percent of the representation on the council, and it is now easier to ignore the City's problems than it once was. For their own part, the City members on the council must be seriously concerned with the demanding problems of the residents of the urban core who are their constituents; accordingly they appear to have little interest in the progress of the Metropolitan Council.

In both the executive committee and the council they take a passive stance towards Metro's policies and program. In 1971, for example, only one chairmanship among the four major metropolitan

---

* On December 1, 1971 the newspapers reported that Metro Chairman Campbell had established a three-member personnel and policy advisory committee under his chairmanship. The newspaper account indicated that the two additional members would be appointed by Mr. Campbell, and chosen from the Metro executive committee. The intention was to provide the elected representatives with more direct influence on the government of Metro. One member of the Metro executive committee, who has since become a member of the new personnel and policy group, described the committee "as necessary to prepare Metro government for future duties as a regional government." Despite this statement the committee appears to be primarily concerned with the coordination of the responsibilities of senior administrative officials.

committees was awarded to a councillor of the City of Toronto. The crucial Social Services and Housing Committee will be chaired, as it has been for several years, by a member of the board of control of a suburban borough. Welfare is, of course, a metropolitan responsibility, and public housing is provided by the Ontario Housing Corporation without reference to municipal boundaries. These facts do not suggest that the leadership will give serious attention to the social problems of the vast number of single elderly persons, mother-led families with dependent children, low-income families, and the families of newcomers from all over the globe, who reside principally in the central city.

THE CITY'S POSITION WITHIN METRO

The City of Toronto has always espoused the principle that Metropolitan Toronto would be far better governed if it consisted of one large unitary city, headed by an elected Mayor, as in New York or Chicago. In the early years following World War II, city officials did all they could to convince the Government of Ontario that there should be one unified City. Support for the concept of "amalgamation" was clearly the dominant position of the central city at that time.

Toronto entered the post-war years with nearly 70 percent of the metropolitan population, and over 60 percent of the assessed valuation within the traditional metropolitan boundaries. In these circumstances it seemed both logical and inevitable that the proper response to the problems of urban growth and development, often described as "urban sprawl," would be the creation of a larger city. The 12 suburban municipalities of the first post-war decade naturally fought hard to forestall "an amalgamation," because they would literally be out of business if the boundaries of the city were enlarged to encompass the traditional metropolitan area.

TORONTO'S COMPARATIVE DECLINE

As the years passed, however, the City of Toronto's position within Metro has weakened significantly. In 1970 it included about one-third of the total population. This proportion will continue to decline as urbanization proceeds, whether or not the present boundaries of Metro are extended. Similarly, the total assessed valuation of the City is approximately 40 percent of the total within Metro

Toronto. It is not clear whether this proportion will continue to drop, since the Government of Ontario assumed responsibility for the entire process of assessment within the province on January 1, 1970. The intention is to reassess all property on the basis of current market values. In view of the nature and quality of both commercial and residential properties in the central city, it is possible that reassessment will raise Toronto's proportion of the total, at least for a time. In any event, the proportion will later decline as construction expands within the three largest boroughs.

The ramifications of the central city's diminution within Metro Toronto could be widespread. Elected and appointed officials, scholars, and researchers throughout the world who are dedicated to the development of metropolitan government must consider seriously the effects of this analysis upon their thinking. The "metropolitan government movement," particularly in the United States and Canada, has certainly faced opposition from officials and residents in suburban municipalities. One argument has been that both groups must give up an important share of local autonomy to attain the objectives of regional planning. If the experience in Metro Toronto is an important indication, local opposition to metropolitan government elsewhere may be strengthened.

THE CITY'S TURN FOR HELP

In the middle 1960's and thereafter, the case for amalgamation put forward by Toronto officials was based on an entirely new principle. Although the changing nature of the City's case for a unitary form of government was not clearly recognized or enunciated by its officials, the basis of the City's new appeal was obviously "survival." The writer has argued earlier that the real test of the so-called "Metro concept," first enunciated by Chairman Gardiner nearly two decades ago, would come when the City was forced to ask Metro for help rather than vice-versa.

In 1963, Frank Smallwood's report for the Bureau of Municipal Research of Toronto presented sufficient evidence to demonstrate that the central city taxpayers were the main contributors to urban expansion within the traditional 12 suburban municipalities.[4] This conclusion was not surprising, since it could be argued that such a redistribution of resources from the wealthier City to the development of underdeveloped suburbs had been the prime objective of metropolitan government, from the very beginning. Within the inadequacies and inequities of municipal taxation based upon property ownership, the property owners of Toronto contributed enormously in helping provide physical and educational facilities for the suburban areas between 1953 and 1965. At that time the Report of the Royal Commission on Metropolitan Government in Toronto emphasized that the newly affluent large townships would soon be required to support the extensive renovation and redevelopment required within the central city.

A SUCCESS: RECONSTRUCTION OF TORONTO'S EDUCATIONAL PLANT

The record has not been entirely bleak. Toronto is one of the very few central cities within established North American census metropolitan areas—perhaps the only one—in which virtually the entire educational plant has been rebuilt, modernized, and rehabilitated. So far as capital facilities are concerned, in the field of education the City does not suffer by comparison with the newer suburban areas. Rebuilding of the educational facilities has gone some way toward attracting teachers as good as those who gravitate toward the new suburban educational systems.*

TROUBLE IN THE SEWERS

On the other hand, there are some kinds of redevelopment in the central city where the issue of redistributing income has not yet been settled satisfactorily. Toronto's sewer system is in urgent need of complete replacement at an estimated cost (in the late 1960's) of at least $300 million. The City is in no position to assume more than a moderate share of the capital expense involved, and it does not receive enough new money annually (from the centralized capital financing within Metro) to permit more than a token contribution to this major task. There has been no real indication of concern on the part of the Metropolitan Council for Toronto's plight in this matter.

---

* The City of Toronto has been unable to complete its program of rebuilding and rehabilitation because the share of capital borrowing available each year to the board has been severely restricted. By 1969 and again in 1970 the City board's request for additional capital was severely dealt with, presumably by virtue of the continued requirements for entirely new capital construction in the boroughs. The discussion often suggested that the City had a responsibility to bear the brunt of the financial stringency.

URBAN RENEWAL: AN UNCLEAR FUTURE

The future of urban renewal, with particular reference to housing and community facilities, is equally unclear within Metro. Although the Metropolitan Toronto Urban Renewal Study identified some areas outside the central city that appeared to require a modern urban renewal treatment, the major areas of blight and slum are within the central city.

The Metropolitan Council will now pay the 25 percent municipal share of both capital and non-capital financial requirements, as laid down in the National Housing Act of 1964. The City has thus technically been relieved of major financial responsibilities in urban renewal, but such relief does not by any means imply favorable action. If anything, Metro's entry into this field, largely as a result of the City's financial straits, makes it more difficult to implement urban renewal programs. After all, if Metro is to contribute financially to the renewal of the deteriorated and blighted slum neighborhoods in downtown areas of the central city, it is clearly the responsibility of the Metropolitan Council to have several assurances: of the need, in the first instance; of the nature and quality of the urban renewal programs to be carried out; of the City's plans, if any, for the relocation of families and businesses from urban renewal areas; and of any existing plans for the involvement of residents in the preparation and implementation of urban renewal programs.

The City has not been without serious fault in urban renewal planning. Certainly no major urban renewal scheme was put forward by the City and rejected by Metro. Perhaps the City was reluctant to put forward some of its proposals because of its secure knowledge that the composition of the Metropolitan Toronto Planning Board and of the Metropolitan Council, particularly after 1967, would militate against approval. On the other hand, the general opposition of citizens' movements and residents of urban renewal areas toward such proposals cannot be ignored. Moreover, confusion within the City government concerning the appropriate roles in urban renewal planning of the Development Department on the one hand, and the City Planning Board on the other, also contributed to what the writer has described as "the crisis in urban renewal in Metropolitan Toronto." [5]

CONCLUDING COMMENTS

Metro Toronto has now nearly concluded its second three-year electoral term since its reorganization on January 1, 1967. The City holds 40 percent of the seats in the Metro Council, and this apparently satisfies the principles of representation by both population and proportion of tax assessments. Nevertheless, the central city remains the hub, the nucleus of activity, and the focus of interest for many of the metropolitan area's 2 million residents.

EYES ON TORONTO

Accordingly, the election campaign for the mayoralty of the City of Toronto occupies more space in the media, and is apparently of greater interest to the residents of the whole metropolitan area than all the other electoral campaigns held simultaneously throughout Metro every three years. Moreover, most citizens pay more attention to the election of a Mayor for the City than the choice of a Chairman for the Municipality of Metropolitan Toronto. Since the election of the Chairman is indirect, it could be argued that Toronto's direct election is much more relevant to the public. But other direct elections go unnoticed. Although the population of the Borough of North York is approaching one-half million, which makes it 70 percent as large as the City of Toronto, reports of its elections are little more than important footnotes in the news media.

The writer has argued that perhaps the City of Toronto was overrepresented during the first 12 years of metropolitan government. But since the reorganization of 1966–1967, it can now be argued that the City is severely under-represented within the Metropolitan Council. The fact that the City has equal representation with the boroughs on the executive committee has not yet significantly influenced distribution of total operating and capital resources, or the attention paid by the Metropolitan Council to the fundamental redevelopment needed in the central city.

THE METROPOLITAN CONCEPT: FROM THE OUTSIDE INWARDS

This argument has been challenged by some observers, who point to the tremendous building boom in downtown Toronto, particularly in the construction of commercial facilities. They insist that the City of Toronto has experienced an unusually large amount of private urban renewal, in comparison with Montreal and certain American cities. This is indeed true, and such activity has persisted, not only in the years of economic expansion after 1963 but also during recent years of restricted growth. It is not private urban renewal that concerns the writer, nor is it merely the matter of rebuilding the sewer system. It is the entire application of "the metropolitan concept"—from the outside inwards, from the suburban municipalities to the central city, from the needs of development to the needs of redevelopment—that is fundamental.

AN EQUAL DEAL FOR THE CITY

In the election campaigns for December 1, 1969, the new basis for the concept of "amalgamation" became quite clear in the view of City officials. The Mayor of Toronto gave unification a high priority in his policy platform. In a new twist he equated "amalgamation" and "an equal deal for the City." Amalgamation, it was argued, is vital to the citizens of Toronto, and must come because "the citizen of Toronto has never particularly benefited from the metropolitan system of government." It was further argued that the Ontario Government's system of grants discriminates against the City, whose needs are greater. Instead of getting more than the boroughs, Toronto gets less, or at best, equal support. Thus under current provincial legislation the City of Toronto receives a grant of 15 percent from the province for educational purposes; the suburban boroughs receive 30 percent. The 15 percent grant is said to reflect Toronto's relative wealth within Metro, as judged by data concerning assessment per capita, assessment per pupil enrolled, and the apportionment of the total provincial grant within Metro on a basis of assessment. In other words, the calculations are pieces of arithmetic based upon the total assessed valuation within the City, as compared with certain boroughs. The total number of elementary and secondary school pupils, for example, is divided into a total assessed valuation, and a "per pupil enrolled assessment" calculated. This is higher in the City than in the boroughs. Frank Smallwood pointed this out in his report for the Bureau of Municipal Research in 1963.

A second example is provided by an analogous per capita calculation. Total population is divided into total assessed valuation, and since the City of Toronto's population is not growing as rapidly as those of the boroughs, if at all, the per capita figure in the City is necessarily higher than in the boroughs. Thus the Provincial Department of Education has justified a proportionate grant in suburban municipalities that is twice as great as that for the City of Toronto.

But these exercises in arithmetic do not take into account the great difference between Toronto and the boroughs in the degree of need and the level of services required. The City of Toronto provides a great many special educational facilities not required in the boroughs. The great majority of non-English-speaking newcomers, for example, settle in the central city. Their children need language classes and counselling. Their families need special adult educational opportunities. These costly facilities, as well as a higher level of "child adjustment services"—psychiatric facilities for emotionally disturbed children, slow learners, etc.—are found in the City rather than in the boroughs. Consequently the City claims that its grant from the province should be far greater. But the province justifies its system, which the author considers to be discriminatory, on the basis of the mathematical calculations.

Until recently subsidies for various public works amounted to 33.3 percent for the City of Toronto; the boroughs received 50 percent. In 1970 the subsidy for public works, particularly for roads, was raised to 50 percent, as in the boroughs. The province is paying 25 percent of municipal health costs in all six municipalities in Metropolitan Toronto. It has offered to pay 75 percent of these costs if the City and the five boroughs were to combine their departments of public health.

A "HAVE-NOT" MUNICIPALITY

Although these arguments were made in the heat of an election campaign, the figures were not refuted. It is fascinating to recognize the complete reversal in the arguments put forward by the City of Toronto in advocating amalgamation over the years 1950–1970. In the early post-war years and into the pre-metropolitan 1950's amalgamation was said to be desirable because of the resources that the central city could make available for the future development of a modern metropolis. In the late 1960's and into the 1970's amalgamation has been called desirable, and indeed essential, because the City of Toronto is no longer a "have municipality," but is now a "have-not municipality." The writer has often said that the real test of the durability of metropolitan government in Toronto is not the clear and impartial sharing of area-wide resources that occurred between 1954–1969, but the transmutation of that process to benefit the City during the 1970's and 1980's.

The central city has become disadvantaged in many respects. Unlike many central cities in North American metropolitan areas, it has not become a vast slum, and its services have not deteriorated. It has not seen violent and bloody confrontations between members of minority groups. Nevertheless, Metro's failure to assume a clear and firm role in urban redevelopment has left the central city with major problems of unfulfilled programs. Although most of its elementary and secondary schools have been renovated or totally rebuilt, its sewer system is totally inadequate and antiquated, and will require at least $300 million (in 1967 dollars) to reconstruct. With each passing year, the demands upon the City for facilities and services that will be of benefit to the entire metropolis and the region beyond it continue to mount, both in magnitude and in cost. But the Municipality of Metropolitan Toronto has shown few recent signs of concern for the disabilities of the central city.

THE QUALITY OF LIFE

We must conclude that the future of Metropolitan Toronto does not lie in a vast expansion—a veritable tripling of its area—through an adjustment of its boundaries to the north and east. Rather, its future lies in a fundamental consolidation of its urban role and a rebuilding of the center.

If Metropolitan Toronto persists in its apparently zoological objective—the creation of an octopus without a heart—the quality of life in the metropolis will suffer acutely as the population grows from 2.1 million in 1970 to an estimated 2.8 million in 1980. Metro's concern must be improving the quality of life for its residents.

Accordingly the quality of life of the future metropolis should now become a central concern of Metro Toronto. If that concern is not given much greater future emphasis than it received in the first 17 years of metropolitan government, and greater budgetary support, some form of amalgamation will almost certainly occur. In that event, the only unknown will be whether the federal system of metropolitan government will have come to an end primarily through neglect at the Metro level, or through political decision at the provincial level.

GLOSSARY

ALDERMAN. Local councillor.

AMALGAMATION. Unification of the municipalities within a metropolitan area by order of the provincial (state) government rather than through annexation.

BOARD OF AUTHORITY. Local housing authorities and other governmental commissions (e.g., Metro Toronto Housing Authority, Ontario Water Resources Commission), whether appointed or elected, are governed by a board of directors.

BOARD OF CONTROL. The Ontario Municipal Act permits cities and towns (as well as boroughs in Metro Toronto) to elect councillors on an area-wide basis. This group of persons, usually four in number, together with the Mayor, becomes a board of control, which considers and prepares policies and legislation prior to full meetings of the municipal council.

BOROUGH. A municipal corporation; an alternative designation to town or city. The term is used in the metropolitan area of New York City and in London, England.

BRITISH SYSTEM. The British parliamentary system and the procedures that have developed to administer government throughout the British Commonwealth of Nations.

BY-LAW. A piece of legislation passed by a municipal or Metropolitan council; a local statute.

CITY SOLICITOR. The chief legal officer of the municipality, usually a full-time civil servant.

COMMUNITY PLANNING BRANCH. A division of the Department of Municipal Affairs of the Ontario Government. This division is responsible for recommending to the Minister approval of all plans of subdivision and is generally responsible for the stimulation of formal physical planning throughout the province.

CONSOLIDATION. Unification of a specific municipal function, e.g., policing, public welfare, etc., previously provided by each municipality within the metropolis and now performed by the metropolitan government alone.

COUNCIL (LOCAL). A government body of elected representatives within a municipality in Metro Toronto. This is to be distinguished from the Metropolitan Council.

COUNTY. A territorial division of the Province of Ontario, which forms an administrative, judicial and political unit. All municipalities in Ontario are part and parcel of a county, unless specifically excluded, as is the Municipality of Metropolitan Toronto.

DEBENTURE. An alternative name for a municipal bond.

EXECUTIVE COMMITTEE. A group of members of Metro Council originally assembled by the Chairman to serve as an advisory cabinet, but later written into the Metropolitan Toronto Act with specific representation from the City and the suburban municipalities.

EXPRESSWAY. An arterial roadway akin to the American freeway, whether elevated or not.

FULL RECOVERY HOUSING. Public housing in which rentals are set at an economic level. Thus all the costs are technically fully recovered over the life of the mortgage. There are no rental subsidies for the tenants.

LICENSING COMMISSION. An authority of three persons headed by a judge, appointed by the Government of Ontario in the first instance, and later by the Metropolitan Council. This commission is charged with the responsibility of issuing licenses to all businesses in Metro Toronto requiring such licenses, e.g., taxis, truckers, and refreshment dispensing vehicles.

MAISONETTE. A small house, usually built in the form of row or terrace housing, and sometimes built vertically in duplex form.

METROPOLITAN COUNCIL. The governing body within a formal metropolitan government. In Metro Toronto members of the Council are first elected in either the City of Toronto or one of the five boroughs, and become members of the Metropolitan Council by virtue of the provisions of the Metropolitan Toronto Act.

NON-WARDS. A child who is in the care of a Children's Aid Society of Ontario or another province, for whom formal legal guardianship (wardship) has not yet been obtained.

ONTARIO MUNICIPAL BOARD. A quasi-judicial body appointed by the Ontario Government to perform certain specific functions which include approval of municipal zoning by-laws and changes thereto, municipal annexations, changes in municipal status, e.g., from town to city, and capital borrowings by each municipality for public works.

ORDER-IN-COUNCIL. In the British parliamentary system, under which the Government of Canada and the provincial governments operate, the decisions of cabinet are issued in the form of Orders-in-Council. Orders-in-Council are akin to Executive Orders issued by the President of the United States, but in the British system they are technically issued by the Cabinet over the signature of the Governor General (for the federal government) and the Lieut. Governor (for the provincial government). They are used, for example, to provide government funds when the legislature is not in session, to make formal appointments to boards and commissions of the province, to initiate commissions of inquiry.

PROVINCE. A geographical and political division within Canada akin to an American state. There are ten provinces in Canada.

ROYAL COMMISSION ON METROPOLITAN TORONTO. A Royal Commission is a formal inquiry initiated by the Government of Canada or a provincial government. The Government of Ontario initiated such an inquiry concerning the future of government in Metro Toronto and named one person, known as the Commissioner, to conduct the inquiry.

SEPARATE SCHOOL BOARD. The elected members of the Board of Education representing supporters of the Roman Catholic schools, designated as "Separate Schools" in Ontario.

TERMS OF REFERENCE. Specific matters to be inquired into and reported upon by a Royal Commission of Inquiry, or any other formal inquiry initiated by the Government of Canada or a provincial government. These terms of reference are outlined in detail in a formal Order-in-Council.

TOWN. An incorporated municipality in the Province of Ontario with a population of less than 10,000.

TOWNSHIP. The original designation given to the large municipal bodies created within the counties of the Province of Ontario.

VILLAGE. The lowest order of incorporated municipality within the Province of Ontario, usually with a population of 1,000 or less.

NOTES

NOTES TO PREFACE

1. Albert Rose, "A Decade of Metropolitan Government in Toronto," *Buffalo Law Review*, Vol. XIII (Spring 1964), 539–556. See also "A Critique of Metropolitan Government in Toronto, 1953–1965," in *Planning 1965*, selected papers from the Joint Planning Conference of the American Society of Planning Officials and the Community Planning Association of Canada (Chicago: American Society of Planning Officials, 1965), pp. 5–22.
2. *Metropolitan Toronto, . . . 10 Years of Progress, Annual Report* (Toronto, 1963).
3. Winston W. Crouch, "Metropolitan Government in Toronto," *Public Administration Review*, Vol. XIV (Spring 1954), 85–95.
4. J. G. Grumm, *Metropolitan Government: The Toronto Experience* (Lawrence: Governmental Research Center, University of Kansas, 1959).
5. Frank Smallwood, *Metro Toronto: A Decade Later* (Toronto: Bureau of Municipal Research, 1963).
6. Harold Kaplan, *Urban Political Systems: A Functional Analysis of Metro Toronto* (New York: Columbia University Press, 1967).

NOTES TO CHAPTER ONE

1. Civic Advisory Council of Toronto, Committee on Metropolitan Problems, *First Report*, Section I (Toronto, November 1949), p. 65.
2. *Ibid.*, Table III, p. 12.
3. Canada, Department of National Revenue, *Taxation Statistics* (Ottawa: Queen's Printer, 1970), Table 1, pp. 8–9.
4. Canada, Dominion Bureau of Statistics, *Census 1941*, Vol. III (Ottawa: King's Printer, 1946), Table 16, pp. 234–235.
5. *Census 1951: Population and Housing Statistics by Census Tracts, Toronto*, Bulletin CT-6 (Ottawa, 1953), Table 1, p. 4.
6. *Census 1961: Population and Housing Statistics by Census Tracts, Toronto*, Bulletin CT-15 (Ottawa, 1963), Table 1, p. 4. The Census of 1961 showed that approximately one-third of the metropolitan population had been born outside Canada. Among this group 404,704 persons had immigrated between 1946 and 1961.
7. *Ibid.*, p. 4.

8. D. C. Masters, *The Rise of Toronto, 1850–1890* (Toronto: University of Toronto Press, 1947), p. 127.

9. Address by Miss Charity Cook, Tenth Canadian Conference of Charities and Correction, Toronto, October 19–21, 1909, *Proceedings*, pp. 10–12. Extracts reprinted in S. D. Clark, *The Social Development of Canada* (Toronto: University of Toronto Press, 1942), p. 420.

10. Bureau of Municipal Research, *What Is "The Ward" Going to Do with Toronto?: A Report on Undesirable Living Conditions in One Section of the City of Toronto—"The Ward"—Conditions Which Are Spreading Rapidly to Other Districts* (Toronto, December 1918).

11. *Ibid.*, Appendix, "Slum Conditions in Toronto," p. 67.

12. Albert Rose, *Regent Park: A Study of Slum Clearance* (Toronto: University of Toronto Press, 1958), p. 37.

13. City of Toronto, *Report of the Lieutenant-Governor's Committee on Housing Conditions in Toronto*, "The Bruce Report" (Toronto, 1934), p. 5.

14. Albert Rose, *Rehabilitation of Housing in Central Toronto*, A Study Submitted to the City of Toronto Planning Board (Toronto: City of Toronto Planning Board, September 1966), p. 11.

15. Ontario, Department of Municipal Affairs, *A Better Place to Live* (Toronto, June 1962), p. 43. The Toronto By-law (No. 14466) was revised slightly in 1941 but was not changed substantially until the late 1960's.

16. Albert Rose, *Regent Park*, p. 42.

17. *Ibid.*, p. 44.

18. Civic Advisory Council of Toronto, Committee on Metropolitan Problems, *op. cit.*, "Foreword," p. v.

19. *Ibid.*, p. v.

NOTES TO CHAPTER TWO

1. The phrase is borrowed from W. W. Rostow, *The Stages of Economic Growth* (London: Cambridge University Press, 1961).

2. Humphrey S. M. Carver, *Houses for Canadians* (Toronto: University of Toronto Press, 1948), pp. 25–27.

3. Bureau of Municipal Research, *Where Are Toronto and Its Metropolitan Area Heading?* White Paper No. 305 (Toronto, December 20, 1945), not paged, 4–5.

4. *Ibid.*, not paged, 1.

5. Civic Advisory Council of Toronto, Committee on Metropolitan Problems, *First Report*, Section Two, Statistical Appendix (Toronto, April 1950), p. 27.

6. Bureau of Municipal Research, *op. cit.*, p. 2.

7. *Ibid.*, p. 3.

8. Toronto and York Planning Board, *Report* (Toronto, December 1st, 1949), pp. 44–48. This report was published following a series of studies of Toronto and the County of York. In April 1948 the City received a comprehensive report from Norman D. Wilson, *A Transportation Plan for Metropolitan Toronto and the Suburban Areas Adjacent;* and in September 1948 a report was prepared by Gore and Storrie, Consulting Engineers, *Water Supply and Sewage Disposal for the City of Toronto and Related Areas*. In the meantime *A County of York Planning Survey* had been completed in June 1948 by Alan Deacon, Eugene Faludi and John Layng. On the basis of these studies the Toronto and

York Planning Board recommended the unification of the City of Toronto and seven adjacent municipalities (p. 47).

9. Albert Rose, "The Challenge of Metropolitan Growth," *Community Planning Review*, Vol. IV (1954), 100.

10. Ontario, Ontario Municipal Board, *Decisions and Recommendations of the Board* (Toronto: Queen's Printer, January 20, 1953).

NOTES TO CHAPTER THREE

1. Albert Rose, "The Challenge of Metropolitan Growth," *Community Planning Review*, Vol. IV (1954), 101.

2. Frederick G. Gardiner, "Metropolitan Toronto: A New Answer to Metropolitan Area Problems," in the proceedings of the Annual National Planning Conference, published as *Planning, 1953* (Chicago: American Society of Planning Officials, 1954), p. 42. Mr. Gardiner's address was originally delivered at the ASPO Conference in Detroit in October 1953.

3. Ontario, Ontario Municipal Board, *Decisions and Recommendations* (Toronto: Queen's Printer, January 20, 1953), p. 69.

4. *Ibid.*, p. 71.

5. Gardiner, *op. cit.*, pp. 45–46.

6. F. G. Gardiner, "Organizing the Metropolitan Administration in Toronto," an address to the Institute of Public Administration of Canada in Ottawa, September 9, 1954 (Toronto: Municipality of Metropolitan Toronto, 1954), p. 13.

7. Municipality of Metropolitan Toronto, *Metropolitan Toronto 1958* (Toronto, 1958), p. 9.

8. F. G. Gardiner, *A Submission to the Commission Appointed by the Lieutenant-Governor-in-Council of the Province of Ontario to Inquire into the Affairs of the Municipality of Metropolitan Toronto*, June 15, 1957 (mimeographed), pp. 1–2.

9. *Ibid.*, p. 7.

10. Municipality of Metropolitan Toronto, *A Submission by the Council of the Municipality of Metropolitan Toronto to the Commission Appointed by the Lieutenant-Governor-in-Council to Inquire into the Affairs of the Municipality of Metropolitan Toronto* (Toronto, 1957), "Preface."

11. *Ibid.*, "Report of the Commissioner of Finance," p. 3.

12. *Ibid.*, "Report of the Commissioner of Assessment," p. 11.

13. *Ibid.*, "Report of the Commissioner of Planning," p. 104.

14. *Ibid.*, p. 106.

15. *Ibid.*, p. 123.

16. Ontario, Metropolitan Toronto Commission of Inquiry, *First Report*, March 14, 1958 (mimeographed).

17. *Ibid.*, p. 2.

18. *Ibid.*, p. 3.

19. *Ibid.*, pp. 4–5.

20. *Ibid.*, pp. 6–7.

21. *Ibid.*, p. 7.

22. *Ibid.*, p. 8. Admittedly a pronounced City-suburban "split" could exist despite the fact that "an exact division" occurred very rarely. The real question is how such splits are resolved between the "City bloc" and the "suburban bloc." On this matter see Harold Kaplan, *Urban Political Systems: A Functional*

Analysis of Metro Toronto (New York: Columbia University Press, 1967), in which there are numerous references to the Toronto bloc in the Metro Council and the Metro executive committee, and an equally substantial number of references to a suburban bloc in the Metro Council. Kaplan's references extend over a wide variety of the functional responsibilities of the Metropolitan Council and the suburban municipalities.

23. Metropolitan Toronto Commission of Inquiry, *First Report,* p. 11.
24. *Ibid.,* p. 12.
25. *Ibid.,* p. 13.

NOTES TO CHAPTER FOUR

1. Ontario, *The Planning Act,* Revised Statutes of Ontario, 1960, Chapter 296. Originally, the administration of this act was the responsibility of the Department of Planning and Development through its Community Planning Branch. In 1960 the branch was transferred to the Department of Municipal Affairs. There was a consistency, therefore, with respect to the manner and the personnel with whom officials of Metropolitan Toronto would deal. Nevertheless, the shift from a Department of Planning and Development (which in the early 1960's was changed to a Department of Trade and Development) to the Department of Municipal Affairs was significant.
2. Ontario, *The Municipality of Metropolitan Toronto Act, 1953* (as amended), Revised Statutes of Ontario, 1960, Chapter 260, Section 179.
3. City of Toronto Planning Board, *Urban Renewal: A Study of Toronto, 1956* (Toronto, 1956). See also a "Short Statement" published by the Community Planning Association of Canada in 1956.
4. "Short Statement," p. 7.
5. *Loc. cit.,* p. 7.
6. City of Toronto Planning Board, *Redevelopment Study Area No. 1,* and *Redevelopment Study Area No. 2* (Toronto, 1957), both distributed in September 1957 for public study and discussion.
7. Metropolitan Toronto Planning Board, *The Official Plan of the Metropolitan Toronto Planning Area* (Toronto, 1959).
8. T. J. Kent, Jr., *The Urban General Plan* (San Francisco: Chandler, 1964).
9. Metropolitan Toronto Planning Board, *op. cit.,* "Introduction," p. i.
10. *Ibid.,* "Introduction," p. ii.
11. Metropolitan Toronto Planning Board, *Report on the Metropolitan Toronto Transportation Plan* (Toronto, December 1964).
12. Metropolitan Toronto Planning Board, *The Official Plan of the Metropolitan Toronto Area, 1959* (Toronto, 1959), p. iv.
13. Metropolitan Toronto Planning Board, *Urban Renewal Study Interim Report,* (Toronto, February 1965); *Inventory of Social Resources, Part 1A, Community Welfare and Health Services,* prepared by the Research Department, Social Planning Council of Metropolitan Toronto, December 1964; *Part 1B, Community Associations,* November 1964; *Review of Publicly Owned Housing in Metropolitan Toronto,* December 1964; *Interim Report,* 1965; *The Role of Private Enterprise in Urban Renewal,* March 1966; *Staff Report,* August 1966. This latter report was, in fact, the *Metropolitan Toronto Urban Renewal Study.*
14. Note 12 above, "Summary," p. F3–4. As pointed out, these eight principles of orderly development are meaningful only if there are alternative

principles of orderly development or contrary principles of disorderly development. It would appear, however, that the nature of the eight statements of principle—their simplicity and acceptability to persons knowledgeable in the planning field—does not make them invalid. It is probable that the writers of the draft Official Plan felt that the simple spelling out of these principles was essential in terms of the lack of planning sophistication that persisted among the members of the Metropolitan Council, if not their sheer lack of understanding of planning, even though the Metro had been in operation for a full six years.

15. Harold Kaplan, *Urban Political Systems: A Functional Analysis of Metro Toronto* (New York: Columbia University Press, 1967). See especially pp. 70–71, 111, 138, 142.

16. "Proposed Official Plan" of the Metropolitan Toronto Planning Area was first issued as a draft dated December 1964. The ultimate version, entitled *Metropolitan Plan for the Metropolitan Toronto Planning Area,* was issued by the Board in December 1966. Nevertheless, the formal letter of transmission from the MTPB to the Metropolitan Council recommending the Official Plan for adoption was dated December 15, 1965. See Chapter Eight.

17. Eli Comay, *A Brief to the Royal Commission on Metropolitan Toronto,* April 1964 (mimeographed), p. 3.

18. F. G. Gardiner, "A Brief" presented to the Royal Commission on Canada's Economic Prospects, 1955–1980, January 23, 1956 (Toronto: Municipality of Metropolitan Toronto, 1956) (mimeographed), pp. 31–32. In the Borough of North York, population reached a half million by 1970.

NOTES TO CHAPTER FIVE

1. Ontario, *Municipality of Metropolitan Toronto Act,* Revised Statutes of Ontario 1960, Chapter 260, Section 217.

2. Joint Advisory Committee on Regent Park South, *Regent Park South Redevelopment Project* (Toronto, January 31, 1955). This committee was chaired by the Assistant Supervisor, Ontario Region of Central Mortgage and Housing Corporation, and included representatives from the Government of Ontario, the City of Toronto, and Central Mortgage and Housing Corporation.

3. Albert Rose, *Regent Park: A Study in Slum Clearance* (Toronto: University of Toronto Press, 1958), pp. 103–170.

NOTES TO CHAPTER SIX

1. Frederick G. Gardiner, "Address to the Inaugural Meeting of the Metropolitan Toronto Council" (Toronto, January 13, 1961) (mimeographed). Mr. Gardiner's statements concerning his impending resignation did not appear in the text of his address, which, of course, was mimeographed in advance for the press and his audience. The statement took the form of a verbal postscript.

2. *Ibid.,* pp. 69–70.

3. *Ibid.,* pp. 73–75.

4. Metropolitan Toronto, *Report Prepared for the Special Committee of the Metropolitan Council on Metropolitan Affairs by the Committee of Metropolitan Department Heads* (Toronto, October 18, 1961) (mimeographed) 283 pp.

5. *Ibid.* This document contains the most comprehensive review of the work

of each department of the Municipality of Metropolitan Toronto prepared since the commencement of metropolitan government on January 1, 1954. The data presented in this report are available in no other document.

6. The breakdown is presented in the report as follows: Part II, departments having metropolitan and local counterparts, in which 15 such functional responsibilities were identified, pp. 21–182; Part III, local departments having no metropolitan counterparts, in which just three major functions were identified, with four additional minor miscellaneous responsibilities, pp. 183–232; Part IV, metropolitan departments having no local counterparts, in which seven functions were identified, pp. 233–252. There were 26 chapters in the report, corresponding to the number of functions or responsibilities identified, plus three introductory chapters.

7. *Ibid.*, pp. 2–4.
8. *Ibid.*, p. 4.
9. *Ibid.*, p. 8.
10. Ontario, Department of Economics, *A Report on the Metropolitan Toronto System of Government*, prepared for the Special Committee of Metropolitan Council on Metropolitan Affairs (Toronto, November 1961).
11. *Ibid.*, pp. 11–14. Mr. Gathercole did not specify that one of the possible solutions might be the retention of the status quo. It is not known whether this was a conscious and deliberate omission. One can speculate, however, that dissatisfaction with the status quo had reached such a point by this time that it was judged wise to exclude it from consideration. On the other hand, the Cabinet may have told Mr. Gathercole that it intended to make changes and welcomed his advice.
12. *Ibid.*, pp. 7–10.
13. *Ibid.*, p. 13.
14. *Ibid.*, p. 14.
15. F. G. Gardiner, *op. cit.*, January 13, 1961, pp. 77–83. However, in later statements to the press and in articles he wrote, the Chairman indicated that he favored a four-city plan to replace the 13 Area Municipalities.

NOTES TO CHAPTER SEVEN

1. Albert Rose, "A Critique of Metropolitan Government in Toronto, 1953–1965," an address to the Annual Conference of the American Society of Planning Officials, April 26, 1965, *Planning* (Chicago: American Society of Planning Officials, November 1965), pp. 5–22.
2. Smallwood, *op. cit.*, p. 35 (Note 5 preface).
3. Ontario, *Report of the Royal Commission on Metropolitan Toronto* (Toronto, 1965).
4. *Ibid.*, "Introduction," p. xi.
5. *Ibid.*, p. 200.
6. *Ibid.*, pp. 200–202.
7. *Ibid.*, p. 204.
8. *Ibid.*, pp. 205–206.
9. Ontario, *Statement by the Hon. John Robarts, Prime Minister of Ontario, Re Report of the Royal Commission on Metropolitan Toronto* (Toronto: Government of Ontario, January 10, 1966).
10. *Ibid.*, p. 10.

11. *Ibid.*, pp. 11–12.
12. *Ibid.*, p. 13.
13. *Ibid.*, p. 14.
14. *Ibid.*, p. 15. The Municipality of Metropolitan Toronto Act was amended by Bill 201 in 1969 to provide that the four alderman members of the executive committee of the City automatically become members of the Metropolitan Council's executive committee. This provision came into effect on January 1, 1970.
15. *Ibid.*, p. 17.
16. *Ibid.*, p. 22.
17. *Ibid.*, p. 22.
18. *Ibid.*, p. 23.
19. *Ibid.*, p. 24.
20. *Ibid.*, pp. 24–25.
21. *Ibid.*, p. 26.

NOTES TO CHAPTER EIGHT

1. *Metropolitan Toronto, 1953–1963: 10 Years of Progress* (Toronto, 1963), p. 2.
2. *Ibid.*, pp. 5–6.
3. *Ibid.*, p. 10.
4. *Ibid.*, pp. 10–11.
5. *Ibid.*, p. 11.
6. *Ibid.*, pp. 28–29.
7. *Ibid.*, p. 30.
8. *Ibid.*, p. 31.
9. *Ibid.*, p. 22.
10. *Idem.*
11. Harold Kaplan, *Urban Political Systems: A Functional Analysis of Metro Toronto* (New York: Columbia University Press, 1967), pp. 137–146.
12. Metropolitan Toronto, *Report No. 1 of the Official Plan Committee* (Toronto, November 10, 1966), p. 2. The report also appeared in the printed documents made available for consideration by the Council of the Municipality of Metropolitan Toronto on December 15, 1966, in an Appendix A to an Executive Committee Report, pp. 2602–2636.
13. *Ibid.*, p. 5.
14. At the end of the publication described as Appendix A the following statement appears: "Report No. 1 of the Official Plan Committee was *adopted as amended* by the Metropolitan Council on December 15, 1966." (Emphasis supplied.)
15. *Ibid.*, p. 34.
16. *Ibid.*, published as Appendix A to an Executive Committee Report, p. 2636. (See note 12 above.)
17. Metropolitan Toronto Planning Board, *The Official Plan of the Metropolitan Toronto Planning Area* (Toronto, 1959), p. 154.
18. Metropolitan Toronto Planning Board, *Report on the Metropolitan Toronto Transportation Plan* (Toronto, December 1964), p. 55.
19. Harold Kaplan, *op. cit.*, pp. 65–66, 164–165.
20. Bureau of Municipal Research, *Transportation: Who Plans? Who Pays?* (Toronto: Autumn 1970), p. 4.

21. *Idem.*
22. Ontario, "Design for Development," Statement by the Prime Minister of Ontario on Regional Development Policy (Toronto: April 5, 1966).
23. Ontario, *Design for Development: Phase Two*, Statement by the Hon. John Robarts, Prime Minister of Ontario (Toronto, November 28, 1968). And "Statement" by the Hon. W. Darcy McKeough, Minister of Municipal Affairs (December 2, 1968).
24. *Ibid.*, p. 8.
25. *Ibid.*, p. 9.
26. *Ibid.*, "Statement" by the Minister of Municipal Affairs, p. 9.
27. Ontario, *Design for Development: The Toronto-Centred Region* (Toronto: Queen's Printer, May 5, 1970), p. 9.
28. Ontario, *Design for Development: The Toronto-Centred Region.* Opening Remarks by the Hon. John Robarts, Prime Minister of Ontario, May 5, 1970, pp. 7, 9 (mimeographed).
29. Ontario, *Design for Development*, pp. 2-3.
30. *Ibid.*, p. 6.
31. *Ibid.*, pp. 10-11.
32. *Ibid.*, p. 15.
33. *Ibid.*, p. 19.

NOTES TO CHAPTER NINE

1. Jean Gottman, *Megalopolis* (New York: Twentieth Century Fund, 1961).
2. Toronto *Daily Star,* Saturday, October 11, 1969, p. 19.
3. Frank Smallwood, *op. cit.*, pp. 36-37 (Note 5, Preface).
4. *Ibid.*, pp. 22-27.
5. Albert Rose, "The Crisis in Urban Renewal in Metropolitan Toronto," *Habitat,* Vol. XI (May-June 1968), 2-8.

INDEX

Allen, William R.: election as Metro Chairman, 79, 89–90; announcement of resignation, 90n; activities and programs, 97–98, 103, 158–160; naming of Spadina Expressway for, 139

Amalgamation: of the municipalities in Greater Toronto, xxii, 16, 33n, 81n, 82, 85, 146, 159, 167; Toronto's first request for, 20–22, 45; Toronto's second request for, 102, 177–178, 182–183; statement of Prime Minister on, 113

Area Municipalities, 22, 25; financing of, 37, 101; functions of, 25–27, 38, 100, 119; representation on Executive Committee, 43, 117; role in planning, 48–52, 61, 108

Assessment, 60; overall assessed valuation, 38, 82, 87–88, 177, 182; uniform, 26–27; responsibility for, 26, 178

Bick, C. O., 36
Bill 80, 21, 24–25, 32, 132. *See also* Municipality of Metropolitan Toronto Act 1953
Bill 81, 122–123
Boards of control, 116–117
Board of Police Commissioners, 36, 80n. *See also* Police
Borough of East York, 93, 114–116, 166. *See also* East York, Township of
Borough of Etobicoke, 87–88, 93, 114–116. *See also* Etobicoke, Township of
Borough of North York, 87–88, 93, 114–116, 181. *See also* North York, Township of
Borough of Scarborough, 87–88, 93, 114–116. *See also* Scarborough, Township of
Borough of York, 93, 114–116, 166. *See also* York, Township of
Borough system, 16, 86–88, 114–116
Boundaries of Metro Toronto, 16, 104, 107, 146, 152–154, 156, 160–166, 184

Bruce, Dr. Herbert A., 8
Bruce Report. *See* Lieutenant-Governor's Committee to Study Housing Conditions in Toronto
Bunnell, Arthur, 58n
Bureau of Municipal Research, xxiv; organization of, 7; publications on housing conditions, 7; on planning, 10, 15–16, 140, 178; submission of its brief to the Royal Commission on Metro Toronto, 104

Campbell, Albert M.: election as Metro Chairman, 160–161; activities and programs, 161–162, 176n
Central Mortgage and Housing Corporation, 52, 58, 67–79, 170
Chairman of Metropolitan Council, 24, 27, 33, 43–44, 62, 115, 142–143, 181; method of selection of, 43–44, 106, 116, 159; election of second Chairman, 89–90, 157; election of third Chairman, 160–161; role, 156–162
Citizen participation: in planning, 63–64, 137–140, 142, 167–170, 180; in regional government, 147, 168–170
City of Toronto: origins, 1–2; as commercial and financial center, 3–4; ethnic and religious composition of, 4–5; early concern with planning and housing, 6–9, 11, 17–20; disabilities within Metro, 176–184. *See also* Amalgamation, Toronto's requests for
City of Toronto Planning Board: district planning of, 53, 63–64; establishment of and early plans, 10–11, 17, 45; development after Metro, 47–53, 63; study of urban renewal, 52–53; relationship to Metro Official Plan, 57, 135
"City-suburban split", 43, 82
CIVAC (Civic Action), 172–173

197

INDEX

Civic Advisory Council of Toronto: Committee on Metropolitan Problems, xxii, 17–20
Comay, Eli, 60
Commissioner of Assessment, 37–38
Commissioner of Finance, 37, 56, 69
Commissioner of Planning, 38–40, 48, 51, 60, 74, 135, 142
Commissioner of Welfare and Housing, 37, 74
Commissioner of Works, 37, 142
Community Planning Association of Canada, xxii, 21, 31, 78, 108
Community Planning Branch (Department of Municipal Affairs), 30, 49, 68
Conservative Party: of Ontario, 23, 143, 154; of Canada, 24n
Crouch, Winston W., xxiv
Cumming, Lorne R., 21, 23, 40, 122

Dakin, John, xxi
Davis, William G., 139, 143, 153–154
Debenture: financing by, 26; assumption of debt by Metro Council, 84, 111, 121
Department of Economics (Ontario), 83. *See also* Regional Development Branch, Department of Economics and Treasury
Department of Municipal Affairs (Ontario): activity in governmental reorganization, xi, 11, 84, 86; responsibility in housing and urban renewal, 67–69 *passim;* commissioning of regional studies by, 144–145; involvement in regional government, 145
Department of Planning and Development (Ontario), 40, 67–68
District Education Councils, 111–112
Dominion Housing Act, 9
Don Planning Area, 53

East York, Township of, 61, 114–115
Educational facilities: need for expansion, 19; problem of financing, 28, 178–179, 182–183; uniform tax for, 111–113; reconstruction within City, 179; future needs in City, 183
Etobicoke, Township of, 30, 45, 61, 75–77, 114–115
Executive Committee of the City of Toronto, 117–118. *See also* Metro Executive Committee
Expressway system. *See* Spadina Expressway, and Transportation planning

Family Service Association of Metropolitan Toronto, 73

Fire protection services, 110, 119, 147
Forest Hill, Village of, 2, 17, 24, 36, 114–115, 137

Gardiner, Frederick G., xxiii, 17, 22, 24, 27–28, 97, 157, 159, 178; concern and activity in public housing, 66–78; resignation and role in Metro reorganization, 82–83, 89, 165–166
Gathercole, G. E., 84
General Welfare Assistance Act (Ontario), 101, 119
Goodhead, Norman, 89
Governmental functions: metropolitan, 25–26; local, 26–27
Gray, A. J. B., 27n
Greater Winnipeg Water District, 20
Grumm, John G., xxiv

Hall, Fred, 37. *See also* Licensing Commission of Metro
Hamilton-Wentworth Regional Area Study, 144
Hardy, Eric, xxiv
Housing: early conditions, 8–10; supply and demand, 14, 29, 31, 62, 126–127; slums and slum clearance, 63, 66; Standard of Housing By-Law, 9; responsibility of government in Metro, 26–27, 65–67, 158; rehabilitation, 52–53, 127; nature of federal-provincial housing authority, 67–68; trend to multiple dwellings, 126–127, 142, 163. *See also* Central Mortgage and Housing Corporation, National Housing Act, Ontario Housing Corporation, Urban renewal
Housing Authority of Toronto, 66, 78–79
Housing Branch, Department of Planning and Development (Ontario), 67–68
Housing Development Act (Ontario), 65

Indirect election, 23, 116, 117n, 147, 157, 159–160, 174, 176
Institute of Public Administration of Canada, 29–30
Interim Housing Committee, 74–76

Jones, Murray V., 47–48
Jones, Victor, xxv

Kaplan, Harold, xxv, 59, 130, 140
Kennedy, J. A., 138–139, 141
Kent, T. J., 55
Kitchener-Waterloo Local Government Review, 145
Kruger, John, 161

INDEX

La Guardia, Fiorello, 97
Lascelles, G. A., 27n, 38
Lawrence Heights Housing Project, 69–77 *passim*
Lawson, M. B. M., 48
Leaside, Town of, 2, 45, 114–115
LeMay, Tracy, 47
Liberal Party of Ontario, 172–173
Licensing Commission of Metro, 36–37, 42
Lieutenant-Governor's Committee to Study Housing Conditions in Toronto, 8
Local Planning Boards, 39, 60–64. See also Planning, local
Long Branch, Village of, 114–115

Magistrate's Courts, 36–37
Mansur, David B., 58n, 69
Markham, Township of, 107, 166
McKeough, W. Darcy, xi, 165
Metro Executive Committee, 27–28, 43, 98, 117–118, 131, 146, 174
Metropolitan Committee of Heads of Departments, 84–86
"Metropolitan concept", xxiii–xxiv, 30, 178; in public housing, 66–67; in reverse, 181–184
Metropolitan Council: establishment, 21–22, 24, 156; functions, 25–26, 41, 49, 84, 119; submission to Commission of Inquiry (1957), 35–40
Metro Toronto Children's Aid Society, 73
Metropolitan Toronto Commission of Inquiry, 32–44, 48, 50–51, 80, 159
Metropolitan Toronto Department of Welfare, 119, 158
Metropolitan Toronto Housing Authority, xxii, 67, 67n; development of programs, 68–79; argument for expanded role, 158
Metropolitan Toronto Juvenile and Family Court, 119
Metropolitan Toronto Library Board, 119
Metropolitan Toronto Official Plan, 38–39, 46–49, 53–60, 108, 130–135, 175
Metropolitan Toronto Planning Area, 26, 39, 46, 49–51, 131–134, 148, 162–166
Metropolitan Toronto Planning Board, 39–40, 76, 162, 180; jurisdiction, 39–40, 61; organization and development, 26, 46–48; review of Metro's programs, 124–130; submission of revised Official Plan, 130–131, 175
Metropolitan Toronto and Region Transportation Study (MTARTS), 148
Metropolitan Toronto School Board, 22, 25, 32, 40–42, 103, 111–112, 120–121

Metropolitan Toronto Separate School Board, 111, 120
Metropolitan Toronto Transportation Plan, 56, 135–136. *See also* Spadina Expressway, Transportation planning
Metropolitan Toronto Urban Renewal Study, 56–57, 158, 180. *See also* Urban renewal
Milner, James B., xxi, xxiv–xxv
Mimico, Town of, 21, 114–115
Minister of Municipal Affairs, 47, 50, 54, 132, 146–147, 153, 164
Minister of Planning and Development, 39, 46
Ministry of Finance and Intergovernmental Affairs (Ontario), xi–xii
Minnesota, Metropolitan Council of the Twin Cities Region, xiii
MTARTS. *See* Metropolitan Toronto and Region Transportation Study
Municipal Act of Ontario, 17, 34, 106
Municipal Board. *See* Ontario Municipal Board
Municipality of Metropolitan Toronto Act, 32, 36, 43, 46, 54, 107, 114, 121–123, 132, 134. *See also* Bill 80, Bill 81

National Housing Act (of 1938), 9; (of 1944), 66–67; (of 1954), 52; (of 1964), 180
New Democratic Party of Ontario, 172–173
New Toronto, Town of, 60, 114–115
North York, Township of, 30, 61, 70–75, 114–115, 137

Official Plan Committee, 131–134
Official Plan: of Metropolitan Toronto, 38–39, 46–47, 53, 108, 130; of Area Municipalities, 39–40, 46, 51; of City of Toronto, 51n. *See also* Metropolitan Toronto Official Plan, Official Plan Committee
Ontario, County of, 54, 147
Ontario Housing Corporation, xxii, 67n, 170; completion of federal-provincial projects, 76n; position relative to Metro, 109, 177
Ontario Municipal Board: powers, x, 39, 106, 121; City's application to, 20, 32, 45, 102–103; Report of 1953, 28–29, 45–46, 65, 122; role in planning, 50, 141–142; consideration of Spadina Expressway, 135, 138–139, 141–143, 170; decision concerning City wards, 116n, 173
Oshawa Area Planning and Development Study, 148, 166

199

INDEX

Ottawa-Carleton, Regional Municipality of, 145

Peel, County of, 54, 107
Peel-Halton Local Government Area Review, 144
Pickering, Township of, 153, 161, 166
Planning: local, 27, 39, 48, 52; regional, 29, 39, 45–64, 107–108; areas, 53. *See also* Metropolitan Toronto Planning Board, City of Toronto Planning Board, Regional planning
Planning Act of Ontario, 45–46, 60, 108
Plumptre, A. F. W., 11
Police: amalgamation of departments, 36, 42, 122, 156; expenditures by Metropolitan Department, 86; regional governments, 147. *See also* Board of Police Commissioners
Population: distribution by municipal units, 18, 114–115; metropolitan, 15, 126, 149, 152, 155; Metro's share of provincial, 164
Port of New York Authority, 20
Public Health services, 110, 183
Public housing, 66–79, 80n, 100, 109, 158, 168; need for social services, 71–72. *See also* Ontario Housing Corporation, Urban renewal
Public transit, public transportation. *See* Transportation planning, Toronto Transit Commission

Regent Park, Community Improvement Association, 170
Regent Park North (housing project), 10, 29, 63, 66, 170
Regent Park South (housing project), 63, 69, 77, 170
Regional Development Branch, Department of Economics and Treasury (Ontario), 145, 151
Regional development councils, 145
Regional government (Ontario), 144–154; studies, 144–145; guidelines, 146–149
Regional planning, 39, 45–63, 107–108, 124–154
Rehabilitation of housing, 52–53, 127, 169–170
Representation on Metropolitan Council, 21, 24, 33–35, 44, 81–82, 87, 98–99, 106, 113, 115–118. *See also* Metropolitan Council
Roads, arterial. *See* Transporation planning

Robarts, John R., 113, 120n, 121–122, 133, 149, 153
Robinette, J. J., 138
Royal Commission on Canada's Economic Prospects 1955–1980, 62
Royal Commission on Metropolitan Toronto, 60, 62, 103, 122, 172, 179; submissions, 103–104; Report, 104–113; statement of the Prime Minister, 113–122 *passim*

Scarborough, Township of, 30, 61, 75–77, 114–115, 161
Scott, Stanley, xxv
Sewage disposal, 25–26, 128–129, 147, 155, 176, 179
Smallwood, Frank, xxiv, 70n, 99–100, 175, 178, 182
Social development, 12–13, 99, 183–184
Social Planning Council of Metropolitan Toronto, 103, 131
Spadina Expressway, 134–144, 170–171; maps, 95–96
Spadina Planning Area, 53
Spadina Review Corporation, 138–139, 170
Special Committee on Metropolitan Affairs (of Metro Council), 83, 86, 89
"Stop Spadina, Save Our City" Co-ordinating Committee, 137–138
Suburbs of Toronto: population, 15, 17–18, 33; finance, 15, 178–179; government, 17; representation on Metro Council, 33, 44, 81–82; opposition to public housing, 71–74 *passim*, 75–77
Swansea, Village of, 60, 114–115

Thistletown (housing project), 76
Thunder Bay, Regional Municipality of, xi, 145–146
Toronto and York Planning Board, 17, 24
Toronto Transit Commission, 25, 36–37, 59, 85, 109, 129–130, 155. *See also* Toronto Transportation Commission
Toronto Transportation Commission, 20, 25, 59. *See also* Toronto Transit Commission
Transportation planning, 46, 49, 55–59, 80n, 109n, 129–130, 134–144, 155
Two-tier system of metropolitan government, vii–ix, xi, 21, 113–114, 144–147, 149, 166

University of Toronto, 17
Urban Development Institute, 131
Urban renewal: need and planning, 51–52, 63, 127; Urban Renewal Study, City

of Toronto, 52–53, 63; future of, 180; Urban Renewal Study of Metro, 56–57, 158, 180; responsibility of governments for, 65, 108, 158; opposition to, 140, 168–170, 180

Vancouver Metropolitan Health Board, 20
Vaughan Township, 107, 166
Voorhees, Alan, 142

Warden Woods (housing project), 76
Waste disposal, 110, 119
Water supply, 25–26, 127–128, 147, 155
Welfare system: inadequacies, 100–102; Metro's involvement, 101, 110, 119, 156, 158, 177; neglect of social services in, 125–126, 177
Weston, Town of, 114–115
Winnipeg, City of and Metropolitan Area of, vii–ix, 81n, 103
Women Electors' Association, 78, 103

York, County of, 12, 27, 107, 147
York, Regional Municipality of, 153, 164, 165n
York, Town of, 2
York, Township of, 37, 43, 61, 75, 100, 114–115, 137
Yorkdale Shopping Centre, 135

Zoning, 40, 45, 46n, 49–52, 56–57, 107